Dear Sisters, Dear Daughters

Words of Wisdom
from Multicultural Women Attorneys
Who've Been There and Done That

Defending Liberty
Pursuing Justice

The poem appearing on pages 244-247 is from *Collective Poems* by Langston Hughes. Copyright ©1994 by the Estate of Langston Hughes. Reprinted by permission of Alfred A. Knopf, a Division of Random House, Inc.

Cover Design by Andrew Alcala, ABA Publishing.

05 04 03 02 01   5 4 3 2 1

Library of Congress Cataloging-in-Publication Data

Dear sisters, dear daughters / Karen Clanton, editor
    p.cm.
    Includes indexes.
    ISBN 1-57073-815-7
    1. Minority women lawyers—United States.   2. Practice of law—United States I. Clanton, Karen, 1970-

    KF299.M56 D43 2000
    340'.082—dc21

                     00-044754

Discounts may be available for books ordered in bulk. Special consideration is given to state bars, CLE programs, and other bar-related organizations. Inquire at Book Publishing, ABA Publishing, American Bar Association, 750 North Lake Shore Drive, Chicago, Illinois 60611.

www.ababooks.org

Acknowledgements

This book would not have been possible without letters from those who've been there and done that. I thank each author for giving her time and advice.

This book would not have been successful without the staff of the Commission on Racial and Ethnic Diversity in the Profession: Sandra Yamate, Cie Armstead, Sharon Tindall, Candace Smith, Douglas Knapp, and former staff members Terryl Mannings and Adriana Damacio. I thank them for their vision in dreaming up such a book, savvy in seeing it through, and expert administration of a potentially unwieldy process.

I applaud Charisse Lillie, Chair of the Commission on Racial and Ethnic Diversity in the Profession, and Karen Mathis, Chair of the Commission on Women in the Profession, for supporting MWAN when this project was simply a grand idea. Their dedication to fostering and honoring the contribution of multicultural women attorneys is evident through their leadership of their respective Commissions.

Many thanks to the 1999-2000 MWAN Committee for their service. We extend a special thank you to the ABA Minority Counsel Program and its Chair, Floyd Holloway, for their gracious support.

On a personal note, I thank Clarence Jones for his invaluable mentoring, encouragement, and support throughout this process. I also acknowledge my parents, Crosby and Myrtice Clanton, whose words of wisdom I live by.

This book is dedicated to those on whose shoulders we stand.

Karen Clanton
Chair, Multicultural Women Attorneys Network

For the American Bar Association

Sandra Yamate
Director of the Commission on Racial and Ethnic Diversity
in the Profession

Ellen Mayer
Director of the Commission on Women in the Profession

Mary Kay Rockwell
Director of ABA Publishing

Adrienne Cook
Director of New Product Development, ABA Publishing

Russell A. Glidden
Director of Design and Production, ABA Publishing

Cie Armstead
Project Manager,
Commission on Racial and Ethnic Diversity in the Profession

Sharon Banks
Product Development Specialist, ABA Publishing

Sharon Tindall
Program Administrator,
Commission on Racial and Ethnic Diversity in the Profession

From the Chairs of

The Commission on Racial and Ethnic Diversity in the Profession,

and

The Commission on Women in the Profession

Dear Colleagues:

The Multicultural Women Attorneys Network (MWAN) is a joint program of the American Bar Association's (ABA) Commission on Racial and Ethnic Diversity in the Profession and Commission on Women in the Profession. In 1989, the two Commissions approved the formation of the entity that is now known as MWAN.

In its groundbreaking 1994 report entitled, *The Burdens of Both, The Privileges of Neither,* MWAN found that, "multicultural women lawyers encounter persistent, pervasive and unique barriers to career opportunity, growth and advancement." The MWAN report concluded by stating in part:

> The next step must be to commit the will and resources necessary to achieve the goal of inclusion by creating more bias-neutral academic and employment environments—environments where merit, energy and talent can triumph over discrimination and disabling stereotypes that inhibit choices, reduce self-confidence and deter professional growth. [MWAN] realizes that women of color must be the primary agents of change and accepts the role of catalyst, guide and inspiration for the long journey over very rocky terrain.

MWAN continues its work as catalyst, guide, and inspiration in this volume, which raises the voices of multicultural women attorneys who graduated from law school more than ten years ago. In these pages, you will read words of wisdom from seasoned attorneys who have written letters to their "sisters" and "daughters." There are some stories that were obviously painful to tell. There are stories and advice about balancing, mentoring and being mentored. There are stories about surviving the trials and tribulations of demanding careers in the law, and overcoming the discrimination and exclusion that unfortunately still exists in the profession.

After you have finished the book, we would like to hear from you. Please allow this publication to begin a dialogue between our Commissions and you. Please join us as we continue to pursue the ABA's Goal IX: the promotion of full and equal participation in the legal profession by minorities, women, and persons with disabilities.

We are grateful to the 1999-2000 Chair of MWAN, Karen A. Clanton, for her diligence, constant attention to detail and expert editing. We also thank Commission members who assisted us with recruiting and nudging contributors to the volume. We appreciate and acknowledge the staffs of our Commissions, and particularly our staff directors, Sandra S. Yamate and Ellen Mayer.

Our final thanks are extended to the contributors. Thank you for your words and for your time, energy, and candor.

Charisse R. Lillie
Chair
ABA Commission on Racial and
Ethnic Diversity in the Profession

Karen J. Mathis
Chair
ABA Commission on
Women in the Profession

Table of Contents

Introduction

Multicultural women attorneys have reached a milepost: 30 years of significant participation and presence in the legal profession. This group will soon comprise almost 5 percent of all attorneys. The road paved by the trailblazers and firsts has become more traveled by a second generation. Through this book project, the Multicultural Women Attorneys Network asked the trailblazers to reflect upon their journeys in the law and through life and to share their stories with future generations. The letters in this book contain the wisdom, wit, disappointments, and triumphs in the sojourns of 84 women.

With few exceptions, the women who penned the letters graduated from law school at least ten years ago. They are diverse in terms of race, practice area, marital status, parental status, and geographic location. Although diverse, what the authors have in common is the grace to give of their time and the courage to dig deep and offer their truth to benefit others. We are made better by their willingness to share in this public manner.

The letters that follow are organized into three groups. The first group speaks to identity as a person and a professional, and explores the concept of success. This group is called Inspiration because the authors share how they have built a foundation that allows them to transcend obstacles and beat odds that to some would have been insurmountable. These women speak of conjuring up the spirit and strength from within to spur them on and sustain them.

The second group details the varied professional paths chosen by multicultural women attorneys. Brilliant careers are charted in this section and useful information about specific jobs is presented. This group is called Path because the authors in this section are pioneers in their law firms, companies, government agencies, law schools and on the bench. Like pioneers, they broke the trail, and in so doing left markers allowing those who follow to know that they are traveling the right route.

The third group of letters examines how one's individual journey fits into the larger context of family and community. This group is called Big Picture because the authors in this section step back from the details of navigating life's daily challenges to attain perspective on the collective well being. This well being begins with the individual but spirals outward to encompass mates, children, friends, mentors and community organizations. The authors here advocate nurturing these relationships as a key to fulfillment.

Following the letters is a section containing author biographies. The biographies are grouped in one section because read as a group, they too tell a story about the accomplishments and contributions of these women. The book concludes with the results of a survey completed by 152 multicultural women attorneys (which include the authors). The survey provides a snapshot of the group's racial, geographical and professional sector breakdown. Importantly, the survey probed the women's attitudes about the profession by asking whether they would become lawyers again if given the chance to live their lives over and whether they had or would encourage their daughters to pursue a legal career.

This book speaks to any sister and daughter: in high school or law school, at the pinnacle of her legal career or simply weighing career options. Men can also find pearls of wisdom in this book: to help shape their attitudes and reactions to their sisters, daughters, mates, and friends who are affected by these issues. They may find that they, too, are affected by the same issues.

The letters here represent only a snapshot of the experiences, feelings, and concerns of multicultural women attorneys. Reading this book should not be the end of the inquiry; this is merely the beginning. Continue the dialogue. Ask a multicultural woman attorney in your life what her letter would say. Better yet, consider asking yourself the same question.

Words of Wisdom
from Multicultural Women Attorneys
Who've Been There and Done That

Inspiration

The letters in this section ask: what defines you?

what is your vision? and what is your success?

All adamantly agree that professional identity

as a lawyer is merely one aspect of self.

They encourage that we shun confining and

ill-suited definitions of success for ones that speak to

who we are as people and what we value.

The women who follow have overcome obstacles

and naysayers to reach a place where they love what

they do, and most importantly, love who they are.

This group of letters is called Inspiration because they

speak to the spirit and strength to transcend and succeed.

"And the power we express is not about making others wrong, but about instilling courage, caring, and love in our work. It is not about being better than others, but about shining brightly and playing big so others will do the same."
—**Peggy Nagae**

"You will be sustained by the internal fortitude of knowing who you are and where you stand. This is the hallmark of the authentic, successful person when the law firm, the corporate community, and even the family does not recognize or appreciate the magnitude of your talents and worth."
—**June Brown**

"The struggle for diversity or equal representation in the profession isn't merely about higher pay, equal opportunity to make partner, or breaking the glass ceiling; it is about something much more profound than that. It is a recognition of the equal value in every human life. If you begin from this premise, no one can ever make you feel less worthy."
—**Macarena Calabrese**

Dear Sisters, Dear Daughters,

Halito. I join my sisters of color in the legal profession in welcoming you to our profession. As women of color, we each bring our own unique spirits to the legal arena. No two of us are alike, but most of us share a common bond that enabled us to persevere through the trials of law school and rigors of practice. To be a "multicultural woman attorney" is to be either doubly blessed or doubly cursed. As you know, we must constantly prove ourselves; we have to be better because we are women and doubly better because we are of color. The bar is set higher for us, and we have to clear it with ease, or we are deemed failures and further curse all of you who come after us.

I look fondly back at my more than ten years at the hallowed halls of the United States Department of Justice. Never before, nor never again will the Justice Department have a more dedicated, grateful, and loyal attorney than Kalyn Free. The most difficult decision I ever made was leaving Justice. I felt like I was severing my umbilical cord. I went to Justice as a baby lawyer, only 23 years old when I was hired. I was trained by the best and the brightest attorneys in the country. I forged the deepest of friendships which I will always cherish, friends who are among the most important people in my life. I loved almost everything about Justice. I especially loved appearing in court and saying, "I am Kalyn Free and I represent the United States of America." Never before have I felt so proud, been so in awe.

What did I not love about Justice? The dual standard and the self-righteous racism. I saw attorneys of color being held to

much more exacting standards than nonminority attorneys. I
served on hiring committees with some of the best-intentioned
and unwittingly racist people one could only hope never to
meet! But I stayed, I played the game, I fought the good fight, I
answered the racist remarks and inquiries as best I could, and I
opened the minds and hearts of the people there for the people
to come after. Why did I do it? How did I do it? This is how,
and why.

I am Choctaw. I am Choctaw first, before I am anything. I am
Choctaw. My allegiance is to the Choctaw Nation of Oklahoma
and flows to my fellow Choctaw tribal members, then to all
other tribes and Indian nations in the United
States, and to all my Black, Hispanic, and Asian
brothers and sisters.

> *Women make
> women stronger,
> oftentimes
> intentionally,
> sometimes
> inadvertently.*

My Choctaw ancestors blessed me with an
indomitable spirit. The same spirit that coursed
through their veins in our Mississippi homeland,
that carried them through the Long Sad March
from Mississippi to Indian Territory, which saw
them survive when all around them were
dying, that gave them the energy and fortitude
to make this wild and foreign land their home,
to rebuild their homes and heal their families,
and to nurture their broken hearts. The same
spirit they instilled in their granddaughter, my
grandmother, an energy and vision that she
passed on to her daughter, who then passed it on to me. It is
this vision and this spirit that informs my being, makes me who
I am, drives me everyday, makes me work harder and fight
longer than any white man and has me reaching for the stars
and vowing never to surrender.

It is this perpetual wronging of my people and yours by the
dominant society which makes me want to right all the wrongs,
stop the injustices, and save the world. This forces me to fight
on and carry on. It is this drive that led me to law school and

into public service. It is my 94-year-old grandmother who greets every day with a smile on her face and hope in her heart that spurs me on. It is my mother who travels 54 miles round trip every day to work at our Indian Boarding School to make a better life for our at-risk children. It is my sisters and cousins who work and teach and counsel troubled children of all colors. It is my mentors and friends in the Choctaw Nation and throughout the United States who believe in me, encourage me, and inspire me to forge a path that will help not only people of color but all disadvantaged and disenfranchised people in America.

I come from a family of survivors, from a family of women, from a matrilineal society. Women make women stronger, oftentimes intentionally, sometimes inadvertently. My grandmother, my aunts, my sisters, my cousins, all are survivors. They each have waged their own wars, whether it be at work, in their families, spiritually, in the home, or in the fields. They have all fought their own demons, each having survived, some more scathed than others, but all sharing the same heart, all caring for each other and for me. Each one has shared in my journey to get me where I am, to allow me to reach for my stars, and realize my dreams. That is who I am. This is why I carry on. This is why I fight the fight.

I am inspired by little boys and girls of color who look at me and see that I'm a girl and I'm an Indian and I'm an attorney and maybe they can be one too. I am inspired by redneck men and oppressed women in Southeastern Oklahoma who told me I shouldn't be running for political office because I am a woman and who told me they wouldn't vote for me because I'm an Indian. I am inspired by purportedly politically correct managers at the Department of Justice who said I shouldn't be working on Indian cases because I was "too passionate." I am inspired by the ignorance and racism throughout these United States that still seeks to oppress people of color. I am inspired by all of this and much more to adopt the mantra of one of my heroes, Kweisi Mfume, "There is no dishonor in defeat, only in surrender."

"You don't look like an Indian. You're an Indian and you don't drink? You are a woman and you should be having babies. Why aren't you having babies? Why haven't you ever been married, what is wrong with you? Why should I vote for you? I won't ever vote for an Indian. Women should be at home. You are going to hell for not staying at home. A man should have that job. A woman shouldn't be a District Attorney. I won't ever vote for a woman."

"You're a woman, I like that. We women have to stick together. I'll always vote for an Indian. I've never had a chance to vote for an Indian before. I think a woman would make a good District Attorney. We Choctaws have to stick together."

People of color came through for me, and I won. Together we made the difference. That was my greatest joy, to see the power of our people at the ballot boxes.

Whatever your career path, whatever your vision, you know what your goals are, only you can set them and only you can reach them. Those who have gone on before you and me broke down some of the barriers, but the barriers are still there, just not quite as high as they were. You still have to clear each of them, and only you can do it. But you have help: you have mentors and you have us. Most importantly, you have yourself. Reach into your soul, listen to your heart, it will always provide guidance, strength, and the right path.

I may not reach my highest dreams, but I can believe in them and follow where they lead. I encourage you to follow your dreams, to join us in the struggle, never to surrender. Kilihoti! (Onward with progress.)

Kalyn Cherie Free

Kalyn Cherie Free *is the first woman ever elected as District Attorney for this two-county position in southeastern Oklahoma.*

Dear Sisters, Dear Daughters,

*Our deepest fear is not that we are inadequate.
Our deepest fear is that we are powerful beyond
measure. It is our light, not our darkness, that
frightens us. We ask ourselves, who am I to be
brilliant, gorgeous, talented and fabulous?
Actually, who are you not to be? You are a child
of God. Your playing small doesn't serve the
world. There is nothing enlightened about shrink-
ing so that other people won't feel insecure
around you. We were born to manifest the glory
of God within us. It's not just in some of us; it's in
everyone. And as we let our own light shine, we
unconsciously give other people permission to do
the same. As we are liberated from our own fear,
our presence automatically liberates others.*
                                   - Marianne Williamson

Reflecting upon the last 25 years, from my first year in law
school, through 10 different job changes, to my current perch as
a consultant, this quote captured my journey and the journey of
other women lawyers of color who I know. We have an enormous ability to be successful in the traditional sense. We also
have an enormous ability to transform the entire legal profession
if we are willing to speak our own truth, to bring our "whole
selves" to our work, and to *own* our heritage, history, and communities. Let me explain what all this has meant for me.

Early in my career Herb Cawthorne, a mentor, told me that if I stopped being the nice, Japanese girl I thought others expected me to be and started expressing my true power, people might not remember my exact words, but they would definitely remember who I was. So I tried it. I was a panelist at a Minority Law Day program; Derrick Bell was the keynote speaker. Another minority lawyer said his firm based their hiring decisions on qualifications, not race. I thought to myself, "Here goes," and challenged his statement as illogical and demeaning. I was uncomfortable, even though I believed in what I was saying. I spoke my truth but was way outside my comfort zone. Several months later, Derrick sent me a letter, said there was an opening at the law school, and asked if I was interested in applying. Did one experience cause the other? I don't know, but I think so.

In another situation, I was meeting with two partners and a senior associate at my firm. The more senior partner made an offhand remark about some recent racial killings in New York that left me uncomfortable. I waited for the other two lawyers to comment. Nothing. Afterward, I sought advice from the only other associate of color at the firm. Nervous but determined, I went back to the partner, told him that while he may not have intended anything negative, his comments could be taken in a negative manner. He turned bright red and stammered out a response. I wasn't sure if I had done the "politically" right thing, but I knew that it was personally right for me.

A third memory comes from attending the Harvard Institute for Educational Management while serving as an assistant dean. One day a senior professor from the Harvard Business School used the word "Jap" during his marketing lecture. I was stunned. I had never heard anyone use that term. I sat up, looked around, and waited for the director of the program or someone else to challenge him. Silence. In the space of seconds, I had to decide what to do. I blurted out words to the effect, "Please don't use that word; it's offensive." He stopped lecturing, looked up and tried to identify who had interrupted him. When he spotted me, instead of apologizing, he said that some of his clients were . . . (naming several Japanese companies), and without another word, he went back to his notes. Sadly for me, no one else said anything either to him or me. It was as though my words had never been spoken, never been heard.

I describe these situations as examples of me speaking my truth. I do not recite them to boast because, on reflection, I could have said things differently, with more love and less right-eousness. I could have been smoother and more skilled. Nonetheless, I have learned something extremely valuable from speaking out. I know I can count on myself to speak my own truth to the best of my ability.

I had never thought of criminal defense, but there I was as the Senior Trial Attorney for the Urban Indian Council, spending day after day in trial. Much to my surprise, I became quite good and won many cases, even though I had no Asian American women role models. Instead, mine were white males or tel-evision lawyers like Perry Mason. While I knew no one would take me for "Peggy" Mason, I did come into my own winning formula. I learned to speak from my heart about my love of democracy, due process, and justice—the reasons I chose a legal career.

> *I know I can count on myself to speak my own truth to the best of my ability.*

And then I realized juries wanted to believe in justice, just like I did. They were common, ordinary people just like me. I also realized that learning Japanese American history and grow-ing up impoverished with parents who had been incarcerated during World War II gave me a huge advan-tage. I had grown up experiencing the pangs of injustice; I had lived with the aftermath of the constitutional betrayal; I had felt the devastation in the wake of their shattered American dream. Coming from my life experience, I could give deeply held, heartfelt meaning to words like justice, due process, and the Constitution. I could also relate to the jurors and the defendants. Aspects of my life that had brought me shame growing up were now the very jewels that caused my abilities as a trial lawyer to sparkle.

I need only remember the mentoring I received from folks like Derrick Bell, who said, "You must do what's right regardless of the personal cost." Or, Minoru Yasui, who said, "I don't know if we're going to win, but we're going to give them hell." Or, Mari Matsuda, who said, "As Asian Americans we must not be used as pawns in the debate against affirmative action."

Derrick, Min, and Mari have lived principled lives based on their heritage, histories, and communities. Among many acts of courage, Derrick resigned his deanship when the faculty refused to hire an Asian American woman professor. According to several professors, she was not qualified and had been ranked as the number two candidate only because of affirmative action. At the end of the debate, Derrick said, "I will abide by your decision, but I cannot represent a school that would do this. I resign."

In 1942, at the age of 26, Minoru Yasui, an attorney and American patriot, intentionally violated the military curfew imposed upon Japanese Americans. He was convinced the courts would vindicate the rights of Japanese American citizens. He lost. In 1943, Yasui's case, along with those of Gordon Hirabayashi and Fred Korematsu, were appealed to the United States Supreme Court, where all three lost again. The Court held that curfew, segregation, and removal based on race was constitutional because of military necessity.

Forty years later, a multiracial group of lawyers reopened those cases, alleging fraud upon the courts. I had the privilege of serving as Yasui's lead attorney. A man of my parent's generation, with daughters my age, Yasui could have been condescending and patronizing to me as a Sansei (third generation) woman lawyer. But he wasn't. He was a model client and a man who possessed more integrity and courage than most. For me, he was a Japanese American hero.

Mari Matsuda is a law professor with real-time expertise that comes from her own intersectionality of race, gender, and class and her experiences as the daughter of socialist parents. Mari has co-authored a book supporting affirmative action entitled, *We Will Not Go Back*. She is a radical in the best and truest sense of that word. She is also an Asian American heroine of mine because she writes her truth with love and soul. She remembers her heritage, acknowledges her community, and has an obvious heart-centered generosity.

We may have been taught that we are inadequate because of our race, gender, class, etc. We know better. If we speak our own truth, bring our "whole selves" to our work, and own our heritage, history, and communities, we can be powerful beyond measure. And the power we express is not about making others wrong, but about instilling courage, caring, and love in our work. It is not about being better than others, but about shining brightly and playing big so others will do the same.

We *can* lead the way, and in so doing, we will forge a purpose worthy of who we are.

Peggy Nagae

Peggy A. Nagae *has served as a Consultant since 1988 and specializes in the areas of change management, organization healing, and leadership development.*

Dear Sisters, Dear Daughters,

I am honored and humbled to have an opportunity to share with you some thoughts that may make you smile and many that will fortify you as you embark on a most exciting journey. To paraphrase June Jordan: you are the ones we are waiting for. Welcome.

My journey began in the small town of Bessemer, Alabama, just outside of Birmingham. It was there that I first began to believe that I was one of the ones that the world was waiting for. It was there, as a young girl, that I learned that there was no objectivity in the meting out of justice—rather, it was based on what the ones in power thought of the ones who were without power. It was there where I knew the face of danger and grew less fearful of challenging the status quo. It is now that I can look at those times and know that I must first see a person and get to know the person before I can accurately assess the situation.

In Alabama in the late 1950s and early 1960s, there was every imaginable challenge to me, a little black girl, seeing myself as a fully entitled citizen of the United States of America. It was also there that I became and proudly remain a realistic optimist. I used those early experiences as an impetus to measure success myself. It is not what someone else thinks you should be or want; it is what you believe and decide. That, my sisters and daughters, is real power.

I remember the old folks who always pushed me to go further, do more, challenge the wrong, and advocate for those who had no voice. They made me aware how important it was that I go farther and do more for myself, those who went before me, and those who come after me. They spoke of the "educated lawyers, who was going to help us get all of our rights." It then became evident to me that in every sustainable action—the law and the lawyers—were always crucial to success. When Dr. King went to jail, the lawyers got him out. When they found that blacks were paid less than whites at the steel mill, it was the lawyers who prepared and won the case to get money damages. I knew that the law was the vehicle for change that most appealed to me. I could teach others to advocate for their rights, heal injustices through the courts, fight for the moral good, and win because it was the right thing to do. Through the years, I have had an awakening that the law is the keeper of the status quo, not a catalyst for change. I still believe, however, that the law, when challenged to protect all Americans, is a powerful agent of change. I also know that those who have suffered from unfair laws are the ones most likely to change the law for the good of all that it impacts.

Dear sister, dear daughters, there remains so much to be done. Race and class seem pervasive in any discussion of the negative impacts of the justice system. Women are entering the penal institutions at an alarming rate and the Sentencing Project is projecting a population of more than two million people in prison in 2000—most of whom are people of color. There are alarming rates of exoneration of death row inmates, most of whom are persons of color, for prosecutorial misconduct. There continues to be a paucity of attorneys and public defenders to ensure that citizens' rights are protected. There are women who sit in prison for double the term of men for the same offense, because they decided to defend themselves rather than risk death as passive victims of domestic violence. There are children who need to see you challenge, advocate, and win on their behalf in civil and criminal courts. As you become the shoulders on which others stand, know that you will win some that you should not have won and that you will lose some cases where there is no reason for the loss. You will encounter those, of a different gender and/or color who will seek to denigrate and marginalize you—but it is all in how you take it. You can either make their difficulties yours, or you can take the time to determine what is best for you.

You must always remember: law may be a calling, and it may be your passion, but it is and will always be what you do, not who you are. That being said, there is no better training in the world for us as women and people of color. You hone the analytical, strategic, public speaking, planning, and resiliency skills.

You also begin to study people—friends and foes. It only takes a few cases—not being paid by a friend to whom you gave a deal in the first place, a few lost jobs because your integrity is not for sale, a few all-nighters only to have the client not show—to give you a strong sense of self and an ability to make a decision about what and who you will continue to deal with.

You will be sustained by the internal fortitude of knowing who you are and where you stand. This is the hallmark of the authentic successful person when the law firm, the corporate community, and even the family does not recognize or appreciate the magnitude of your talents and worth. Admittedly, there will be barriers, unfairness, and delays. But if you have internalized that you are and will always be a capable and contributing member of society, circumstances are just that—a circumstance in the moment. You will also learn that whatever occurs is cyclical and that, "This too shall pass." I am emphasizing that this is how to fortify yourself because in this work where you are a leader and an advocate, you will oftentimes be lonely and unappreciated. Look inwardly and then act outwardly with a consciousness that compels you to act—not because of the anticipated rewards, but rather despite the lack of tangible rewards.

Never limit yourself—always be fearless, set the standard for yourself. Always know your boundaries, set them after you have studied the situation and made a decision based on what you stand for. Never let the stature of the person with whom you are interacting determine what you will and will not do. I promise that this will bode you well in the long term. You will be able to go anywhere and meet anyone, take on jobs that others would unequivocally refuse, and refuse opportunities that some would sell their souls for. Allow for the mistakes, because the successes are awesome. It is the journey, no matter how circuitous, lived in the moment that is a well-lived life. Lead with passion and know that great leaders are great servants whose ultimate goal is to develop more leaders—not more followers. This life will require you to share your time, talents, and treasures with others as you must be a visual example rather than one who says what they can do.

Finally, my sisters and daughters: you are the warrior-princesses who are unafraid of challenge and confrontation, but capable of negotiation and compromise. This is the season for which you were born to change, for it is the young who have always led with energy, commitment, and selfless sacrifice. As you forge ahead, please allow yourself to serve without fear of what others will say or think about career and social standing, communicate with as diverse an audience as you can. Look globally, interact without regard to the social-economic status of your counterpart, find balance in all that you do, and take good care of yourself, spiritually, physically, emotionally, and financially.

If you do these things, you will have the ingredients for success and winning on every front. Sometimes you will win, even when you don't know that you have won. You will eagerly seek challenges and explore new paths, then you too will have real power.

June Brown

June A. Brown *is an Attorney in Chicago, working as a Consultant on technology and strategic development issues.*

Dear Sisters, Dear Daughters,

The most important advice I can give is to set your own goals for what you want to achieve. The opportunities for minority women attorneys are far greater today than they were when I graduated from law school. We do not yet compete on an even playing field, but we will eventually succeed and we must continue to prepare the way for those who follow.

My initial dream was to become a physician. Despite excellent grades, I was not allowed to enter any of the medical schools I applied to because they were not accepting women. Refusing to accept rejection, I applied to the University of Chicago Law School. Remarkably, I was admitted. There were only three women in a class of nearly 200. I was the lone woman to graduate in 1951.

I looked for employment in the Chicago area, but none of the law firms wanted to hire a woman, let alone an Asian. So when our daughter was six months old, my husband and I moved back home to Hawaii.

I became the fist Japanese American woman admitted to the bar in Hawaii. Even in Hawaii no law firm wanted to hire a woman. The government refused me a job when others, male, were eagerly recruited. Most said, "You should be home taking care of your baby."

Without the prospects of a job, I had only one recourse left and that was to open my own law firm. I didn't get many clients, and those I did get couldn't pay me much. I taught part time at the University of Hawaii and became active in the Democratic Party of Hawaii. Having determination and resilience in the face of defeat and rejection is what it takes to fight against barriers and glass ceilings.

When I look back over the challenges of my career so far, I know that I was extremely fortunate in the support I received from my family. When I returned to Hawaii to pursue my law career, I had a loving mother who helped to care for our young daughter. My husband John has always been an equal partner in caring for Wendy and running the house. He has wholeheartedly supported my political career and, in fact, ran all 20 of my campaigns.

Another key ingredient to my success is that I love what I do. I work long hours, seven days a week, but I am doing what I want to do. I take a great deal of satisfaction from working to pass laws that will improve the lives of people and fighting against laws and regulations that are unfair or discriminatory. As a Member of Congress, I can help make government work for my constituents. Among my proudest accomplishment are passage of Title IX, which prohibits discrimination against women in educational programs that receive federal funding, and reducing government secrecy through the Freedom of Information Act. Like the other architects of the Hawaii's "bloodless revolution" of 1954, I have tried to do my part to advance social justice in our nation and state.

Having determination and resilience in the face of defeat and rejection is what it takes to fight against barriers and glass ceilings.

I have few regrets because I always went after what I wanted even if I did not always succeed. My campaign for president of the United States in 1972 was the most audacious. I did it to call attention to the need to end the war in Vietnam.

Finally, my advice to young minority women attorneys is to find work that inspires you and that helps to define who you are. I am glad that my political career did not prevent me from taking care of my parents when they needed me, enjoying a happy and fulfilling marriage, and raising an accomplished and independent daughter. There is still so much I want to accomplish, and I am looking forward to the challenges and opportunities the future will bring.

Patsy Mink

Patsy Takemoto Mink *has been a Democratic Member of Congress from Hawaii since 1990 and previously served in the position from 1965 to 1977.*

Dear Sisters, Dear Daughters,

When I was asked what advice I would give women of color who are lawyers, my first thought was the standard: always be prepared, competent, professional, and maintain your reputation. This is good advice for any lawyer. On further thought about what is really important for women of color who face competition as well as discrimination in the practice of law, I decided to take the direct approach. My advice is: GET A LIFE! GET A VISION! AND GET A GRIP!

I know you're saying what kind of advice is that? Well, it is important that women of color who practice law have a sense of humor and a sense of perspective. Often we are in situations where our first response is to get angry or offended, and we fail to use the situation for educational purposes.

For example, as a supervising attorney in a city law department, I was in court to observe a person I supervised. As the case progressed, it was clear that my help was needed. The young attorney asked me to talk with an elected official who was involved. When the official saw me, a black woman, he demanded to see the person in charge. I indicated that I was in charge and that I was the person who would and could make the final decision. The official refused to accept my statement and continued to act as if I wasn't there. All of the other parties to the case were clearly embarrassed because I was the only person of color in the room. After I informed the official that the matter could only be handled by me and that I was the person he had to deal with, he left court to avoid working the situation out with a black woman lawyer.

It was his loss and my opportunity. I showed class and professionalism and solved the problem. Most importantly, I didn't lose perspective and start screaming about stupid, racist behavior. I handled the situation in a way that provided a lesson to the individual I supervised, as well as the parties involved—proving racism and sexism don't have to impede progress.

In a similar situation, the offending party kept demanding to see the person in charge. He was not accepting my authority and demanded to see my boss, who just happened also to be a black woman. Not to be outdone, he then demanded to see her boss, who turned out to be a black man! At that point he demanded to see the ultimate boss, a white male, who refused to talk with him and directed the person to deal with me or else there would be no settlement. These situations provided many laughs about racism and sexism in today's society.

Believe me—you will encounter discrimination based on your race and/or gender, but it should not create such anger and bitterness that you cannot function. Yes, it is hard to deal with injustices, but you cannot let it get a stranglehold on you, compromising your effectiveness, professionalism, and integrity.

When I was a new and young lawyer, I joined with five other lawyers of color and sued our employer for race and gender discrimination. Before the suit was settled, I was often confronted by white male and female coworkers asking me, "What do you want?" After the suit was settled and it was shown that women lawyers made less than men performing the same job, the reaction was not very different. The women were happy to be fairly paid; the white males feared affirmative action; and the office became a union shop, with seniority as the basis for any promotion. This, of course, meant that women and people of color were the last hired and, consequently, rarely had enough seniority to be promoted. I left the office and headed in a different direction, but fate had other plans.

Two years after I left the office, I returned to it as the chief deputy with the responsibility of day-to-day operations. Four years later, I became the first woman chief public defender in my jurisdiction. The lesson to me and I hope to you, is that anger, bitterness, and hostility can motivate action, but they cannot sustain personal growth and development. So, if you're bitter, angry, and disappointed, deal with it, get over it, and GET A GRIP!

Family and community are vital to your success in life and in the profession. You will always need the support of others, especially in times of stress or disappointment. Family and friends are your foundation, and you must always appreciate them and their support. When you are so busy developing your career that you forget those who helped get you there, you will feel the effects of this loss for the rest of your life.

When I was in law school, I was a wife and a mother. I had to take care of my husband and son and do my homework. I am blessed with a supportive husband who helped with the house-work, childcare, and homework (even though he was not a lawyer). My parents and siblings also helped with babysitting, errands, and pep talks. Because I had friends whose journeys were down many different career paths, I was always given advice and updates concerning the rest of the world, unrelated to the law. Faith and church are equally important. The faith community is a nourishing resource for those dark days when you feel no one hears or cares.

Family extends beyond blood relatives. Friends are also family and they, like your biological family, need your input to keep the relationship flowing. Stay in touch with old school chums and make new friends at work, church, and the health club. Travel is a great way to meet new people and get rid of stress. So pick a location, get going, and get a life!

Community involvement allows you to make new friends and give back to those less fortunate than yourself. There are many opportunities for you to mentor children, work with neighborhood programs, run for local school boards, and raise funds for charities. The most important thing to remember is that this life is not about you. It is about what you contribute. We are in a service profession and our mission is to be of service to others.

Do you see things beyond yourself and your own world? If you don't have vision, how can you expect to be happy, fulfilled, or accomplished? Visions are what help you set and reach goals. The world you live in provides many and varied opportunities to fully participate in what life has to offer. Many people can tell you what they think should be your goals, dreams, and ambitions, but it is up to you and only you to make those personal decisions.

One of my heroines is Fannie Lou Hamer, a strong, black woman from the civil rights movement. She said, "I am sick and tired of being sick and tired." With these words she moved from being a poor, black woman in a small Mississippi town, to a strong, active black woman who became involved in the movement that opened up the right to vote for all poor and disenfranchised people in America.

I believe Fannie Lou Hamer's statement should be used as a call to action for you and all women of color. This call-to-action statement is the basis for my advice to you about how to succeed as a woman of color, as a lawyer, and as a committed person.

In closing, my sisters in law, if you want to know what to do and how to do it, remember—GET A LIFE! GET A VISION! AND GET A GRIP!

Rita Aliese Fry

Rita Aliese Fry *is in her second six-year term as Chief Executive of the Office of the Cook County, Illinois Public Defender.*

Dear Sisters, Dear Daughters,

Timing is everything! If I had been offered this opportunity to write to you two years ago, I'm not sure that I would have anything useful to say (although that would not have stopped me from saying something). During the past three years, however, something wonderful and exciting has happened. First and foremost, I have learned to acknowledge that I like the woman I have become. As a result, I no longer measure my success through the eyes of others. Second, I have accepted the fact I am where I am because I am supposed to be here.

I have been associated with the firm of Laner, Muchin, Dombrow, Becker, Levin, & Tominberg, Ltd. for 12 years. In January 1994, I became the firm's first minority and first female nonequity partner. By the time this letter is published, I will have become the firm's first minority and first female equity partner. Although I am quite proud of my professional accomplishments, I am most proud of the things that I have learned about myself and how I have used what I learned.

As an associate, I wanted the partners to perceive me as a "superstar." (Naturally, if I were a superstar, then I would be successful.) What I soon realized was that being a superstar meant practicing law in their image. It meant doing things the way they did things. It meant thinking the way that they thought. It meant saying the things that they said. It meant having my priorities mirror their priorities. In other words, it seemed to me that for me to become successful, I was going to have to become one of them. Unfortunately for me, for the first nine years of association with the firm, I tried to do exactly that—become someone I am not.

It was only after yet another in a series of disappointing end-of-year reviews and after I failed to receive the compensation I believe I deserved, that I realized I had been going about everything the wrong way. For nine years, I had defined my success in terms of what the partners perceived me to be. I had defined success using other people's values. Consequently, I had been measuring my success through the eyes of others.

I have learned that I am the only one who can define my success. I have learned too that the most important thing is not what other people think of me but rather what I think of myself. I like the woman I have become and the woman I am always trying to be. I am kind. I am loving. I am giving. I am devoted. I am compassionate. To the extent that I have these qualities and that these qualities are evident in how I work, how I live, and how I interact with my friends, family, and others, then I am successful. I have at long last discarded the burdens attached to believing that my success depends on whether others deem me to be successful. And, for the past three years, my success has been virtually automatic.

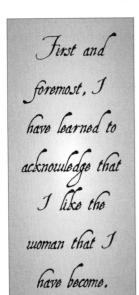

First and foremost, I have learned to acknowledge that I like the woman that I have become.

I have also learned that I am in the place that I am because I am supposed to be here. What this means is that I've stopped asking why my professional and personal path has taken the direction it has taken. I no longer concern myself with what I perceive to be the unfairness of things that have happened in the past. I realize that every day I make choices. For the most part, the choices I have made and continue to make are good ones. Consequently, I am in the place that I am because of the choices I have made.

I like the place I am in. I am surrounded by people who love me. I am a wife. I am a mother of three daughters. And, I am a friend. I cannot complain about this place. When I look at where I have been and where I am going, everything I see is good.

I am excited about the opportunities that are sure to present themselves because I am in this place. I am confident because I now know who I am and what is important to me, so that when opportunities arise I will make very good choices. I will then end up in another place and will face even more new opportunities. Then I will be in another place with even more opportunities. If I am lucky, this endless circle will go on and on and on.

As you continue to pursue whatever your success is, take some time to learn who you are and what you want. Learn to take advantage of opportunities that are present because you are in the place that you are meant to be. Only then will you truly be successful.

Violet M. Clark

Violet M. Clark *is a Partner with Laner, Muchin, Dornbrow, Becker, Levin and Torninberg, Ltd. in Chicago.*

Dear Sisters, Dear Daughters,

It's hard to know what to say to you in this letter. I've started it several times, only to start over when its tone (completely on its own) grows flippant, or cynical, or angry. I want to strike the right balance—to encourage you, to inspire you, to make you laugh—but I keep coming up with things that might discourage you or make you mad.

Don't get me wrong. I love being a lawyer. Every day I thank my Maker that I stumbled into a profession that interests and challenges me. I love the power that the law has to help people, to change things, and to give people hope.

But in the 18 years since I passed the Georgia Bar I've learned a few things. I'll share one brief lesson with you: don't get caught up in other people's definition of success. As a new lawyer, I confessed to my hairdresser that I'd taken a job with Atlanta Legal Aid at an annual salary of $13,700. Every woman in the beauty shop took it as a personal affront that I hadn't chosen a job that paid more! "Girl, I know you didn't pay that school all that tuition to make less than I do" and "Well, maybe you'll find something else soon" were the kinder remarks aimed my way. It was disappointing that the sisters in the beauty shop didn't understand that for me that low salary, low prestige spot was literally a dream come true.

Eighteen years later, I realize that my time at Legal Aid gave me things I would never have received in one of those fancy law firms. It was there that I learned how to be a lawyer. I established a sound basis in the fundamentals of practicing law, and I got hands-on experience in helping people resolve problems. I was encouraged to participate in bar activities, and I received invaluable mentoring from more experienced lawyers. As a result of litigating all those eviction cases, I got to know all of the judges and many of the litigators in my county. As a result of serving on all those bar committees, I was elected president of the 6,000-member Atlanta Bar Association. I'm now able to help my profession and my community in ways that I never dreamed possible.

My wish for you is that you find your way to a career that makes you happy. Yes, there are people who expect less from you simply because you are a woman of color. There are even people who want you to fail. But there are also people who expect wonderful things from you and who will be disappointed if you don't excel. You are not alone.

Paula Frederick

Paula J. Frederick *is Deputy General Counsel for the State Bar of Georgia, where her primary duty is interpreting and enforcing the ethics rules for lawyers.*

Dear Sisters, Dear Daughters,

Is it easy to be a successful minority female attorney? No, but it can be worth the sacrifices that you have to make to achieve success. Hard work and long hours are the hallmark of a successful attorney. As a minority female attorney, however, that is often not enough. You likely will encounter colleagues and clients who question your abilities just because of your gender and/or the color of your skin. On the other hand, you also will encounter people (male or female, black or white) who assess your skills fairly and are willing to help you become a better attorney. These are your mentors, whether or not they are officially recognized as such. Seek them out and develop relationships with them on a personal as well as professional level.

You will also have to learn how to define success and not rely on other people's definitions of success. I prefer to define success by attainment of personal goals such as developing a skill or conquering a challenge. I also include in my definition of success the notion of giving back to the community because I believe that to whom much is given, much is expected. Whatever success means to you, have faith that you will achieve it, and you are sure to succeed.

Laura A. Wilkinson

Laura A. Wilkinson *joined the antitrust practice group of Rogers & Wells LLP in Washington, D.C. as Counsel in 1996.*

Dear Sisters, Dear Daughters,

Through the joys and traumas of my life I have internalized one lesson: the importance of being true to oneself. Some told me that I could not be successful if I was true to myself. As I discovered, however, the reality is otherwise. One must actually pay a dear price for not being true to oneself.

A friend of mine, Kata (not her real name), learned this lesson too. Kata was a hardworking summer associate at a large law firm. When the firm organized a weekend retreat for summer associates, Kata hesitated to go. Kata did not drink. She also knew that the attorneys at her firm drank and that she would not be comfortable. Kata was also reluctant to go because the retreat was taking place at a special time when her husband was incapacitated and needed her care. To increase her chance of getting an offer, however, Kata ignored her truth and decided to go. She wanted to show that she was a "good firm citizen."

During the retreat, and as Kata had anticipated, the lawyers drank. Some were so drunk that they lost control. Amidst this crowd, Kata felt unsafe. She also felt lonely. She had nothing to share, not even their common bond with alcohol. The lure of a potential job offer forced Kata to attempt to engage in superficial discussions. Not much came of it.

After the retreat, at the end of the summer, the firm discussed the offers to summer associates. The partners who had attended the retreat voted and convinced others to vote against Kata. "Even though her work was excellent, Kata had appeared ill-at-ease during the retreat, a sure indication of her inability to be a team player," they said. Kata did not get an offer. Kata had paid a dear price for not being true to herself.

The ability to be true to oneself requires values. Values define an individual. Anyone can have values when everything goes well. This is why many people claim to have values. These people do not realize, however, that values are not values unless they withstand the test of challenges. The world can actually assess an individual by observing the behavior of that individual in difficult times. You may, for instance, hear some minorities claim to support diversity efforts in the workplace. "It is the only right thing to do. We must develop and provide the best opportunities for our personnel of color," they will tell you. When left to their own devices or when placed in a position of authority, however, these minorities will often be the first to justify the unjust treatment of other minorities. Obviously, one needs to use discernment in presenting one's point of view in the workplace. There is, however, a difference between expressing one's truth with diplomacy and lacking values. During challenging times, a person with values will present her point of view in a manner that fosters respect for all, including remaining true to herself, while a person who lacks values will settle for the convenient and will lack the strength to live up to her highest potential.

Dear sisters and daughters, you should know that there is a price to pay for lacking values. People notice people without values. Most may choose to be silent about what they see. And some may even like what they see if it suits their needs. But the wise know not to trust people without values. An employer who is concerned about liability on diversity issues may like and use the minority employee mentioned above. But this employer (if advised) will hesitate to entrust such an employee with certain responsibilities. In condoning the unjust treatment of another human being, that employee has actually sent an unspoken but powerful message to her employer that she is not to be trusted to stand up for what is right. Her employer may like her but will not respect her. Rarely do human beings engage in serious business with people they do not respect. A dear price to pay.

Being true to yourself is actually an asset because truth pierces the veil of illusion. From my own experience, I have found that it is difficult to remain in a destructive environment without living the life of a lie. With honesty, illusion has no home. And without illusion, there are no excuses, just actions. This is why honest people have the strength to face life on life's own terms, yet live to their highest potential. Fearless, they will not deny the realities that life is handing them. They will simply work around them. They will not, for instance, date and marry someone whom they know "not to be the right pick," just to discover many children and financial commitments later, that they paid a dear price for not being true to themselves.

Being true to yourself is also an asset because your inner truth will support you during difficult times. President Nelson Mandela is an example. Imprisoned under the apartheid regime for more than a quarter century, the first black President of South Africa was able to survive under very difficult conditions. He emerged from what could have been a traumatic experience, not only a hero, but also one of the wisest and most cherished men that this planet has known. President Mandela planned for the worst and expected the best, but the unexpected happened. He lost his loved ones. He lost his freedom. He lost his job as a lawyer and politician. He also lost his earthly possessions. But President Mandela also knew that unless he allowed it, the apartheid regime could not take his truth from him. It was always within. President Mandela's inner truth carried him throughout. It was his friend. It was also the reservoir of his energy. His truth built him when the world was trying to destroy him. His truth even reconstructed him into a stronger and better man. When all else failed, when all else died around him, President Mandela's inner truth represented the immortal within himself. It was his essence. The choice that President Mandela made in choosing this highest path for himself, in following his inner truth, explains why he was awarded the Nobel Peace Prize in 1993. A constant companion, his inner truth had provided the light that carried him through the tunnel, even when he could not carry himself.

The example of President Mandela shows that the best time to discover one's truth is not in times of need. As the "Mandelas" and gold medalists of the world have discovered, for important goals, preparation must be made in advance, with determination and consistency. This requires a vision. As President Mandela found, the journey is a long, long solitary walk. The world will not applaud progress made. It matters little, however.

The rewards are worth it. They range from material gains like jobs or social recognition, to intangibles like inner strength, valuable friendships, and the respect of others. Despite these rewards, however, we have a duty to be true to ourselves. As minority women lawyers, much was given to us. Through the self-discipline of gaining our legal education, we were given the gift of learning the process of living to our highest potential. A true gift indeed. A law degree for minority women is more than an achievement about reading books. Like President Mandela's Nobel Peace Prize, our law degree is the symbol of a victory over what could have destroyed us. But this gift carries a responsibility. As indeed, to whom much is given, much is required. It is therefore our responsibility to lead others, by our example, to take ownership of the same gift and live to their highest potential.

In being true to ourselves, we are showing the way and doing just that.

Marie-Flore V. Johnson

Marie-Flore V. Johnson *is an Associate in the corporate department of Dorsey & Whitney LLP in Minneapolis.*

Dear Sisters, Dear Daughters,

If there is one thing that I wish someone had been able to tell me long ago (and I would have been able to really hear), it is that the most insidious burden of discrimination and stereotypes is too often self-created. What do I mean by that—not to have a chip on your shoulder? No, nothing so simplistic. It is critical to be aware that you have accepted and internalized some of the messages about who you can and cannot, or should and should not be that the society around you inflicts upon you unceasingly. And, despite those messages, you have found within yourself the strength and fortitude to move forward and become something more than what was or is expected. But in the process, you have unwittingly accepted a burden that is not yours to bear. It is the burden of perfection, of being the showpiece both for your race and your gender. "Mama always said you have to be twice as good as them . . ." No one can or should expect to always be twice as good as anyone else. And anyone who tries will find that the life she has carved out is too exhausting and burdensome to be satisfying.

Which brings us to the central question—why have we chosen this profession and these lives? Is it to be a showpiece? The role of multicultural woman lawyer is inherently a stab at perfection. Is it to impress some faceless (or not faceless) others with our accomplishments? To give our parents something to be proud of? To show the world what people who look like us can really do? Or, is it because you are doing something you truly want to do? That you enjoy? That you do in a way no one else would? That gives you a life that is full of unending joy because each day you do something that is what you want to do? Want to spend the precious days of your life doing?

Oh, please, everyone knows that women of color are too "down to earth," too much the salt of the earth to search for eternal joy in a career. There are mouths to be fed, educations to be paid for, and retirements to be funded. Ah, but in that belief itself is the greatest limitation. I am a woman of color, the foundation, the rock. How dare I consider stepping outside of that role to consider joy and fulfillment that comes not from fulfilling (or refuting) the expectations of others, but from fulfilling my own destiny?

When I was growing up I didn't know people of color who played tennis or skied, and so I thought it was something only "they" did. And I suppose, in part, I am a lawyer because my father was a lawyer, and it seemed an attainable goal for "us." But what if I had not accepted those implicit limitations? What if I do not accept them now and believe that I can be exactly who I am—writer, guru, corporate attorney, physicist, educator, nurturer, family lawyer—those things least expected and most expected of me if they bring me joy? If I can do that, then I do not continue the perpetuation of racism and stereotypes.

So I would encourage you to be diligent in finding your unique path. The law itself affords a breadth of possibilities, and the analytical skills borne of legal training afford a wealth more. But be vigilant in examining your motivations with brutal honesty and finding the path that is uniquely yours. For there alone lies the possibility of true greatness.

With a profound belief in your real possibilities,

Roni Michele Crichton

Roni Michele Crichton *is an Attorney working for Xerox Corporation in El Segundo, California.*

Dear Sisters, Dear Daughters,

I am one of those over-50 women who attended college when career choices were limited to the three main women's professions: nurse, secretary, and teacher. So I became all of them sometime in my life. My story echoes that of so many of my sisters of Asian heritage growing up in a white society.

We were the first Asian family in Glendale. I was one of a handful of nonwhite faces at our parochial school, and I grew up with no Asian friends and very little Asian influence other than that of my immediate family. It was important to be an American and emulate what was acceptable in the world that I knew. I was the double minority—a woman and a person of color. And the women's issues were much more important before the color issues were clarified. My husband says I was General Patton in the kitchen, and that was the last place I wanted to be.

Because the time (yours and mine) is not available for a long conversation, I thought I would share one piece of advice: Never give up on your dreams. My favorite saying is: Success is never final, failure is never fatal, courage is always crucial. Keep that hope and courage alive.

Your sister,

Ruthe Catolico Ashley

Ruthe C. Ashley, RN, MSN, J.D., *is a Nurse-Attorney and Consultant on medical/legal and risk management issues to health care facilities across the nation.*

Dear Sisters, Dear Daughters,

Where does one begin? There is so much I wish I could say and share with you to make your journey just a little less burdensome than that of those who came before you. Unfortunately, there is no teacher like experience. I only hope that my words serve as a spark to fuel the fire within you to persevere and pursue your dreams.

I'd like to share with you an experience in my life that helped define the person and professional I am today.

My family immigrated to the United States in the early '70s. Although both of my parents are intelligent, educated professionals, they struggled with some basic concepts of everyday American life and were sometimes preyed on by unscrupulous businessmen who thrived on unsuspecting immigrants. I decided that when I was old enough, I would find the answers to all these "how it is done in America" questions by becoming a lawyer. Now I just had to find out how that too was done in America.

During my senior year in high school, I went to see the guidance counselor to discuss my plans after graduation. At our meeting, I told her I wanted to attend one of the major universities in the area, major in political science and Spanish, and go on to law school. In her sweetest, most condescending voice and never allowing the smile to leave her face, she told me it was wonderful that I had such high hopes for myself, but I should look to a local community college if I wanted to continue studying. If law interested me, perhaps I would consider a career as a court reporter or paralegal. After all, she said, becoming a lawyer required great intellect and command of the English language and surely I wasn't up to the task. I explained neither interested me; I wanted to be a lawyer. Flustered that I had challenged her, she ended the conversation and told me in no uncertain terms that unless I applied to the community college she suggested, she would not help me or give me a letter of recommendation.

With a name like Macarena Rocio Tamayo Romero, this wasn't the first time I'd felt the sting of the tongue lashes uttered by racists, but this was a defining moment in my life and my future depended on it. I could either accept the limitations she imposed on me and realize that a Hispanic—an immigrant at that—would never be good enough to be a lawyer or I could go on without her assistance. I chose the latter. Now, I just had to find out what was an SAT, why some insisted on calling it an ACT, and who was and where could I find this Mr. Stanley Kaplan who could help me pass the entrance exams. It was an interesting few months, but I entered the university of my choice without her assistance or letter of rec-ommendation. Actually, I never saw her again.

> *The struggle for diversity or equal representation in the profession . . . is a recognition of the equal value in every human life.*

I became a lawyer, practiced law, and currently hold the highest and most visible position of any Hispanic in the American Bar Association.

It's been nearly two decades since I had that conversation. I can't say that it hurts or angers me any less today, but it has been a blessing in many ways. It taught me not to be fearful of standing alone when justice demands it. It taught me to explore and acknowledge my own limitations, but never allow others to affix them, regardless of their position or authority. Most importantly, it taught me to never sour. Experiences like these will come and go throughout our lives. With each encounter we are stronger and more prepared to meet the next one, but never allow them to decide the person you are and limit your horizons.

Moreover, for every racist and male chauvinist I have encountered, I have had the pleasure of knowing at least one other decent, compassionate, and open-minded human being. Remember there are many professors, lawyers, administrators, and mentors out there with a great desire to help and guide you. Look for them. Be sure to search outside your own zone of comfort; they may not be wrapped in the same skin tone or gender as you. I have received good advice and support from white males and females, as well as African Americans and Hispanics. Don't limit your possibilities to those within your race and gender alone.

The struggle for diversity or equal representation in the profession isn't merely about higher pay, equal opportunity to make partner, or breaking the glass ceiling; it is about something much more profound than that. It is a recognition of the equal value in every human life. If you begin from this premise, no one can ever make you feel less worthy.

BUENA SUERTE!

(Good luck!)

Macarena Calabrese

Macarena Tamayo-Calabrese *is the Special Assistant to the Executive Director of the American Bar Association in Chicago.*

Dear Sisters, Dear Daughters,

I am so pleased to be one of those whose voice of experience you are seeking. My experiences will not be yours. My path will not be yours. Please take from my words whatever will help you to continue on the path towards your dreams and your goals. I hope that my words will help to light and ease your way.

I was born in the mid-1940s into a family of American Indians and "Coloreds." At the tender age of seven, I announced to my family that I would go to college one day. That was a very big dream for a minority child in Amityville, Long Island, N.Y., where I grew up. Although our schools were integrated and most considered themselves to be "liberal Northerners," a strict racial divide ran through our little town. Whites lived on one side and the rest of us lived on the other side. In the midst of the racism and discrimination there, I dreamed of becoming a lawyer. I wanted to find ways to seek justice and racial harmony.

I do not recall exactly when I decided that I would become a lawyer. I do recall the day when I shared my aspirations with my white fourth grade teacher, Mr. Hicks. He was shocked and warned me that girls like me should aim more realistically and not "go reaching above myself." I was crushed and I carried that hurt with me for a long time. As I grew older, I learned to use that hurt to strengthen my resolve. The desire to prove him and others wrong became strong medicine for me. Sometimes, I had to take it in great gulps, but it never lost its power to spur me onward.

Like so many of us, my path to my goal was full of detours. I married at nineteen, had my first child at twenty and my second child at twenty-two. My husband and I had a plan. First, he would earn his Ph.D. and then it would be my turn to get back into school full-time. It sounded good in theory. It was difficult in practice. I wanted to be a good stay-at-home mother and wife, but it was difficult to think of putting my education off for several more years. I had to keep reminding myself that my turn would come eventually and that I would not have suffered "brain atrophy" when the time arrived. Finally, both children were in school full-time, but then my husband's military career required frequent moves.

Who was it who spoke so eloquently of "a dream deferred"? How many of us have had to defer our dreams? Yet, somehow, we manage to keep going. I drew from the strength of my religious beliefs, my family, and from others who offered advice, encouragement, or just kind words. I also drew from the naysayers like Mr. Hicks. Repeatedly, I had to turn a deaf ear to accusations that I was trying to be better than everyone else by attempting to reach higher than most expected that I could go. I had to remind myself that, by pursuing my own dreams, I was modeling for my own daughter and son. I had to remind myself that I had been given intelligence and drive for a reason and that I should not waste those gifts.

After my children were successfully raised to young adulthood, I finished law school and began to practice. What should have been a fairytale ending to my story became a chapter of loss. Unexpectedly, I began to lose what was most important to me: my marriage. It began collapsing under the unanticipated weight of the role-reversal that occurred as my legal career began to arch upward and my husband's illustrious military career began to glide steadily toward an early retirement and the uncertainty of finding a second career. To save my marriage, I cut back my billable hours and eventually stepped off of the partnership track hoping that it would make a difference if I removed myself temporarily from the pressures of trying to make partner "on time." Neither approach helped.

I would not have planned it this way, but, while I was off the partnership track, my firm offered me an opportunity to head our attorney recruitment department. It was to be temporary. Once in the position, however, I saw ways to improve my firm's efforts to recruit, hire, and retain attorneys of difference. From the vantage point of being a law firm manager, I learned how large law firms really work, how important decisions are made, and how to get things done. Through observing our recruitment and retention successes and failures, I developed a solid understanding and expertise in the area of coaching a law firm to hire, retain, and promote a diverse attorney workforce.

I never returned to the practice of law. Today, I am the Director of Diversity and Professional Development at my firm. As a part of my responsibilities, I am an "Executive Diversity Coach." That means that I am hired by other law firm leaders and by the executives of our business clients to coach them on how to begin thinking about issues of diversity all the way through to the successful retention of a diverse attorney workforce. No other position quite like this exists. I am creating it! Amazingly, I have found another way to seek justice and to work toward racial harmony.

My advice to you: Do not fear either the unconventional path or the detours. Sometimes it is the unconventional path and the detours that take us to where we belong. Keep dreaming dear Sisters, dear Daughters.

Susani N. H. Dixon

Susani N. H. Dixon *is Director of Diversity and Professional Development at Holland & Hart in Denver.*

Dear Sisters, Dear Daughters,

The first figure of authority who told me what society expected of me was a woman named Sister Julia, the Vice-Principal of my high school—a woman who would not write me a letter of recommendation to Harvard College because Harvard did not want "people like me." I did not understand why an institution such as Harvard would not want bright students, eager to learn and looking to be challenged. So, I sent my application anyway, and four years later, I sent Sister Julia an invitation to my graduation from Harvard College.

I share this story with you: (1) because the road to success and fulfillment for a multicultural woman attorney is paved with Sister Julias; and (2) because there are lessons to be learned from the women who have walked that path before you. I believe it is important for you to understand that the women "who have been there and done that" have experienced a few bumps in the road along the way.

Lesson Number One: Believe in Yourself and Be Comfortable with Who You Are. Maintain your confidence, your sense of self, and your motivation to keep working towards your goal-- even when the world around you doubts you. As a woman of color, the world around you may indeed question your talent, your motivation, and your commitment from time to time, but that should serve as a reminder of how important it is for you as a woman of color to hold your head up high and reach each of your goals. If you do not believe in yourself and are not comfortable with who you are, why should anyone else believe in you or be comfortable with you?

Lesson Number Two: Cross the Finish Line. Everytime I set a new goal, I like to view my successful attainment of that goal as I would view crossing the finish line at the end of a long, hard race. Ultimately, it does not matter: (1) how long it takes me; (2) whether I go over, or under, or around obstacles; or (3) whether or not I stop for a rest along the way. As long as I do not give up or quit, I will eventually cross that finish line. A legal career can be a demanding and grueling career, but it can also be an enlightening, rewarding, and fulfilling experience.

A successful legal career has two essential ingredients: (1) finding an environment where you like the legal work you are doing and, equally as important, if not more so; (2) finding a job where you like and respect the people with whom you will be working. I have found that lawyers or other professionals who settle for only one of these two criteria eventually get bored or frustrated and leave their jobs. Do not settle for only one of these two criteria; demand both.

Lesson Number Three: Cross-Gender and Cross-Racial Mentoring are Necessary. As the only hispanic female partner in a large, majority law firm, I can assure you that while there may be a great deal of "people like me," there certainly are not very many "people who look like me." As such, it was important for me, and will be important for you to identify cross-gender and cross-racial mentors. Two of my favorite mentors look nothing like me—or each other, for that matter. One was a left-leaning, internationally prominent African American male lawyer and lobbyist in his 50s, and the other is an ultra-conservative, right-wing white male corporate lawyer, respected by his peers nationally as a lawyer's lawyer. Both of these men have shaped my development as a lawyer, and I likely would not be the lawyer I am today without their influences. Please note that had I waited around to be mentored by somebody that looked just like me, I would still be waiting for that mentor. I believe a collection of mentors serves the same purpose and may even be a better option due to the variety of perspectives and backgrounds available to you as a resource. Mentors can serve different purposes, work in different locations and look nothing like you. Do not underestimate the value of a good mentor or mentors and realize that they all do not have to look like you .

Lesson Number Four: Dare to Dream. The last bit of advice I can offer you relates to your overall attitude and personal philosophy for success. As for overall attitude, always maintain a positive mental attitude. Never waste your valuable time and efforts creating your own, or perpetuating someone else's, negative energy. And, lastly, do not be afraid to work towards a goal that seems a little far-fetched—something no woman of color has done before. For if we do not strive to keep reaching new heights, we will never advance the status of women of color in the legal profession.

I hope you find the above lessons useful as you begin your walk down that path. Remember: Believe in yourself; Strive towards your goal; Learn from those around you; and most importantly, Dare to Dream! Good luck and much success!

(P.S. Do not forget to hold the door open for those women who will follow in your footsteps!)

Clarissa Cerda

Clarissa Cerda *is Vice President and General Counsel for Open Port Technologies, Inc. in Chicago and the former Assistant Counsel to the President of the United States in the White House.*

Dear Sisters, Dear Daughters,

When I think about where I am in life and how I got here, I realize that I am not where I had planned to be (and I did have a
plan), but I am happy and probably a better person for it. My
husband of almost 20 years and two teenagers are constant
reminders of what is really important in my life. I have learned
to be grateful for and to enjoy each day as it comes and not to
dwell on my past mistakes and the disappointments I have
encountered. I have also learned not to let the prejudices and
ignorance of others stand as obstacles to my goals. The keys to
my personal happiness and professional development are in
the words "flexibility" and "faith." Many of the choices I made
over the last 20 plus years (law school, law practice, marriage,
children) depended on my willingness to compromise or to follow a slightly different course and my having faith that the alternate course that I pursued offered just as much, if not more,
than my original plan.

For example, I started college intent on becoming an elementary school teacher or counselor working with children. After
three months of student teaching when Boston implemented its
infamous busing plan, I had a change of heart. I decided that
law school could also offer me an opportunity to work with
kids, perhaps as a public defender in the juvenile justice system.
Needless to say, after three years of law school I had another
change of heart. I graduated law school intent on becoming a
criminal prosecutor in the (Chicago) Cook County State's
Attorney's Office. I accepted a position in the Criminal Appeals
Division of the office. Was I working with children? No. Was I

prosecuting? Not in the traditional sense. Was I happy? Yes. My willingness to consider an alternative to my original plan provided me with a wonderful professional experience. The research, writing, and oral advocacy skills I developed in this position have served me well throughout my professional life.

This same willingness to make certain adjustments in my personal life led to my next job and getting married sooner than I anticipated.

In 1980, my husband (my fiancé at the time) was working in Boston where we decided that we would live. (Again, I was being flexible here: five years before, I had determined that I was not going back to Boston after college.) I started interviewing for jobs in February. Our plan was to get married in May, with the hope that I would find employment by the fall. Wrong again. I received the perfect job offer with an administrative state agency with a starting date in April. I would be able to continue the same type of work I did as an Assistant State's Attorney. Of course, the September wedding we had so carefully planned was now in jeopardy, but after consulting with family and friends, we changed the date. In April, we had a small wedding ceremony in the minister's chambers in Boston and in August, we had a grand affair in Chicago. This satisfied everybody; my bridesmaids got to wear their dresses and our parents and my family minister participated in the church wedding that had been planned.

I have not always been so ready to consider the alternative or to trust in my faith. I have also faced adversity on the job. At one point in my life, about six or seven years ago, while working in the private sector, I decided that I was not really happy in my job. I did not know what I wanted to do, but the thought of working in state government again intrigued me. Some of my colleagues, however, noted that public sector employment was not the way to find fame and fortune. Shortly after this soul-searching event, I received an unsolicited job offer from a government agency that I turned down. It was an excellent position, but the "money was not right." It was the one of the few times in my life that I would not compromise on my position and, furthermore, I did not believe that my family could sustain a reduction in my salary. About a year later, I was part of the downsizing effort of my employer and the government job I had rejected suddenly looked very good. My inflexibility and lack of faith in this instance taught me a lesson on being true to myself. In my heart, I knew that I should have taken the government job, but I did not view it as an opportunity.

Fast-forwarding to the present, there are times when having a plan for any given situation does not always mean that matters will go my way, but maintaining my flexibility and my faith usually put me in a good position to pursue my interests. You have to believe that things happen for a reason and look at every disappointment as an opportunity to take another path to the same goal. In fact, the expertise on ethical issues that I gained from my first job in Boston is exactly what I needed to qualify for my current position: Legal Counsel to the Massachusetts Attorney General. Who could have guessed where my flexibility and faith would lead to?

The closing remarks of a speaker at an event I attended a few years ago have stayed with me and I want to leave them with you: Yesterday is history, Tomorrow, a mystery. But today is a gift from God. That's why it is called the present.

Do not harbor regrets, but learn from your missteps. Stay focused and keep moving forward even if you have to take a detour along the way and you will accomplish all that you set out to do.

Pamela M. Dashiell

Pamela Moran Dashiell *serves as Legal Counsel to the Attorney General of the Commonwealth of Massachusetts.*

Dear Sisters, Dear Daughters,

You shouldn't have to do it alone, but you should be tough enough to do it if you have to. The unfortunate reality of my generation still holds true for today's women of color in the legal world, but it ought not be your deterrent. There will not be an abundance of women of color mentors readily available to you in your law school or law firm. Legal mentors in my generation were even fewer and farther between. But I cannot relate enough the significance of mentors in your lives. It is their experience that will provide you with a foundation for your own career, as their support will inspire you to maintain that energy for your convictions. In my life, I learned from several important individuals, but my parents were my career's first mentors. Even though they were not in the legal field—and were actually farmworkers who worked in fields—I could not ask for better mentors than them.

My parents taught me high standards. By this I mean that my siblings and I had to do well in our studies even though we had to work after school and then do homework. We had to be presentable even though we were poor and without expensive things. When I became the head of legal organizations, I maintained the high standards for myself that my parents had taught me and showed my employees, by way of example, what I wanted from them. One of the most difficult decisions I ever made had to do with firing many committed staff members in my first managerial position. My philosophy remains that even poor non-profits must provide the same quality of service as any other legal firm. In such a way, I will ensure that the campesino who walks into my non-profit will receive the same quality of representation offered by any law firm in Beverly Hills or the Upper East Side. This is critical if we are to truly assist the community we seek to defend.

I thank my parents for this standard of excellence, a combination of the best competence with the best commitment, that inevitably wins my cases.

For today's generation of minority female lawyers, mentors are as necessary as ever. You need mentors because they will become your career's biggest advocates. When I was at UCLA Law School, there were not any minority female faculty to benefit from. In my perseverance to find supporters in the administration, I did establish wonderful relationships with professors and fellow students who were empathetic to my issues. They would become my mentors and were the ones I eventually asked for recommendations and legal career advice. They also became great friends: people who taught me how to balance my life and not base my entire identity around being a lawyer; how to make up for the experience I lacked when I lacked it, and how not to regret my everyday choices. These relationships grew into strong support networks for us. From my parents, I found mentors; from my mentors, I have my friends; and from my friends I have the biggest supporters of the issues closest to my heart, like civil rights.

Being competent and committed will get you to many doors, but having people on your side will finally get them open.

Antonia Hernández

Antonia Hernandez *is President and General Counsel of the Mexican American Legal Defense and Educational Fund in Los Angeles.*

Dear Sisters, Dear Daughters,

As I write this letter, I am in mourning for the death of my grandmother, Mrs. Reffer Lillie, who died a month ago, at the age of 89 in Houston, Texas. She had truly "been there and done that," and she often shared pearls of wisdom that I have found useful in charting a successful career in the law.

My grandmother often spoke to me about the perils of "starting something that I could not finish," and she reminded me "to count my blessings, to be gracious, and to be grateful for every door that closes, because another one was sure to open."

And so it has been. I attended a *de jure* segregated elementary school in Houston, Texas, and received an education from teachers who were unparalleled in terms of their knowledge, skill, and determination to educate the first generation of children in Texas who would live in an integrated world. In addition to my parents, who were talented artists (my father, a musician and teacher, and my mother, a theatrical producer, actress, and teacher), my earliest role model was a young attorney named Barbara Jordan, who was a family friend, and a rising star in the legal and political worlds.

I will never forget my third grade teacher at Turner Elementary who smiled gently when I told her that I wanted to be a lawyer like Barbara Jordan when I grew up. She told me that Barbara was "different" and that girls were supposed to be teachers, like my mother, and that was what I should do. Thankfully, my parents never placed any limitations on the dreams that my sister and I had, and that is my first piece of advice for you.

Define your own vision of success, and do not let anyone or anything stand in your way. Seek out mentors and get all of the advice that you can, but never, ever adopt someone else's vision of what success in the law and in life will be for you.

As my grandmother would tell you, don't start something that you can't finish. If you are going to be successful, you will have to take some risks. But it is so important to keep your perspective and to try to have some balance in your life. So if you plan to start 12 projects and the result is that you can only finish seven of them in a less than exemplary fashion, you really may want to consider starting and finishing five projects, which can be completed on time and in an exemplary manner.

Each of my jobs as a government lawyer taught me important lessons about life, the law, and the power of the individual to effect change. As a young lawyer in the U.S. Department of Justice Civil Rights Division, I was involved in at least two significant pieces of Voting Rights Act litigation that were basically initiated by citizen letters, written to the Civil Rights Division about perceived inequities in the results of elections in two southern states. As an individual, you have the power to effect change in your community, your law school, your law firm, your corporation, and your governmental agency.

Many people get frustrated when change is not sweeping, immediate, and instantaneous. My life in government taught me that change, even incremental change, is good and valuable and is contributory. So learn to be patient, but not too patient, as you seek to make your mark on the world.

I was trained by experienced and highly trained lawyers who were dedicated to the Rule of Law. These lawyers had tremendous integrity and adhered to the highest standards of ethics and morality. I wish the same for you. And if you are not blessed to have early supervisors of such good quality, do not use their shortcomings as an excuse to slip into bad habits.

Remove yourself from their sphere of influence at the earliest possible time in your career.

Despite everything that you read about lawyers leaving the profession in droves there are a number of us who love what we do. I love the challenge of assembling the pieces of a defense of a case. I love learning about the ins and outs of a new client's business, and understanding how the business has an impact on the facts of the case. I love going to court and arguing and advocating after I have massaged a brief and learned the law of the case. I love handling and supervising my pro bono cases and hearing the satisfaction of a client who tells me tearfully that no one has ever stood up for him like that before. I love supervising associates who are handling pro bono cases, who learn how the law can really work for a person who has never been properly represented in a legal dispute and who realize the value of public service and giving back to the community. Even after a week like the one that I just had, with billable hours to spare, sleep deprivation and nothing that could possibly pass for balance in my life, I can tell you that I love the law, and I am grateful that I am a member of the profession.

I urge you to squeeze every ounce of value from the law degree that you have received. Work hard and play hard. Give something back to your community. Be a mentor to a lawyer with less experience than you in your firm or institution. Give this profession a chance. The rewards are many.

I wish you prosperity, peace, joy, and fulfillment.

Charisse R. Lillie

Charisse R. Lillie *is a Partner in the law firm of Ballard Spahr Andrews & Ingersoll, LLP, in Philadelphia where she is a member of the Employment and Labor Law Group of the litigation department.*

Dear Sisters, Dear Daughters,

What does some one say to a group of young, enthusiastic lawyers, just starting their careers? The initial response by the jaded might be "nothing." Don't spoil it for them, let them hold on to the "dream" as long as possible. But when we sit back and think—what is clear is that everyone's dream is not the same, so there is always something to share.

Professionally, the most important piece of advice that I can offer you is to remember that the only person you are competing with is yourself. As lawyers, you are trained to look at the facts, so let's look at them. You were in the top 1 percent of the top 1 percent of the students in the world, and you have survived to become practitioners. So the first hurdle has already been met. The critical question of "Can you do this?" has been answered—and that answer is yes. (Of course, the question what is "this" still has to be answered, but you'll find out soon enough, and you will find that it changes day to day, moment to moment.) So now that you know that, stop assessing yourself in terms of the other people around you and start remembering what you have known your entire life—you owe it to yourself to be the best that you can be. You do not owe it to the firm, the partners, the company, the clients—you owe it to yourself first. So when you wake up in the morning, and you get to the office, and you see the "less than sexy" stuff sitting on your desk that has to be done, remember that from the smallest task to the most critical, you give it its proper due and DO IT WELL! If, at the end of every day, as you evaluate what didn't get done, and what has to be done tomorrow, you know that you gave the very best you had to give, there is nothing more you can ask of yourself. Therefore, there is nothing more anyone else can ask of you. If you remain true to yourself and honest, your integrity will be unquestionable.

Second, cherish the relationships you develop with people along the way. There is a philosophy in the workforce that you can't have "friends" at work. I won't debate that point here. But what I will say is that I know there have been times in my practice where I have questioned my decisions—careerwise and casewise—and there are other lawyers, now friends, whom I look to for a reality check! They understand, listen, offer guidance, or just an ear, which I trust, because over time they have shown that they have my best interest at heart. We may not always be lucky enough to find a mentor—if you do grab the coattails, and hang on for the most valuable ride of your life—if you don't, remember that we can and do mentor each other. I look at my friends and classmates who graduated from law school with me, took the bar with me, or have crossed my path, both personally and professionally, and I am humbled by their successes and greatness. I marvel at all we have been able to do. I gain encouragement from their achievements and strive to continue to be better myself. And I look to them for support.

You owe it to yourself to be the best that you can be.

Third, remember that you never know so much that you cannot continue to learn. In the beginning, you should view yourself as a dry sponge, looking to soak up all the practical knowledge and wisdom that people want to share with you. This also means, never be afraid to ask a question – the only person who will regret it if you don't is you! As you become more seasoned in your practice and learn the ins and outs, remember that seeing the "same old thing" in a different light, through someone else's eyes, may add a new and helpful perspective.

Remember that you are not perfect; you will make mistakes. Own them, learn from them, and move on.

Lastly, I would like to offer some personal advice. What makes each of us good at what we do is the different perspective we bring to our work because of the incredibly diverse lives we lead. Therefore, don't forsake your life for your practice. Listen to that inner voice. If it says, "I need time, space, sleep, vacation. . ." don't wait too long before you answer it. Practicing law is what you do, not who you are. Remember where you came from, and give back whenever you can. I am Barbara's daughter, Ethel's granddaughter, Christopher and Crisandra's sister, Sandra and Chris's aunt, Alpha, Dotti, Carolyn, Sharon, and Lisa's friend. And for that, I am truly most proud and grateful!

Good Luck, enjoy, be happy and God bless.

Crystal Ashby

Crystal Elizabeth Ashby *is In-house Counsel for BP Amoco in Chicago.*

Dear Sisters, Dear Daughters,

Sitting down to write this, I'm asking myself what I can possibly tell you to affect your career success. What I'll do is tell you the things that made a difference for me. First, let me warn you—I spent 14 of my 17 years as a lawyer practicing in the same large law firm in Chicago. I only left the firm 18 months ago to join Ford Motor Company. While I hope that much of what I have to say will be relevant to any lawyer, I know that my advice is necessarily colored, and somewhat limited, by that experience. And, like everybody else, I'm still learning. As you read, you should begin to see that all of the points are interrelated in a very real sense.

TOP TEN THINGS I WISH SOMEONE HAD TOLD ME ABOUT THE PRACTICE OF LAW

10. PRACTICE DOES NOT MAKE PERFECT
There is always something to learn, and sometimes we learn through our mistakes, or if we're really lucky, we learn through observing the mistakes others make. And others DO make mistakes. One of the greatest burdens we can put on ourselves is the burden of attempting to be perfect. Even worse is believing that we are the only person to ever make a mistake, or that we're the first person to make a particular mistake, or that any mistake we make should be a career-shattering event.

When I was in my fourth or fifth year at the firm, the head of the litigation practice of the world's largest law firm told me what he considered to be the major key to success in the practice. For any young lawyer to be truly successful (translation: to make partner in a large firm), the lawyer must have the opportunity to make a mistake (fall on her butt, as he put it), suffer the consequences (be kicked in the butt), and be given a chance to recover and move on to the next level. According to this partner, who was refreshingly honest with me, one of the obstacles facing us as women and minorities in large firms is that often supervising partners, who are largely white males, are afraid to go through this developmental process with us. They are afraid of the implications or consequences of "reading us the riot act." As a result, instead of offering that crucial constructive criticism and guidance, the supervisor may be tempted to avoid the confrontation and avoid working with the minority lawyer altogether.

I was always fortunate to work for partners who would give me the criticism I needed, yet recognize that my mistakes were like anyone else's: a part of the development process that any successful lawyer must endure. This is the true definition of the level playing field. You must have the opportunity to take your lumps like everybody else. Otherwise, you can be "protected" into career oblivion. If you believe you are not being treated on an equal basis with your peers in terms of both praise and punishment you may have to initiate this conversation with your supervisor. Don't hesitate to do it.

9. YOU ALONE ARE RESPONSIBLE FOR YOUR CAREER DIRECTION

Early in my career, I made the mistake of believing that "The Firm" was some benevolent, omnipotent organism that worked behind the scenes to guide my career development, make sure that my workload was manageable, and assure that I would be treated fairly in assignments and evaluations. That was not the case, and I learned some important lessons from my mistaken belief. Managing your career development is a job unto itself. You must at all times be aware of what the firm's expectations are, what your immediate supervisor expects, and what you and others are doing to meet those expectations. This is an ongoing responsibility. I can't tell you how many times I had long, sobering talks with friends who had been blindsided by developments that they should have seen coming. If your firm requires 1900 billable hours, but everyone routinely bills 2100, you need to know that and plan accordingly. It's up to you to learn both the spoken and unspoken rules of the game.

8. NINETY NINE PERCENT OF THE TIME, IT'S NOT ABOUT ME
This one is crucial. Human beings have a tendency to believe the world revolves around them, both for better and for worse. It does not. Not for better, not for worse.

In my first year at the law firm, I completed an assignment for an important client, whom I had never met. A few weeks after the work was completed, the client wrote an unfavorable letter to a very powerful partner (whom I had never met), criticizing the work. I was devastated. I was sure that my career was over [see number 10 above], and I couldn't figure out what I had done to incur his wrath.

Upon reading the letter, my own supervising partner came to me and told me that this client was in the habit of writing a nasty letter every time he received a project from our firm. I learned that the evil client ran a subsidiary of a much larger firm client, and he had been trying for years to send legal business to another firm where his brother was a partner. My supervisor intervened with the powerful partner in charge of the client and explained that I was a very good young lawyer who had been thrust in the middle of an ongoing battle with this client. [see number 5 below]

Over the years, I faced many situations where something way beyond my control had a very real and palpable impact, both positive as well as negative, on my career progress. The true art is learning to tell whether a situation is of your own making or something much different.

7. SET CLEAR GOALS . . .
Studies over the years have shown that nine out of ten people do not set career goals, but of the 10 percent of people who do

set them, nine of ten achieve them. Try it. Even if I'm wrong, you'll be better off. At the beginning of each year, I write a personal business plan setting forth my goals for the year. As an associate, to assure that I had a buy-in from my supervisor, I shared that plan with him. During the year, I made sure that I documented all of my accomplishments.

A written plan, no matter how simple, is a powerful tool. Check your progress often. Don't be caught in the ninth month trying to do a year's worth of development in the fourth quarter.

6. . . . BUT BE FLEXIBLE
Once I started to get the hang of the planning process, I quickly learned that, while the planning may occur in a vacuum, so to speak, life stands still for no one. I can truly say that I accomplished just about every goal I ever set, and believe me—some of them were really aggressive. In at least 75 percent of the cases, I had refined, or even redefined, the goal before I achieved it. I think my greatest breakthrough came about when I learned that continuous evaluation is practically its own reward.

5. NEVER UNDERESTIMATE THE IMPORTANCE OF A MENTOR
I believe that every truly successful person has had at least one mentor. I've had several. My thoughts on mentors:

Mentors can be the difference between glowing success and flaming disaster. A good mentor can help you to get out of trouble. An excellent mentor will keep you out of trouble in the first place. I was lucky enough to learn early on that mentoring is really a two-way street. It sounds unfair, but nobody wants to mentor a loser. On the other hand, don't losers need mentoring more than anybody else? Whatever the case may be, I think mentors instinctively hedge their bets; they look for a mentee (or "Tormentor," as I like to call them) who they believe will be successful.

How do you find a mentor? Sometimes you choose the mentor; sometimes the mentor chooses you. No matter how much you may feel this way, what you don't want to do is portray yourself as a "basket case," desperately in need of guidance. What a mentor is looking for is a winner, or at least a winner in the making. Be creative in your thinking about mentors. Don't limit yourself to the management of your firm or organization. Two of my most valued and truly valuable mentors are female partners at other large firms in Chicago. Each one of them became a mentor after I had received some press about some accomplishment or another. They didn't seek me out in my darkest hours, but they were there for me in the dark hours that followed. In addition to those two, I count among my mentors several of my former partners, a CEO of a publicly traded company, two executive recruiters, a federal judge, a retired law professor, and several insurance executives.

4. NOTHING BEATS A STRONG SUPPORT SYSTEM

This goes without saying. Everybody needs to have somebody in her corner. Now, I'm not just talking about mentors, but all of your means of support: family, friends, colleagues, clients, etc. The more you are surrounded by supportive folk, the better off you are. I'm not talking about people who will simply agree with you on everything and reinforce negative or destructive patterns that you may fall into from time to time. I mean true friends, who will offer encouragement and criticism at the appropriate times and in your best interest. [see number 10 above]

3. IT'S ALL ABOUT ME

This is not in contradiction to number 8. The well-worn cliché is well worn because it's true. You must be true to yourself. No job is worth sacrificing your values, your health, your family, or your sanity. You have to maintain some balance in your life [see numbers 2 and 1 below] or nothing will work for you. At the end of the day, you have to answer to your conscience, look at yourself in the mirror, and be able to say, "it's worth it to me," or "it's important to me," whatever "it" may be.

2. GET A LIFE !!!

One night in February of 1997, I was sideswiped by a speeding 18-wheeler on my way home from work. It was about 10:30

p.m. I had been working late because I was planning to leave in two days for a long-anticipated ski trip. Although my car was nearly totaled, miraculously, I escaped without a scratch. It was 1:30 a.m. by the time I made it home. And, true to the stoic characteristics that run through the women in my family, the stark reality of a brush with death did not hit me until about an hour later. When it hit, it hit hard.

For some unknown reason, I decided to rate my day on a 10-point scale. In a real sense, that could well have been my last day on earth, and I suddenly needed to know how I would rate my last day. After taking stock, I determined that the day had been a seven. Even though I was pretty shaken, I was tremendously relieved to think that I might have died that night, but I would have died a happy person, one who had had a good day, and who was looking forward to a well deserved week of fun.

What's the point?

The point is that on that night, I thanked God for all of my MANY blessings. I thanked Him for sparing my life, I refrained from beating myself up for being at work until 10:30 at night, and I declared that I would strive each and every day of my life to live at a level seven or above.

I've kept that promise.

My day today was an eight at least. At the very least.

1. NO, REALLY – GET A LIFE !!!
I mean it. Get a life. Good luck. And you go, girl!

Muzette Hill

Muzette Hill *is in the General Counsel's Office of Ford Motor Company and represents Ford on all emissions-related warranty issues.*

Path

The letters in this section pave a pathway
through the various sectors of the legal profession.
The women explain how they got from
point A to point B to point Z and then back to C.
Learn what it is like to counsel one of the
nation's busiest airports or how one can become
a federal administrative law judge.
Learn how some began as poverty lawyers
and ended up partners in large corporate firms.
Being open to opportunity, welcoming change, and exercising
flexibility are the traveling shoes worn by these authors.
This group of letters is called Path because they speak
of forging your own way even when that means
creating an opening where none existed.

"After one tax season of sorting through the bits of paper and receipts of someone else's life, I found that my practical plan had turned into a nightmare and I moved on to a new career . . ."
—**Vickie E. Turner**

"Have the faith and courage to follow your conscience, and your career will be blessed in unexpected ways."
—**Dorothy Roberts**

"If we aren't making mistakes from time to time, we are probably spending too much energy executing other people's ideas of the world at the worker bee level rather than thinking strategically at management levels. We must not be afraid to make the right mistakes."
—**Kathryn Kimura Misna**

Dear Sisters, Dear Daughters,

There is so much that I want to share with you that it is difficult to know where to begin. I want you to know that unlike many lawyers, I did not always dream of being a lawyer. In fact, it was not until my junior year at Wellesley College that I seriously started thinking about what I wanted to do after I graduated the following year. Four of my closest friends were all registering for the LSAT, and I asked one to pick up a package for me too. By surrounding myself with phenomenally focused women, I was inspired to pursue a legal career and have not regretted my choice at all. In fact I feel very blessed . . . I love being a lawyer, and my career has been on an upward momentum ever since.

For those of you who are in law school, don't believe the HYPE —"all lawyers must graduate in the top 10 percent and work at a large law firm in order to have a financially rewarding career!" You do not have to be in the top 10 percent of your class nor work for a law firm to have a financially and intellectually fulfilling career. Of course, you should strive to achieve academic excellence. That goes without saying. But where you work when you graduate is a very personal and important choice. From the experiences of my friends, large law firms allow you the luxury of paying off your student loans earlier and acquiring some fancy toys. Also, the client contacts may lead to future in-house employment, or the clients may follow you to any subsequent firm if you decide to leave your current firm. The "firm life" (billable hours, atmosphere, and grunt work) and dream of partnership, however, is not necessarily the goal of many lawyers today. I quickly learned this during my second-year summer when I split my time between two large firms.

Also, it is okay not to know exactly what type of law you want to practice—trust me. I never took a labor law or an employment law class. Yet, the majority of my career has been centered on employment litigation. There are numerous legal specialties (e.g., mergers and acquisitions, health care, corporate, real estate, government contracts) and the best way to find out what type of work lights your fire is during your law school summer employment and the jobs you embark on during your legal career.

Let's talk about the infamous job search for a minute. The legal job market has always been extremely competitive. But, you must have faith in yourself, your intellect, and legal skills to know that you will secure the right job. You have to have tenacity to persevere. I received my strength from my family, friends, and faith.

Let me backtrack for a moment. I had a very orderly approach in the beginning of my legal career. While in law school I focused on my grades and graduation. During my third year, I focused on securing employment with or without the help of my career office. After graduation I focused on passing the bar exam. What I am trying to say is don't put the cart before the horse. There is no need worrying whether you will find a job after graduation when you are in your first year of law school. Similarly, there is no need to worry if you will pass the bar exam before you graduate. Trust me—you will!

Now back to the job search. After my clerkship, I focused on the next job opportunity. I received an offer for a staff attorney position with the Connecticut Commission on Human Rights and Opportunities (CCHRO). The CCHRO was understaffed and had tons of cases. It was great. While I was there I focused on learning employment law, trial skills, and doing the best job I could for the clients we represented. In fact, my first administrative trial in my legal career received media coverage because it was against the Guardian Angels (private "law enforcement" group) who declined to allow women to join its Connecticut troops. Of course I was extremely nervous, but intense overpreparation allowed me to calm my nerves and helped guide me through my first trial. I learned a lot and was able to help people who had been grossly discriminated against on their jobs. If you want immediate trial work then you should attempt to find a job with an agency, federal government, or smaller law firm.

I always knew I wanted to live in Washington, D.C., so I began my job search by joining a predominantly African-American women's bar association to make connections. It was the best decision I have made in my legal career for numerous reasons. First, I was able to secure employment, via a job announcement attached to the bar association's monthly mailing *before* moving to D.C. Second, I made some great friendships with other female lawyers and judges. Third, through these friendships I was quickly able to navigate through D.C.'s legal establishment.

The most important advice I can give is that your reputation, legal acumen, and knowing how to get along with a diverse group of people are keys to your professional success. Also, don't let racism or sexism define you. Yes, racism and sexism exist, and will continue to exist, but you have to decide when to fight your battles and when to ignore the distractions to achieve your goals.

After my first legal job in the District, a Caucasian coworker and friend left to go to the FBI's Civil Litigation Unit. She knew that I had employment law litigation expertise and that the FBI was hiring attorneys in its Employment Litigation Law Unit. The lesson: your coworkers may lead you to new job opportunities.

My ultimate goal was to work in-house in the private sector. I shared my goal with a bar association colleague who was at a firm (she is now a partner!). Needless to say we shared our ideas and goals and have helped each other during our careers. She was the person who informed me of the opening at my present job (Children's Hospital). Through this job I have been able to gain significant labor and healthcare law experiences. I am deliriously happy! Of course, I have hired her and her firm to handle some of our employment litigation cases. Similarly, I have declined to use attorneys who were rather snooty toward government attorneys, or firms that were less than gracious to other minorities or me in their hiring and recruitment. So remember—be nice to your colleagues, opposing counsel, and others in the legal community because you never know who knows who or who you may need a favor from in the future. You must help others as they strive for new opportunities and you should acknowledge when you have been helped along the way.

I hope you will seek to find a mentor on your job who can help you strategize for your future career growth. If you can't find a mentor on your job, then ask a colleague from a similar institution, or a contact from a bar association. Strive to stay abreast in your area of legal expertise by attending relevant conferences. These conferences are great networking opportunities. In these days and times, it is not unusual for you to make four to six significant career moves to obtain the utmost career satisfaction. Also look for upward mobility within your organization. Last, do not feel that you are alone. There is always someone who has been in your position or who is currently dealing with the same issues you are faced with everyday. Women of color must continue to dialogue with one another to learn from each other, draw on our collective strengths, and strategize for the year 2000 and beyond. I wish you the best of luck.

Truly yours,

Elicia Pegues Spearman

Elicia Pegues Spearman *is the Associate Counsel at the Children's National Medical Center and represents management in labor and employment litigation matters.*

Dear Sisters, Dear Daughters,

Being asked to write this letter has provided me a wonderful opportunity to take stock of the past quarter century of my life and reflect on my career in the law. To begin, let me *cut to the chase* and provide the punch line: given the opportunity of turning back the clock, I'd do everything all over again with few, if any, changes.

I pretty much stumbled into law as a career. In my senior year of college, I began to have misgivings about my intention to teach math or history in some midwest high school. It wasn't for lack of interest in teaching or the subject matter. I had a visceral fear that if I stayed in the midwest and taught school, I would never experience some wider world that existed beyond the fairly parochial borders of my life to date. But without teaching as a goal, I felt rudderless. It had never occurred to me that I might pursue a career in anything other than the traditional careers for women of teaching or nursing, and I had no mentors or role models to point me in another direction. I was, after all, the first woman in my extended family to attain a bachelor's degree, and I knew no women in the professions.

Purely by serendipity, I landed my first legal job as a corporate paralegal for Pepper, Hamilton & Scheetz, a large law firm in Philadelphia. The year was 1973. I loved my work and thought I had a pretty wonderful life, paying my own way in a big city on a salary that after a few years reached the magical five- figure mark of $10,000. I was a very good paralegal, completely dedicated to my job and a quality work product, yet had no higher aspirations. I simply couldn't visualize myself in the attorney's seat. Fortunately, I had a few mentors who thought otherwise, and to them I am deeply indebted. One, Cary Levinson, is to this day a good friend. The other, John McLamb, died far too young of ALS or Lou Gehrig's Disease, as it is known, but the things I learned from him had staying power. They double-teamed me to provide the not so gentle push that I needed and were a source of encouragement and motivation while I was in law school.

Cary and John had a profound influence on me, which brings me to my first major piece of advice: pursue relationships with mentors and be open to finding them in unexpected packages. Many women of color assume that a mentor has to look like them. Were that true, my colleagues in this book and I would have been doomed, because so few women of color preceded us in the law. My mentors—Cary and John and several who followed them—happened to be white men with whom I clicked and who formed their first impressions of me based not on my gender or race, but on the quality of my work.

I, in turn, have mentored many law students and young professionals. Few have been Asian American women like me, which has not been for lack of interest on my part. It has more to do with people who have gravitated toward my areas of practice and with whom I've clicked, which is to say that good chemistry is critical. Perhaps because of my specialties in corporate finance and securities law, many of my protegees have been white men. Still others have been white women, and a current protegee is Sidney Smith, an African American male law student with whom I correspond by e-mail. In every instance we have enjoyed a special relationship that cannot be forced, which is why I am dubious of formal mentoring programs in which mentors and protegees are assigned to each other.

I suppose I should tell you what I've been doing since attaining my J.D. in 1979. I've had a number of really great jobs and have done just about everything that one can do with a law degree except sit on the bench. Immediately out of law school I served as law clerk to Justice Stanley Mosk of the Supreme Court of California, and can't say enough for this experience. From there I went to O'Melveny & Myers, a large corporate firm where I was a member of the corporate department. There, I learned to represent clients in complex business and financing transactions and worked with people who had the highest ethical and quality standards. It took me awhile to learn that not all attorneys embrace these standards, and I feel fortunate that they were instilled in me from the very beginning.

After five years of private practice, I suffered the burnout that is not uncommon among large firm associates. A conversation with the dean of my alma mater while I was on campus interviewing students led to my becoming a law professor, teaching Contracts, Corporations, Banking, and Advanced Corporate Problems. Leaving private practice was a frightening prospect, yet at the time I thought it a matter of survival. I loved the work but not the extreme sacrifices it required, and I couldn't imagine my life always being that way.

My years in academia were both rewarding and frustrating. Fundamentally, I loved teaching and the many opportunities it afforded to provide professional and community service in a meaningful way. But I also felt cloistered and missed the highs of representing clients and doing deals. That, coupled with my distaste for academic politics, ultimately led to my departure. I survived the promotion and tenure process, then took a two-year leave of absence to work in the new administration for the city of Philadelphia.

Mayor Ed Rendell had just been elected and had appointed Judith Harris as his City Solicitor, which is the chief legal officer for the city. Judy recruited me as Chair of the Corporate Group and, together with her Chief Deputy and the Chair of the Litigation Group, we administered the City Law Department. It was exhilarating to be practicing law again, and I also enjoyed the challenges of managing and supervising. A unique aspect of my job was working for Judy, a brilliant attorney who happened to be an African American woman. This was a completely new experience for me and, in ways I can't really put to words, it was different in a very positive way. Maybe it's because we felt more comfortable with each other or weren't worried about saying or doing the right or wrong thing. Or maybe it's because it was just so wonderfully empowering.

With about half a year remaining in my leave of absence from the faculty, the opportunity to work for my current employer came along. Well, it didn't just come along. My former mentor, Cary, represented a company in need of a corporate secretary and identified me as a candidate for the opening. The company was Bowater Incorporated, and the job was at corporate headquarters in Greenville, South Carolina. This was a rather dramatic move for someone who had spent her professional years in San Francisco, Los Angeles, New York, and Philadelphia.

Today I am Vice President, Secretary, and Assistant General Counsel of Bowater, which is a New York Stock Exchange listed company and a global producer of newsprint and other forest products. Professionally, I'm doing what I've always loved, which is to practice corporate and securities law in a high-quality environment and to serve on the boards of nonprofit agencies about whose work I am passionate. Ironically, I am now as acutely aware of my status as a woman of color as I have ever been because I am the only female and minority in the senior management group of the company. After years of taking diversity somewhat for granted, I felt unexpected qualms on certain occasions. Now, after six and a half years, I generally enjoy a mutual comfort level with my male colleagues that serves me well in doing my job effectively. But I'd be less than honest in not revealing that at times I feel invisible or alienated, which has led to sadness or anger. Fortunately, for the most part I feel like "one of the guys," with a shared mission of getting a particular job done and doing it well. I would like to believe that I can be an agent for change in the company, though it is not my primary agenda because it's been my observation that women and people of color with agendas so often aren't heard. I think you have to lead by example and pick your battles wisely.

The evolution of my career from job to job provides the basis for a central theme of my career advice to students and young professionals, which is always to be open to new opportunities and to embrace change as an energizing force. I used to think that one graduated from law school, joined a firm, became partner and worked until retirement. What a life I'd have missed for not pursuing the alternatives. My career has been very much a building block process with each of my earlier positions contributing to the foundation of knowledge and experience that equip me to do the job I hold today.

Beyond my philosophy that change is good, the prescription I offer as you enter the profession is to pursue excellence in all that you do, always take the high road and never, ever burn a bridge. I should add that it helps a good deal if you can maintain a sense of humor. I could give you countless examples of how these practices have served me well, and I hope never to abandon them. Because after all, an attorney's professional reputation is her most cherished asset.

During my career I've been heartened to see ever-increasing opportunities for women of color in all facets of the legal profession. The outlook for your future is bright, and I wish you strength, success, and fulfillment, both personal and professional.

My very best wishes,

Wendy Shiba

Wendy C. Shiba *is Vice President, Secretary and Assistant General Counsel of Bowater Inc. in Greenville, South Carolina.*

Dear Sisters, Dear Daughters,

My father, Edgard Armando Rosales, was a passionate man who firmly believed the United States was the land of opportunity. Although he only had a sixth-grade education in his native country, Nicaragua, and spoke little English, he sensed his daughters could be very successful in the U.S. with a strong formal education. "I did not come to this country to work like an animal so that my daughters would end up stupid like me," he would often say (in Spanish). My father has been the driving force behind my decision to be an attorney, my interest to be well established in my career, and my continuing desire to advance towards professional excellence.

When he died unexpectedly at the age of 39, leaving my mother a young widow with five girls, I learned a valuable lesson at the tender age of 13: a woman cannot depend on a man for her financial security. It is against this family background that I became the first attorney in my large extended family.

When I began my studies at Hastings College of Law in San Francisco in 1979, I believed, perhaps naively, that hard work was the only ingredient to a successful law experience. After graduation, I discovered that hard, exemplary work is a necessary component for success, but other factors such as luck, good contacts, solid interpersonal skills, and some risk taking are also important.

I started my law path as a research attorney for the California Supreme Court. My duties consisted of reviewing approximately

100 criminal petitions for hearing (e.g., murder, rape, and robbery cases) and making recommendations to the Supreme Court as to the disposition of the cases. Good work and contacts helped me land that job. It was a wonderful experience. I learned about the inner process of the appellate system, which has assisted me tremendously in my appellate practice. It was through this experience that I knew criminal law was not the practice area in which I wanted to specialize. That realization caused me to turn to public law practice, my current field.

For the past 16 years, I have been a Deputy City Attorney for the city and county of San Francisco. I have handled more than 200 trial court matters, and have been the attorney of record in approximately 15 published appellate decisions. Three of these cases were decided by the California Supreme Court. I have also had the privilege of serving as Assigned Legal Counsel to several San Francisco City departments: the Recreation and Parks Commission (1983–92), the Human Rights Commission (1983–89), the Police Commission (1989–92) and presently, the Airport Commission (1992–present). All of these assignments have allowed me to face intellectually stimulating legal issues of public importance in the areas of affirmative action, free speech, municipal law, aviation/airport law, and employment law, to name a few.

I believed, perhaps naively, that hard work was the only ingredient to a successful law experience.

Notwithstanding all of my litigation-related victories, I must say that my greatest challenge as an attorney has been serving as General Counsel of San Francisco International Airport, the nation's fifth busiest airport. I accepted the promotional at the age of 37. At the time, I had practiced law for 10 years but had no management-level or aviation-related experience.

As General Counsel of a public entity, which operates both as a small city and highly successful business enterprise, I am ultimately responsible for all of the airport's legal matters. I was able to gain the confidence of very demanding airport managers and policymakers through, again, hard work, self-confidence, effective interpersonal skills, common sense, luck and a solid legal team of attorneys and support staff. Today, after almost seven and a half years, my team and I (including a roster of highly qualified outside counsel) are at the forefront of every legal issue and every significant business/policy matter that concerns San Francisco International Airport.

This *Dear Sisters, Dear Daughters* project has allowed me to reflect on the people, beyond my family, who have been instrumental in my rewarding law journey. Interestingly, the three main advisors I had along the way have all been nonminority, older men. Each tendered his unsolicited advice and guidance with no ulterior motive other than to help me succeed in my career. To each I owe much gratitude, and they remain my friends today.

What is my best advice to fellow women attorneys, especially women attorneys of color? First, listen to your heart regarding what area of the law most interests you. Then get a job in that field. That decision will make you a happier lawyer. Second, find a mentor and consult with him or her often. Third, work hard and take chances with new opportunities. Fourth, maintain good contacts by dealing with others fairly and openly, whether they are clients or colleagues. Fifth, don't take yourself or your power too seriously.

If good things can happen to me, a San Francisco Mission District Latina girl who started out clueless in the legal profession, good things can happen to you too!

Mara E. Rosales

Mara E. Rosales *is General Counsel for the San Francisco Airport Commission and the Director who manages the San Francisco International Airport.*

Dear Sisters, Dear Daughters,

My mother inspired me to pursue the practice of law. She showed me, by example, that I could be anything I wanted to be despite the adversities in life.

As a child I remember being asked what I wanted to be when I grew up. In my youthful innocence I responded I wanted to be the president. Even when I tried to change my answer to something I believed was more attainable, my dad jumped in and stated I could be president if I wanted to be. At an early age, my parents had instilled in their children that they could achieve anything they wanted. I am the middle child of an older sister, brother, and two younger sisters.

On a family road trip home from Ohio, I asked my mother the name of the university we were passing on the highway. She told me it was Purdue University and she would be proud of me if I attended that school. I graduated from high school on a three-year program and began attending Purdue University in West Lafayette, Indiana, the summer before freshman year began, it was the only college I'd applied to. My high school guidance counsel tried to persuade me not to graduate early. He also advised me I would be better off attending a trade school, rather than college. They should have dropped the "guidance" from his title.

Taking advantage of opportunities helped me reach my educational goals. Purdue University offered me the opportunity to attend college prior to freshman semester; I took advantage of

79

it. Once in college, I became determined to graduate. I knew I could not leave without graduating. In May 1980, I graduated from Purdue University with a bachelor's of arts degree in psychology. Being president seemed farther away.

Back at home, with a degree in psychology, I was still not clear as to what direction my life would take. I watched night after night as my mother spent countless hours studying her law school material at the dining room table. She encouraged me to apply for law school and the Council on Legal Education Opportunities (CLEO). As I waited for my acceptance, I asked her many times if she thought I was capable of getting into law school and completing the program. Each time she replied I was certainly capable and would surely complete the program if I studied as I had seen her study for so many nights. I received my acceptance into CLEO, and from there, I was offered the opportunity to study law at the University of Missouri in Columbia, Missouri.

I had been on a waiting list for CLEO and didn't believe I would be accepted once the first day of the summer program came and went. I was at work when I received the call. On the second day of the program I was told I could join the program if I reported to the University of Iowa School of Law that evening. My family immediately telephoned me at work. When I spoke to my employer about having to leave because of this opportunity, I remember the boss asking me whether I really wanted to leave a job making as much money as I made to join a profession that was "already saturated." I replied, "Yes." With the assistance of my father, I packed my little car and arrived in Iowa City, Iowa, that evening.

CLEO was instrumental in preparing me for the vigorous study of law that was still to come. Nothing, however, could prepare me for one of the biggest losses of my life. During my second year of law school, I lost my brother in a car accident. While back at home with my family attending the funeral, I considered ending my law school tenure. I did not want to return. It was my mother who instructed me to go back and finish. She reminded me how important it is for us to finish what we start.

I have been a public servant my entire legal profession. After graduating from law school on May 6, 1988, I began employment with the Attorney Registration and Disciplinary Commission as I studied for the bar exam. I was fortunate to pass the bar exam on the first sitting. After approximately two years, I began working for the Illinois Department of Human Rights. Being a public servant can be very rewarding. You can take great pride at the end of the day knowing you have been able to help so many people. Additionally, it gave me time to study for my masters of laws degree (LL.M.). After completing the program in two years, I graduated from IIT Chicago-Kent College of Law with an LL.M. in financial services law. Later, the opportunity for me to become an adjunct professor at Chicago-Kent College of Law became available and, once again, I took advantage. Today, I serve as legal counsel to the Cook County Recorder of Deeds. I saw it as an opportunity to continue serving the public while learning new things.

I hope to continue to strive for even higher goals. Everyday brings new opportunities and challenges. I've learned it's about being okay to just be you. I always keep trying to improve myself and keep God in my life. While I may never be President of the United States, I still believe there is an office somewhere out there with my name over the sign that says "President."

Sincerely,

Paula Bouldon

Paula K. Bouldon *is Counsel to the Recorder at the Cook County Recorder of Deeds in Chicago.*

Dear Sisters, Dear Daughters,

I was born in India and was raised partly in India, partly in Canada, and partly in the United States. Since my parents were among the first wave of East Indians to move to America, I did not grow up knowing any East Indian children who were older than me and living in the United States. Thanks to my parents, I led a relatively sheltered existence. I was expected to set a good example for my younger sister and for my parents' friends' East Indian children.

Ever since I was a toddler, I knew that I was going to be a doctor. I had many aunts, uncles, cousins and family friends who were physicians, or were in the process of becoming physicians. I don't recall being rebellious or arguing with my parents about anything significant in junior high or high school. All that changed in college. I graduated one year early with high honors from Harrison High School in Farmington Hills, Michigan, so that I could get a head start on college and medical school.

I didn't count on having so much fun in college, and I didn't count on the experience being so culturally different from the way I was raised. When I changed my major from Biology to Business to Engineering to General Studies, it created quite a stir in my family on both the North American and Asian continents. And as I dated throughout college and law school, it became the source of much conflict and heartache within my family. At that time, my parents believed that only "loose women" opted for the dating scene instead of a nice, arranged marriage. My relationship with my parents weathered some pretty rough times even as the realization dawned that there could remain a rift between us forever. There seemed to be no getting around the fact that our cultural values were becoming increasingly divergent.

At the conclusion of my senior year in law school, my parents had come to grips with the idea of me dating. By the time I began working as a lawyer in Chicago, they no longer cared whether I married an Indian, they just wanted me to get married! So we had made some progress. At age 26, when I married, my parents joyfully welcomed my husband into our family with open arms.

I have now been happily married for 12 years. Playing with my beautiful and intelligent three-year-old daughter, Kristen, rejuvenates me. While taking care of her is time-consuming, it is also extremely rewarding. Whenever I start getting bogged down in juggling my work, bar, political, and community activities, I pull out of my slump by doing something extra special with my little girl. I am fortunate that she is a bright child with an easy and outgoing nature.

While Kristen is in our church preschool during the work week, she often accompanies me to some of my evening activities. I am also lucky to be able to split the household chores and child-rearing responsibility with my husband. Matt is the love of my life—even when he complains about me scheduling too many activities! The greatest times of my life are when the three of us participate in fun activities together—walking, shopping, eating at a restaurant, swimming at the beach, reading Dr. Seuss over chocolate milk and coffee at the bookstore, or running around the nearby Chuck E. Cheese. At times I regret that we didn't have Kristen earlier!

Much of my focus in the early days of my career was solely on my job. I learned a lot in my 12 years as an Assistant State's Attorney in the second largest prosecutors' office in the country. I was initially assigned to the Criminal Appeals Division, writing briefs for and arguing in the Illinois Appellate Court. After a year, I was promoted to the Juvenile Division where I served in both the Delinquency Courts and the Abuse and Neglect Courts. After trying hundreds of cases, I was promoted to the Felony Review Unit, the Preliminary Hearings Division, the Night Narcotics Division, and to the Grand Jury Unit where I indicted defendants accused of Class X felonies such as murder, armed robbery, and aggravated criminal sexual assault. When I finally reached the Felony Trial Division, I had the opportunity to try numerous felony bench and jury trials.

When a position became available in the Medical Litigation Division of the Civil Actions Bureau, I was chosen to fill it. When I interviewed for the position, I did not have much civil experience because I had only worked for one year in private practice before coming to the State's Attorney's Office. I stressed to the interviewer that I had many physicians in my family and that my cultural background could prove especially helpful in representing some of the Asian physicians from Cook County Hospital. Cook County Hospital has a high percentage of nurses and physicians who are from many different ethnic and racial backgrounds. I found this assignment especially fascinating because I was forced to learn various aspects of medicine to defend complex multimillion dollar lawsuits. During the course of this assignment I tried and won a number of jury trials that some of my colleagues believed were losers only because the clients had heavy accents. Helping ethnic physicians was personally rewarding and made my parents, relatives, and parents' friends particularly proud.

In 1995, some of my friends from the Asian American Bar Association pointed out that I lived in a judicial subcircuit that had one of the higher percentages of Asian Americans. They inspired me to try to get elected to the bench. I decided to run for judge even though I had no political support. I discovered that at that time it was impossible to win in that subcircuit on the Asian American vote alone. Although I lost the race, it was

an incredibly rewarding experience. I was touched by the kind
words and the heaps of encouragement from the Asian
American community. My high risk pregnancy slowed me down
a bit—I found out that I was pregnant a few days after filing my
papers to run. Because I did run, my husband, my daughter,
and I have formed deep friendships with Asian American community members that will last for the rest of our lives.

After losing the election, I became more involved in a variety of
activities in the Asian American community. I also began getting
involved in the campaigns of politicians who were good for our
community. This was easy to do. I quickly discovered that there are many more worthwhile
causes and politicians than there are people to
support them.

Thanks to the support of the Asian American
community, I was chosen as a finalist associate
judge candidate in 1997 and again in 1998. The
list of finalists was compiled from a list of several hundred candidates both times. The associate judge selection is a process whereby the
Chief Judge of the Circuit Court selects twice the
number of finalists than there are vacancies to
be filled. Then, each of the full circuit judges
casts one vote per vacancy. The top vote getters
are sworn in as associate judges. While I did not
get enough votes to win in either attempt, I did
build even more bridges in the process. I also learned that while
qualifications and community support were important, the people who were ultimately successful in the process were the ones
who had invested the time to make strong political connections.

> By
> affiliating myself
> with various
> organizations,
> I was no
> longer a lone
> voice.

I discovered that politicians who were genuinely interested in
helping our community would listen to me because I had firsthand experience with some of the issues facing Asian
Americans. By affiliating myself with various organizations, I
was no longer a lone voice. My advice and input began carrying

more weight because I was part of much bigger things—powerful organizations within our community! For example, when I voice an opinion in my role as President of the Asian American Bar Association, many people tend to give it more weight than if I voiced the same opinion as an individual.

I currently serve as Special Counsel to Daniel W. Hynes, the new Illinois State Comptroller. As one of his directors, I supervise about 20 people. I am also working on drafting legislation and getting it through the General Assembly while simultaneously serving as the *de facto* Asian American liaison in our office. My job is hectic, yet fascinating. I have a great liking and respect for my boss. He is bright, hard working, ambitious, talented and a rising star. At age 30, he is the youngest Illinoisian to hold a statewide office. He appreciates that we need to diversify more governmental offices, and he takes action to do so. With my assistance, I was thrilled that he formed the first-ever Asian American Advisory Council to the Comptroller. Shortly thereafter, the Hispanic American Advisory Council came into existence. We still need to form the African American Council, the Gay & Lesbian Council, and the Women's Council.

I love my job. However, sometimes I miss the days when I dealt exclusively with legal problems in a courtroom setting. I haven't stopped dreaming about attaining a judgeship at some point in the future. But I intend to keep my options open. Perhaps I may have a shot of being special counsel to Governor Daniel W. Hynes some day!

Rena M. Van Tine

Rena M. Van Tine *is Special Counsel to the Illinois State Comptroller and she is the President of the Asian American Bar Association of Chicago.*

Dear Sisters, Dear Daughters,

I have often considered writing a book but have never found the time or courage. The book would not be intended to preserve the memory of my experiences for days ahead when my recollection begins to fade, but would be more of an opportunity for me to reflect upon my blessings and my challenges. In so doing, my hope would be to learn as I continue to develop as a law partner, mother, daughter, wife, and an active community and bar association volunteer. Although my book will have to wait, I hope that through this brief synopsis someone can learn from, relate to, or simply rejoice in our shared experiences.

After graduating in the top of my high school class and receiving a four-year academic scholarship to college, I decided to forego additional education. After all, I was now "grown" and my high school counselor assured me that despite my high grades I should set my sights on vocational school where I would be less likely to fail. With my confidence slightly shaken, I secured a job transcribing tapes that were dictated in the midst of traffic by real estate agents. I quickly reclaimed my confidence, quit the job after two weeks, and went to college. I learned my very first important career lesson: Believe in myself and trust my family and friends who believe in me.

I attended the University of Nevada, Las Vegas, and earned my place in the academic honor society. Despite the fact that I had little interest in being an accountant, I majored in accounting because after all, it was a practical major that guaranteed job security. I then accepted a job in a large accounting firm that I instantly disliked. After one tax season of sorting through the bits of paper and receipts of someone else's life, I found that my practical plan had turned into a nightmare, and I moved on to a new career as a Nevada Gaming Control Board Agent auditing casinos and periodically working undercover. After two years, the thrill of that job was gone.

Next, I was blessed to receive encouragement from a friend who was attending law school and to have the good fortune of receiving a full scholarship to attend the University of San Diego School of Law. In law school I was active with the Black American Law Student Association (BALSA), tutored students in civil procedure, made law review, and received the International Academy of Trial Lawyers Award for excellence in trial advocacy.

Always be visible, stay involved, and keep your options open.

After graduating, I realized that my goal of being a civil rights attorney for the U.S. Department of Justice was unlikely. Timing is everything and given the political climate at that time, the Civil Rights Division was no longer a viable option. I shifted my focus and decided to summer clerk for a large law firm. I parlayed that into a 16-year position, first as a summer associate, then six years as a litigation associate and nearly 10 years as the firm's first and only African American partner. I will always value the opportunity I was afforded through that experience. It was wonderful training and allowed me access to people and places that would otherwise have taken years to accomplish. I learned how to be a strong litigator, but I also made sure I was not just another invisible attorney in the maze of a large firm. I joined bar and community organizations. I chaired committees and often served on executive boards. This experience was my second important career lesson: Always be visible, stay involved, and keep your options open.

Over time, I wanted more control over my life, which now

included the blessings of a husband and three sons. After tremendous soul searching I stepped out on faith to join a law firm of highly-visible, experienced litigation attorneys with whom I had developed relationships over the course of my career. They were also refugees from large law firms. I was fortunate to be invited into the partnership as a name partner. The move from a nearly 200-person majority law firm to a predominantly women and minority owned 10-attorney law firm accompanied by my supportive clients, secretary, and paralegal was neither traumatic nor disappointing. I am in control of my destiny. I have a rich foundation on which to grow based on relationships formed across the United States with both in-house and outside counsel. Those relationships are fostered by a commitment to bar associations that gave me the confidence to step out of my comfort zone. If I can offer my fellow sisters and daughters any words of advice they would be to first learn your trade well which will always provide you with opportunities, build relationships, have faith, and most importantly, never, ever lose sight of who and what you are.

Vickie Turner

Vickie E. Turner *is a Partner with Wilson, Petty, Kosmo & Turner LLP and focuses on defending clients in general business litigation, product liability, warranty, and First Amendment rights.*

Dear Sisters, Dear Daughters,

As you embark on your legal career, let me share with you some of the lessons I learned on the path to the job of my dreams with the intention of smoothing your path to the job of your dreams.

As a law student, my dream was to be a labor lawyer. This was truly a dream because, in 1972, there were few women practicing labor law and fewer courses in the law school curriculum that addressed labor law than there are now. What I did was to create opportunities to learn as much about labor law on my own as possible. For example, I convinced the dean of the law school to send my friend and me to a seminar in New York City on Title VII to compensate for the absence of courses that included Title VII in the law school.

Looking back I am clear that one of the most important things I did to get to where I am was to become active in local and specialty bar associations. They provided a context in which I became known in the legal community. I found every job I have ever had as an attorney in the "old girls network."

When I graduated from the University of Michigan law school in 1975, I was a single parent of a five-year-old and one of the few people in my class of 360 people who did not have a job. Two weeks before the bar exam, my telephone rang. When I answered it, the man on the other end introduced himself as Jack, the General Counsel of a local insurance company. He explained that he had recently attended a dinner party where he had mentioned that he was planning to hire an attorney for his office. One of the women at the party challenged him to hire a woman. To which he replied, "I would if I knew one." She gave him my name and telephone number. And so, he was calling me to invite me for a job interview. I went the next day for the interview, and he hired me on the spot. Although he told me the name of the woman at the party, I did not know her. Apparently, she was a friend of someone I had met at a women's rights meeting. Although the duties of the position did not include pure labor law, I did have the opportunity to become familiar with ERISA, an important new piece of labor legislation that had just become effective. I was willing to defer my dream temporarily so that I could support my son.

I found every "job" I have ever had as an attorney in the "old girls' network."

After I began working for Jack, I became active in the Women Lawyers Association and attended their meetings and conferences where I met many local attorneys. One Sunday afternoon a few months later, my telephone rang. It was a local attorney whom I had met at a Women Lawyers Association function. He was calling because his law firm was looking to hire an African American woman attorney, and they wanted to come over to interview me for the position. I was not looking for a job because I was satisfied with my position with Jack; but I invited them over. Within a few minutes, four of the partners of the law firm were sitting in my living room getting acquainted with me. They offered me a position with one of the most prominent plaintiff's law firms in the country. I accepted it and worked there for five years. Again, while it was not labor law, I did have the opportunity to learn to litigate plaintiff's employment discrimination cases.

After awhile, I was overcome with curiosity about how it would be to have an all-woman law firm, so I left and joined with three other women attorneys. We handled plaintiff's employment discrimination cases and women's rights issues. We made a difference for a lot of people and had a lot of fun in the process. But, after five years, I was not earning enough money. So, I closed my practice and began to look for a job.

After a few well-placed inquiries, I heard about a special project that the director of the Michigan Department of Labor was beginning. It was a wonderful opportunity to obtain a close-up view of the inner workings of state government. I applied for it and she hired me. The project lasted six months. When it was completed, she promised to keep me on her staff, although it was not clear what I would be doing. The very next day, I was sitting in her office working at her desk because I did not have one of my own, when the phone rang. It was the General Counsel of the International Union, UAW, whom I had met at a Women Lawyers Association function. He had a vacant position in his office and had heard through the grapevine that my temporary assignment had ended. He invited me for an interview. I went. He offered me the job,and I have been there for 13 years living my dream of practicing labor law.

In closing, I think it is important to create goals for yourself to provide direction for your career. Yet, allow yourself the freedom to take a temporary detour from your long-term goals if necessary. Along the way it is important to network and take advantage of the many opportunities that participation in bar associations provide. I hope you find my experiences valuable. Please do not hesitate to call if I can support you in some way.

Best wishes,

Connye Y. Harper

Connye Harper *is an Attorney in the legal department of the International Union, UAW, where she litigates labor law issues on behalf of the union.*

Dear Sisters, Dear Daughters,

Dare to dream. When I graduated from college, I never imagined that I would have the exact career that I now enjoy. I wish I could tell you that I planned strategically with foresight and single-mindedness to become a law professor. Unfortunately, I can't. I can tell you, however, that I always dreamed of finding my spot in the sun where my mind would be challenged, my opinions would be considered, and the impact of my work would benefit society as a whole.

I am a tenured faculty member at the University of Pennsylvania as a Professor in the Wharton School and the Law School. I teach real estate law to undergraduates, MBAs, and law students. My research focuses on the legal issues confronting community development and urban planning. I am married and have one son.

When I entered law school in the fall of 1982, I had no idea what a lawyer did other than what I observed from television. All I knew was that getting a law degree would allow me the luxury of flexible career paths, while making my family proud that I had walked the hallowed halls of Harvard. As a graduate of a small women's college (where I was nurtured and where I excelled), I was in no way prepared for the fear-based pedagogy of law school instruction. My self-confidence (always my strong suit) vanished the moment I stepped into Langdell Hall. But, as my grandmother says, (I am sure yours says it too) what doesn't kill you makes you stronger. That sums up my law school experience.

Harvard opened up a world to me that I never knew existed—Wall Street corporate finance. I loved the deal making; I was awestruck by the sheer magnitude of money moved in one transaction. But in the back of my mind I knew that I could never be satisfied just making money. I had to find a way to make a difference. Having said that, I must be honest with you. I could never be a public interest lawyer. God bless them and the work they do but that life is not for me. I faced a career dilemma of trying to straddle two worlds—deal making and public service.

I have worked in large and small private law firms. I found the most important predictor of my happiness in a law firm was the skill, intelligence, and professionalism of the people surrounding me. In this regard the partners, of course, were important indicators of office compatibility. But every bit as important were the other associates. I guess my bit of advice for those looking for law firm jobs is to try to find someplace where you might find a friend. Law firms can be very lonely places.

I could not have tailored a better professional situation for myself than the one I am in now. Serendipity took me out of the law firm and into academia, but hard work has kept me here. My business school side indulges my passion for deal making (albeit as an observer now rather than a participant). My research builds the platform upon which I hopefully can influence urban policy issues. My teaching connects me with an extraordinarily talented, inquisitive, and smart pool of tomorrow's leaders. I am truly living my dream. My greatest professional joy is when someone, a reader, student, or colleague, tells me that my research, teaching, or service to the academic community has made a difference in his or her life.

Along the way I have learned to keep my dream at the forefront. While I have never sat down and plotted out my career path, I have held fast to the values consistent with achieving my goals. Some opportunities I have sought out, such as leaving a large firm and moving to a boutique. Some opportunities just landed in my lap, such as my present job at Penn. But with each career move I have learned something about myself. Knowledge, in turn, informed the next step.

Once someone asked me which was a bigger career obstacle for me: race or gender. As an African American women how do I separate the two? When the white guys get invited to the partners' houses for dinner, and my invitation gets lost in the mail, is that racism or sexism? (Or maybe they just didn't like me as a person!) Who knows and who cares? I enjoy who I am—a driven, caring, and intelligent person who happens to be an African American woman.

I also realize that career is just a fancy way of saying job. I do not define myself solely by my title. My family is, by far, the most important thing in my life. I derive more happiness from a cock-eyed, sloppy, good-morning-mommy kiss than any real estate deal could ever supply. My job is a way to help provide for my family in a manner that I find stimulating and rewarding. It is a means to an end—not an end unto itself.

In closing I must confess that I am no Pollyanna. There have been numerous unpleasant situations I endured directly stemming from issues of race and gender. But to dwell on them takes my eyes off of my dream and focuses them on other people's reality. Don't let them have that power. Dare to dream.

With the warmth of sisterhood,

Gigi Poindexter

Georgette C. Poindexter *is an Associate Professor of Real Estate at the Wharton School and an Associate Professor of Law at the University of Pennsylvania Law School.*

Dear Sisters, Dear Daughters,

I was born in Cape Town, South Africa, and now I am a Law Professor in New York City. My legal career has been more rewarding than I ever could have imagined growing up in South Africa. In the next few pages, I want to share with you why this has been so and also to indicate to you some ways of over-coming the pitfalls that certainly will befall you in a profession that is slowly moving away from its largely-white and largely-male edifice and history.

I happened on the law when I studied at the University of Natal in Durban, majoring in Economic History and African Politics. While pursuing my B.A., I was employed as a coordinator at the Legal Aid Clinic at the university. The experience there piqued my curiosity about law and its possibilities and limitations. I obtained a scholarship to study law, and when I graduated I joined a public interest law firm in Johannesburg.

From my vantage point as a student activist in South Africa, the civil rights movement in the United States excited my views on the possibilities of law. I was energized by the civil rights move-ment, by the way it challenged the fundamental underpinnings of American society and forced Americans to come to terms with the civil rights demands of black Americans, and later women and other minorities. I was particularly struck by the impressive array of legal leaders this movement generated. All these fueled my desire to spend time in the United States, and I obtained a scholarship to do my Masters in Law at Columbia Law School.

With my LL.M. in hand, I started an internship with the NAACP
Legal Defense Fund in New York City. As I had expected, the
caliber of the attorneys working there and the kinds of cases
that engaged them was admirable. Mostly I was proud to be at
this historic place and thrilled at the cachet of being at the major
civil rights legal organization in this country. After a brief stint at
the NAACP Legal Defense Fund, I went back to Columbia Law
School as the Chamberlain Fellow in Legislation, where I
researched worker rights and public interest legal possibilities in
South Africa.

What I found most beneficial during the time that I spent in law
school in South Africa and the United States was the advice and
guidance I obtained from mentors. I have been mentored by
men and women, black and white, and their counsel smoothed
the way for me as I negotiated my professional identity and my
place in the world of law. For women entering the profession,
mentoring is essential.

In early 1986, I moved to Australia to teach law. By then,
although the practice of law was of great interest to me, the
possibilities of teaching law suddenly appeared quite extensive,
and I decided in a moment of adventure to go to Australia to
teach law.

Teaching law in Australia turned out to be quite exciting. I was
exposed to a new legal environment and accumulated skills and
knowledge that would stand me in good stead as my research
and scholarship became more comparative and international.
From the comparative experiences of the United States and
South Africa, I began to analyze and appreciate Australia's troubled issues of race relations and the search to find a solution to
the problems confronting indigenous people and other minorities there. Although I enjoyed living and teaching in Australia,
and acquired valuable insight into the intersection of race, gender, and the law, I was drawn back to New York City, with its
tremendous cultural, intellectual, and political challenges. In
1992, I moved back to New York City to take up a professor-

ship at the City University of New York School of Law.

Leaving a tenured law teaching position in Australia was a frightening prospect, but it provided another challenge and one that I have not regretted. Teaching at an institution committed to training public interest lawyers, and teaching students the ethical values in lawyering that I treasure dearly, have been rewarding experiences. Amongst others subjects, I teach International Human Rights Law, which seems so appropriate at this stage of my career. The experiences, comparative and international, to which I've been exposed, have not only furthered my understanding and knowledge of the universe of International Human Rights Law, but have also confirmed my belief that all our struggles for equality and social justice are international in character.

My coming of age as a lawyer coincided with the emergence of the era of globalization, so confident and ubiquitous now. At the same time that legal practice has become more specialized, it has also become more globalized. And as contested as the notion of globalization may seem, legal norms (both human rights and trade and economics) have become so internationalized that all of us engaged in lawyering are implicated in these developments. I belong to many international organizations and have traveled to many countries on all continents. I am the secretary of the International Third World Legal Studies Association. I belong to the African Studies Association of Australia and the United States and I am a member of the American Society of International Law and the Law and Society Association. For those of you entering the profession, or seeking to expand your law practice, there are a host of international organizations with local counterparts that provide valuable human and legal resources.

I am a single woman with no children, and I'm not sure whether these are active, predetermined choices, or whether they just happened. I suspect, though, that my career choices, and particularly the requirement to be mobile, have contributed to my current status, which I enjoy. It allows me to mentor law students in ways that may have not been possible if I had family commitments. The most rewarding and the happiest times for me are when students graduate or obtain satisfying jobs and come back to share their experiences and their new lives as lawyers. The saddest times are when students do not live up to their potential, or when as lawyers they succumb to the cynicism of law practice generated by excessive and stressful workloads.

All of the above is a way of saying that the best advice I can give to you, prospective lawyers, is to maintain a sense of openness, be flexible, and continue expanding your legal and intellectual boundaries. My travels and my experiences on three continents in many ways mirror what the legal profession has become, a community linked by international trade and international concerns. I do believe that to succeed in the legal profession, whatever our indicators of success, we need to be flexible and willing to adapt to change. These are cliches, but they are also true. I find myself now a tenured law professor, very satisfied and mostly optimistic about the possibilities for law graduates, particularly female law graduates of color. Optimism is a key to excelling in the profession. For women of color, the twin processes of racism and sexism, often lurking in unexpected places, can be deleterious. The kind of optimism that I refer to is one that recognizes the need to challenge invidious attitudes where they surface, but also to overcome in the face of them. The universe of law for minorities and for women is a much more accessible and exciting one than it used to be. The challenge for you is to find your place in the profession and to attempt to do the ordinary things of law extraordinarily well.

Penelope E. Andrews

Penelope E. Andrews *is an Associate Professor of Law at the City University of New York School of Law.*

Dear Sisters, Dear Daughters,

My experience is varied and interesting. A tremendous advantage was clerking prior to becoming an attorney. One year of clerking was in criminal court and one year in civil court. I gained invaluable experience in legal procedure, insight into legal practice, exposure to judges, knowledge concerning motions and pleadings, and finally familiarity with the nuances of the courthouse.

Through practicing on my own, I developed some useful tools that will carry me into the millennium. An attorney is a salesperson. I can sell my "legal wares" if given the opportunity. I've learned how to meet people in a strange environment and talk to them in an impromptu manner. Certainly, I wouldn't categorize myself as "Cool Hand Luke," but I have learned to wing it.

Law school taught me to sink or swim. The same applies to being an attorney; you must be a quick study. In court, the judges are your teachers, and once again you must rise to the occasion. I was not and I am not afraid of embarrassment or mistakes. You just wipe the dust off your shoulders and try again. This doesn't sound like a significant attribute to possess for an attorney but believe me, it's very important. Every mistake is a learning experience, and you must turn it around and make it into a success. When in doubt, just call an attorney for guidance. Attorneys love to talk to attorneys. Basically, they have big egos and love giving wisdom and advice on legal issues.

Being a solo practitioner for seven years had its advantages and disadvantages. As a general practitioner, I gained experience in family law, juvenile law, criminal law, probate law, foreclosure law, administrative law, civil law, trial litigation, appellate law, office management, and last but not least "how to run a business." I became computer literate and learned how to perform all functions of a law firm from secretary to paralegal to billing to collections agent.

I made myself marketable in many areas of the law. The "top law firms" want corporate law experience that I don't have. I have not been tainted by the big firm syndrome, however. There are stories through the grapevine of many women of color leaving these firms because of unknown and "hush" reasons. The grass is not always greener on the other side.

After running my own business and going solo, I thought I could conquer the world. I must confess, I am quite fearless and willing, ready, and able to take on any challenge. Of course, my path is not for all attorneys. I am definitely people oriented and have the gift of gab. The most important people in my career are judges and clients: judges because they can make or break your case and clients because they are paying your salary. If you don't do a good job, clients won't come back. You are your best advertisement. If your legal services are good, the clientele will follow.

You truly must be a rainmaker if you run your own firm. A good and bad consequence of working for yourself is that you get used to being your own boss. A warning to the wise, you may have a problem working for other people in the future.

I like to say that my father taught me a valuable piece of wisdom while I was in law school. He told me I was successful. I asked him how could I be successful when I wasn't even a lawyer yet. He responded "You're successful right now today. It doesn't matter what you'll be ten years from today; you're already successful even if you didn't do another thing in life."

I had three mentors when I first became an attorney. I am still connected to one of those individuals today. One person was a friend from law school who was well connected in the community. That person was my first partner and his family and their affiliations supplied me with my first clients. The second mentor was an attorney who became my confidant and friend for the next seven years. I leased space at his law firm (a small family business with only one other attorney). I was taught to charge my worth and not to sell myself short. The third mentor is a law professor, judge, and friend who helped me tremendously over the years since our acquaintance in law school. He opened many doors for me and gave me tremendous legal advice. There were several other professional people who gave me legal advice and support when I was a solo practitioner. Every attorney who has any degree of success must have at least one mentor. I also was a mentor to two students—one is now a solo practitioner attorney and the other is a computer analyst.

I have practiced foreclosure law in New York and Connecticut. Currently, I am doing law guardian cases in New York and I previously had performed hundreds of Juvenile Matters in Connecticut.

The attributes of networking and being somewhat of a social animal are assisting me in adjusting to upstate New York's legal arena. I am co-chair of the program committee with Greater Rochester Association of Women Attorneys (GRAWA) and a member of the Women's Bar Association of the State of New York (WBASNY), which I find rewarding professionally. Never let anyone break your spirit. As an attorney, I consider myself fortunate. I love being an attorney. I can always hang out my shingle and practice law. And I'm not afraid to do it.

Valerie R. Johnson

Valerie R. Johnson *is a Staff Attorney at the Legal Aid Society in Rochester, New York.*

Dear Sisters, Dear Daughters,

I write to you during a time of tremendous transformation. I have spent 12 years in the law, finishing my career as a name partner in a firm based in Los Angeles. It was a wonderful, challenging, and satisfying period in my life, and I may find myself returning to the work again someday. At present, I am engaged in a national and international lecture tour that permits me to pursue my passion for examining race relations in America and the implications for peace. About a year ago, I left full-time practice to do the work I am doing today. But for now, I wish to share with you some of my experiences in deciding on the law as a course of training, developing my skills as an attorney, and building a practice with a boutique firm that was (and continues to be) one of the most highly respected firms in Los Angeles.

In my college years, I had no idea that I would eventually pursue the study of law. It was only after I finished my masters degree in public health that I realized that legal training was something I wanted to pursue. I knew no lawyers. My parents were first generation immigrants from Korea who really did not know much about the legal profession, and those people who were lawyers and to whom I turned to for advice, discouraged the idea. I was told that it was a miserable profession, that there were long hours, lots of headaches, and few opportunities for women to advance. Of course, the discouraging comments from the lawyers only enhanced my desire to check out law school. My view was that the training would give me insight into one of the most powerful institutions in society—the court system—and help me to learn about history. It would show me how to analyze issues in a new way, and possibly give me the chance to learn about creative ways to resolve disputes. I applied to one school, UC Davis, because it was close to my job in Sacramento and it was a public institution (i.e., affordable). When I was admitted, my employer worked with me so that I could fulfill my duties at work and go to law school. The first year was a killer. By the second year, the challenge was less daunting in part due to the fact that my job went part-time. I finished law school with a bang—an arrest for civil disobedience in support of the antiapartheid student movement; an honor from my fellow law students; and a full three years never having looked at my grades (and never regretting not picking them up).

> *I wish for you . . . the chance to spread your wings, dream large and loving dreams, to seek justice and dignity through your work and to counsel others.*

When I finished law school and passed the bar, I found a job with a labor law firm. The people were great but unbeknownst to me, the firm was about to split, and I was not sure with whom I'd end up. I found another job fairly easily, before the first firm broke up. I didn't enjoy the work in my second job, so I put out the word to friends that I was looking again. Many people counseled me that I should stay in a miserable job because moving around so much in the early part of one's career "wouldn't look good on the resume." For me, the job was going to be a big part of my life—at least 10 to 12 hours a day—so I wasn't about to stay miserable. I kept looking and found a wonderful place to land; good people, good values, and excellent quality work. I ended up staying at the same firm for 11 years.

The development of my practice was part me, part luck, and part good support. I worked hard, but I also knew that the partners in my small firm were not in a position to train me to do trial work. So, I found a program that allowed attorneys in private firms to work in the office of the local prosecutor and try cases for about a month. The training before getting to trial was several months; evenings at the courthouse after work. But, in the end, trying cases was the goal. I convinced the partners to support this effort, and when I finished, I was able to take a leave, try cases, and qualify to pick up appointed cases out of the criminal courts. My partners were experienced federal practitioners, so I was able to pick up both state and federal trial advocacy skills. It was hard work, long hours, and great training. Then, in 1992, there was a crisis in Los Angeles.

The implosion of Los Angeles in the spring of 1992, produced a billion dollars worth of damage, destroyed thousands of small, family-owned businesses, and was recorded as the worst civil disaster this century in the nation. My activities outside of work included involvements in the Korean American community; I was President of WORK (the Women's Organization Reaching Koreans), and President-elect of KABA (the Korean American Bar Association of Southern California). It was in the aftermath of four days of burning, looting, and vandalism that I voiced a message of reconciliation. It was picked up in the national news in an interview I did with Ted Koppel's *Nightline* and suddenly I found myself in the middle of enormous media demands. I have no doubt that the media created an awareness of who I was and clients began to call. My practice grew, and the work load began to reach impossible proportions. My partnership was offered to me a year later.

In developing and maintaining my practice, I remained committed to staying involved with the organized bar, students, and the community. My service on various commissions and boards enhanced my opportunities to help others and expanded my base of knowledge, contacts, and skills. It is always a delicate balance: self, family, and career. But there is nothing that I regret having done. Nothing that I can say I would have changed about my decisions or my involvements.

I wish for you, my sisters and my daughters, the chance to spread your wings, dream large and loving dreams, to seek justice and dignity through your work and counsel to others. In many ways that go unnoticed, it is a noble profession that you are pursuing, and it is one that will give you the chance to meet extraordinary, caring, and committed individuals who you will cherish as friends and colleagues for the rest of your lives.

Angela Oh

Angela E. Oh *joined UCLA in January 1999 as a Lecturer, Visiting Scholar and Lawyer-in Residence and was previously a Partner at Beck DeCorso Daly Barrera & Oh.*

Dear Sisters, Dear Daughters,

I confess that in my career as a corporate lawyer I took the road "more traveled," but it still made all the difference! In the beginning, though, I never intended to become an international corporate lawyer. When I left Hawaii to attend Yale, I majored in Asian Studies. I won a Bates Fellowship to study under Yasunari Kawabata, a Japanese novelist and Nobel Prize winner I greatly admired. After graduating in the first class of women at Yale in 1971, I then survived three cold winters at Harvard Law School in the class that broke the 10 percent barrier for enrollment of women, but enrolled only three Asian Americans. My part-time work for the federal Office for Civil Rights in Boston and my research work for Professor Derrick Bell on affirmative action during law school made me realize that despite my idealism and desire to change society, there were no simple legal solutions to racial and gender discrimination. I was not sure I had the perseverance to endure the frustrations of a public interest law practice. Public international law at that time seemed bureaucratic and limited to the United Nations, the Hague, and a few international agencies. Private practice, however, involved business; and I had been raised in an Asian academic family that abhorred commerce and thought lawyers ranked just above embezzlers. Moreover, in 1974 there were no Asian American partners at any of the top law firms in the major cities.

The international business world had one irresistible appeal— the possibility of combining my knowledge and enjoyment of Asia with my desire to correct the misconceptions Asians and

Americans had of each other. I had grown up in an all-white Pentagon suburb in Virginia, an American military base in Japan, the predominantly Asian population of Hawaii, and the Vietnam War and Cold War era when Asians were the enemy, so I had seen firsthand the problems of conflicting cultural assumptions and racism through ignorance.

Opportunities for lawyers interested in Asia were still limited, but the opportunity to be involved in the earliest stages of Asian business development seemed to me an exciting pioneering prospect. The chance to travel to Asia and keep up my language skills were also important considerations. So, despite my trepidations, I packed away my aloha shirts and the chance to return to Hawaii, and joined the ranks of the lowly first-year associates in an internationally known New York law firm. Within a few months, I was sent to Tokyo, and then sent to Hong Kong to help expand the firm's three-lawyer branch office. I learned how to work in a satellite office, be resourceful, and, most importantly, how to get and keep clients. It is more art than science, and a lot of hard work, but essential for women and minorities to succeed.

How did I get clients? I spoke at numerous conferences, met executives at business receptions and dinners, served as trustee or board member, or was part of negotiating teams with accountants, bankers, or investment bankers who liked my legal and business judgment and my work ethic. Because I had a solid client base and energy to spare, I was given the chance at the age of 31 to open the New York branch office of a California law firm as founding and resident partner. I later moved to a Wall Street firm when clients needed a firm headquartered in New York, and subsequently moved to another New York firm that had more growth potential in Asia. Nothing was planned, but successful projects began new projects.

The difficulties of my chosen career path are numerous—the frequent political changes in Asia and the U.S. that can dramatically change both the legal and business considerations, the lack of continuity in management of companies because of personnel and ownership changes, the perception of a lawyer as a cost rather than as a benefit, the increased competition from the increased number of lawyers, the subtle discrimination that women and minorities face, the time difference with Asia that swallows up my evenings, and the extensive travel requirements away from my children and spouse, despite the convenience of laptops, e-mail and faxes. When I traveled or was in the office late, I had to tape record the lullabies I usually sang to my children at night. It is not possible to have everything.

The rewards, however, are easy to list. The Asia Pacific practice gives me a chance to use my knowledge of Asian and American laws, politics, customs, and people to create legal structures and relationships that I hope will endure well beyond my involvement as a lawyer. Because it is still a growing field with few experienced practitioners, I have been able to participate in projects in almost every industry sector. I am being paid to learn about industries as diverse as satellite television hardware and programming, the Internet, resort hotels, apparel, emerging markets funds, insurance industry regulations, cosmetics distribution, automotive manufacturing, Broadway show and film financing, supercomputer technology, oil refinery facilities, mass transportation systems, and the pharmaceutical industry. Many of the men (and a very few women) I met in Asia who were bright young leaders in business and government 25 years ago are now senior business executives and government officials in those countries. Because of the network of government, business, and academia I have developed over the years, I am frequently asked to identify potential business partners or discreetly advise on how to restructure existing business

> *When I traveled . . . I had to tape record the lullabies I usually sang to my children at night. It is not possible to have everything.*

relationships. Through these assignments I have been able to develop a closer rapport with my clients as a counselor and business advisor, rather than merely as one of many technicians and specialists. Clients range from large conglomerates to entrepreneurs with many business interests to non-profits to an individual with one good idea. And now clients are women and minorities, which certainly wasn't the case in 1974.

What keeps me interested is that no two projects are ever identical. The laws and market conditions change so rapidly in Asia that even consecutive projects can have slightly different outcomes. Moreover, cross-border transactions always require at least two sets of laws and rules, which adds an additional layer of intellectual complexity and challenge. I feel fortunate that part of my job requires keeping up with the latest news about Asia, attendance at seminars at the Asia Society and Japan Society, and discussing foreign policy issues at the Council on Foreign Relations. Inasmuch as I am constantly teaching associates to think creatively along parallel and intersecting lines of legal and cultural systems, I am also constantly learning new approaches from industry sources, clients, and foreign policy experts. Boredom is not possible in the U.S.-Asia legal practice. And my two teenage children and husband are proud of my achievements and my activism in the Asian American community. My daughter thinks she might even want to be a lawyer someday. Nevertheless, I am hopeful that in the future I will eventually have time to take the road less traveled at slower speeds, be it teaching, writing, a different use of my skills, or something entirely different, and yet still make a difference in the world we live in.

Alice Young

Alice Young *is a Partner in the New York office of Kaye, Scholer, Fierman, Hays & Handler, LLP and is Chair of the firm's Asia Pacific Practice Group.*

Dear Sisters, Dear Daughters,

I write this having been named just two days ago to lead the new west coast legal office of BP-Amoco, the second largest oil company in the world. Within the 250-attorney BP-Amoco Legal Department, I have suddenly become one of the highest-ranking female lawyers. And so, it is a good time to reflect on how and why I was offered this position by senior legal managers who had never met me before last month.

First, my background. I have worked at Atlantic Richfield Company (ARCO), the eighth largest oil company for the past 18 years. I started in the Litigation Department, having come from two years of practicing litigation at a major law firm.

In January 1989, I was asked to provide corporate legal work to ARCO Marine, Inc., the company that owns and operates tankers transporting Alaskan crude oil to refineries along the West Coast. Three months later, the Exxon Valdez oil spill occurred, which changed the lives of thousands, including me. Because of the magnitude of the spill, the entire industry was under a magnifying glass. The way in which the industry responded to the outrage caused by the extensive damage done to the pristine environment in Alaska was going to be seen by millions of people. No oil spill of this magnitude had ever occurred in the United States. Extensive and reactive laws were being proposed and passed to regulate the industry. Solid legal advice was critical at that time. The business people were constantly turning to me for guidance. In short, during the year succeeding this event, I was tested on a daily basis, not only

my legal advice, but my communication skills, business judgment, reaction time, and stamina.

Eventually events calmed down, yet I continued to advise this
client for 10 years. I can truly say that it has been my most
rewarding legal experience. I quickly became a part of the business team—advising on all aspects of the company, from operations, to human resources, to policy issues, government
affairs, and even ship christenings. My fondest compliment, was
when my clients would tell me that they forgot that I was a
lawyer. Many would come not just for legal advice, but for a
sounding board, a critical thinker, a devil's advocate, or just an
empathetic ear. As I became more experienced and more comfortable with this role, I extended it to the ARCO Legal
Department as a whole.

Last year, I founded the ARCO Legal Women's forum, which was
a group of all female attorneys who would come together on a
quarterly basis to discuss issues and share in fellowship. I was
active in revamping the staffing review system where each attorney would be reviewed on a developmental basis to assess his
or her future opportunities. I was able to embark on these projects because I was trusted and respected by those around me.

I feel that the offer for yet another great opportunity came just
this week. It was made clearly on the basis of reputation and
past performance. I had gained the respect of not only ARCO's
legal management, but that of my colleagues and peers, who all
recommended me for the job.

The bottom line for me and my advice to you, is that it is all
about your credibility. That is all you come to a job with, and
that is all you leave it with. It is your conduct toward others,
your honesty, and your respect that sets you apart. I have one
basic rule, "Treat everyone with dignity and respect." Said
another way, "Treat everyone the way that you would want to
be treated." Those simple mottos, told to me and lived by my
mother, have been the hallmarks of my life. It is amazing how

many people (including most lawyers) fail to follow them. It is disappointing to see how many people treat people poorly, and at the same time, would never tolerate others treating them the way that they treat some.

I have discovered that it is not how brilliant you are, it is not how many awards you have received or your grade point average that makes you successful. Sure, those things can give you opportunities and may open some doors, but once given a chance, if you don't have the highest reputation for honesty and respect toward others, then you will never go anywhere.

I recognize that what I say is not always easy, particularly when you encounter someone who does not practice those values. I also know that it can sometimes be downright exhausting—giving people your time, your advice, and your ear takes a lot of hard listening and patience. For me that has meant less than optimal nights' sleep, less personal time, and a constant balance as to what can realistically be achieved in a day. Is it worth it? Absolutely. Why? Because I have to be able to look myself in the mirror each day. The only way that I can do that is to know in my heart that I have treated everyone with dignity and respect—the very same way that I want to be treated.

On a final note, I have three young sons (age 7 and twins age 5) who I watch in awe each and everyday. Although there are exceptions, for the most part I see them living these values. The feedback that I receive from their teachers and their playmates' parents is that they are the nicest, kindest and most courteous boys that they have seen. I take great pride in those compliments, because I believe that is truly my legacy to pass on to them. I hope I have passed these thoughts on to you as well.

Susan Liebson

Susan D. Liebson *has been named to lead the new west coast legal office of BP-Amoco.*

Dear Sisters, Dear Daughters,

Unlike a number of sisters who long aspired to practice law, I entered the field of law quite unexpectedly and based on a split-second decision. After receiving my masters degree in Electrical Engineering, I worked as a fiber optics engineer for Bellcore (now Telcordia Technologies). During that time, I studied network architectures and transmission strategies for delivering high-bandwidth services to the home (e.g., video-on-demand). I have always been drawn to the cutting edge of technology, and after working for a couple of years, I developed an insatiable yearning for more knowledge.

I realized that my return to academia was inevitable. About this time, I received an offer from the University of Virginia to serve as the Assistant to the Dean of Electrical Engineering. This position was salaried and included teaching responsibilities and a full scholarship to obtain a Ph.D.

I toiled long and hard over whether I should accept this position, and I kept asking myself the same difficult questions: Could I endure the challenges associated with being the only African American female faculty member in this department? Would my long-term relationship survive the distance between Virginia and New Jersey? What do friends and family members think is the right decision? Friends and family members with whom I shared my dilemma thought this was a "no-brainer." In their view, this opportunity was a chance of a lifetime that I should pursue without hesitation.

After much introspection, I decided that, while I wanted to build on my engineering background and experience, I did not want to go deeper and narrower into the field of electrical engineering. Instead, I longed to broaden my knowledge base through exposure to new disciplines and different ways of thinking. I decided to forego what most considered to be a once-in-a-lifetime opportunity.

My decision-making process taught me a great deal about gaining clarity about what I wanted and the questions that were really relevant to reaching the right decision. I realized that many of the questions that caused me the most turmoil were not really relevant to my decision. Yes, I could endure being the only African American female, as I had previously in many similar situations; the harsh reality was that I was likely to be the only African American female in most professional situations in which I would become involved. My long-term relationship was what it was, and distance alone could not make or break the relationship. Family and friends can be excellent sounding boards, but only when their advice is a reflection of your wants and needs and not theirs. The pinnacle question was what's good and right for me. Ultimately, I realized that a good opportunity, including this one, should be left on the table if it is not the right opportunity for me.

My thirst for more knowledge became stronger with each passing day, and I became frustrated because I had not found the right avenue to realize my untapped potential. I became unsure, hesitant, and unfocused, and I involved myself in every activity imaginable searching for any sign of what my next endeavor should be. I envisioned myself doing great things, but what? How? I had more questions than answers.

About this time, a coworker and good friend informed me that Bellcore had launched a new patent attorney training program. Under this program, two engineers from the corporation would be selected to work full time in the law department to train to become patent attorneys and receive full scholarships to attend law school at night.

This opportunity was perfect for me. Patent law, a specialized field open only to scientists and engineers, entails writing technical descriptions of innovative, leading edge technologies for the purpose of seeking patent protection. The basic academic training for aspiring patent lawyers is the same as for those pursuing other areas of law. The field of patent law was an avenue for me to be exposed to another discipline, build on my background and experience in electrical engineering, and learn a new perspective and approach to solving problems.

On learning of Bellcore's program, I immediately called the Assistant General Counsel to express my interest in being considered. I was informed that applications were no longer being accepted and that five finalists out of over 30 applicants had been selected (my coworker was one of the finalists).

I continued to express my interests and began to sell why I was the best candidate in the program only to be told, "Sorry. Send us your resume and we'll consider you for next year's program." Not taking sorry for an answer, I immediately faxed my resume to the Assistant General Counsel with a full explanation of why I should be selected for the program.

Very shortly, I received a telephone call from the Assistant General Counsel's office to schedule an interview for the next day. Shortly after the interview, I learned that the final five had been expanded to the final six, and I was being considered for the program.

There was no time to celebrate. I had two weeks to study for the Law School Admissions Test (LSAT). Considering my past performance with standardized tests, I was not encouraged, but I was clear that this opportunity was for me and I just needed to stay the course.

My lowest point in this process was when I had to present the Assistant General Counsel with my LSAT scores, which were less than adequate. But I argued my strengths. I pointed out that I had excelled scholastically at the undergraduate and graduate levels, and standardized tests had never been indicative of my scholastic performance or ability to excel in the workplace. The lesson here is rely on your strengths and be slow to explain your weaknesses. To do otherwise could demonstrate weakness.

The rest is history. I was selected as one of two engineers to participate in the patent attorney trainee program. My only regret is that my coworker was not selected for the program. Some criticized her for sharing with me information about the program, their rationale being that doing so led to her own unsuccessful result. Her response, which spoke volumes to her impeccable character and clarity, was that her role was to lead me to this opportunity which, in her mind, had resulted in a successful outcome. For this, I will forever call her sister and friend and admire her clarity and sense of self.

Law school was one of the most thought-provoking and rewarding experiences that I have ever had (second only to my experiences as a wife and mother). I have thoroughly enjoyed the practice of patent law, and currently, I serve as Assistant General Counsel of Intellectual Property in the Aerospace Division of AlliedSignal Inc. I have been particularly fascinated by the practice of law in the corporation because I am able to partner directly with corporate leaders and define legal strategies to achieve business objectives.

I urge women with strong aptitudes in math and science and the desire to be on the cutting edge of technology to consider patent law as a career option. I believe it could prove as satisfying for you as it has been for me.

Loria B. Yeadon

Loria B. Yeadon *is Assistant General Counsel—Intellectual Property for AlliedSignal Inc. of Morristown, New Jersey.*

Dear Sisters, Dear Daughters,

I am delighted to write to you about my position as a Federal
Administrative Law Judge (FALJ). For those of you who are
interested in public service, this position is very rewarding.
Historically, the appointment of African Americans to these positions has been few and far between. In 1972, Paul A. Brady
became the first African American to be appointed as a FALJ. He
was with the Occupational Safety and Health Review
Commission until his retirement several months after my
appointment in 1996. I am the second African American judge
appointed to this commission. African American females consti-
tute a very small percentage of the approximately 1,400 such
positions nationwide—approximately 1,100 positions are with
the Social Security Administration. I know of only five African
American FALJ's in the Washington, D.C., area, and approximately two others outside of this area. My introduction to this
field came about as a result of my having litigated cases as an
attorney with the U.S. Department of Labor. At that time, I
appeared before judges in both federal district courts and federal administrative law forums. My face was certainly a novelty in
locations such as Big Stone Gap, Norton, and Abingdon,
Virginia, where I tried cases before the Federal Mine Safety and
Health Review Commission. There were occasions when the
courtroom would be filled to capacity with spectators who
wanted to observe the government's attorney—a black female.
During this time, the early 80s, I was impressed by the fact that
I never appeared before an African American FALJ. This led me
to inquire about the process of becoming an administrative law

judge. I learned it was a very competitive process wherein one received a numerical score and was placed on a register with the Office of Personnel Management (OPM), after completing a four-part process that included a written examination. One aspect of the written exam that prevented large numbers of women from ranking high on the register was the additional veterans' preference points added to scores of veterans, who were mostly males. Furthermore, by the time most women generally embarked on this process, they had spouses and children, which could make the relocation aspect of such an appointment more difficult. Thus, those of us choosing such a career had many difficult choices to make. I know of one African American woman whose husband and son followed her from Seattle to Dallas. At the time of this move, her husband had no employment in Dallas. At the time of my appointment, I had just finished major renovations in my home. It was my belief that I would narrow my relocation choices to commutable cities, and thus, I could still maintain my home in Philadelphia. I subsequently realized, however, that to be assured of an appointment I had to be willing to relocate to any city. As I looked at the big picture, I was single and had no children, and my family and friends all had the ability to come and visit me. Furthermore, I realized that such a move did not have to be permanent. At this time, my narrow geographic preference prevented me from an appointment. I decided to enlarge my geographic preference to indicate my willingness to go anywhere in the nation. Once I faxed OPM this revised geographic preference, within 30 days I received a call from OPM that I had been appointed to a position with Social Security in Hattiesburg, Mississippi! With that appointment came the excitement of selling my home and relocating for at least the next two years. I am proud that I became the first African American FALJ in the state of Mississippi. The folks there were elated at my presence, and I was made to feel at home. I could not have received a better assignment. After a year, I was appointed to my present position with the Occupational Safety and Health Review

Commission in Washington, D.C. This move brought me within a couple of hours of my home as well as to an area of the law which I had really enjoyed.

As exciting as this work is, I am confronted with challenges as a traveling judicial officer. As a single African American woman, I have been mistaken as the court stenographer on several occasions. There was the occasion where I was hearing a case in the courtroom of a federal agency at the World Trade Center in New York City, and at the conclusion of day I discovered that I had locked myself out of the judicial chambers. It was 6:00 p.m., and the support staff had left for the day so I searched the hallway hoping to find someone who might assist me. I recognized a gentleman whom I had seen on the elevator that morning. I inquired of him where I might obtain a key. He asked me what business I had on that floor that day. I was a little surprised by this inquiry in light of the fact that I was wearing my judicial robe and we were standing in front of the bank of elevators where there was a signboard that contained information pertaining to the case I was hearing. He explained that it was June and there were a lot of graduations going on in the city, thus he assumed I was a recent graduate of some school and was perhaps visiting someone on that floor. I found this explanation incredulous, but then I recognized that as a black woman such an assumption was not beyond the range of possibilities. I assured this gentleman that I was not a graduate and then moved on in search of someone else who would assist me. Such incidents, however, are balanced by the warm greetings and expressions of pride that I receive from others, especially from those of color, when they learn that I am the judge assigned to the proceeding.

> *I would like to relay to you the importance of exploring opportunities that expose you to lifestyle changes.*

In closing, I would like to relay to you the importance of explor-
ing opportunities that expose you to lifestyle changes. Such
rewarding opportunities will create new opportunities for those
who follow you. I would also like to emphasize the necessity of
maintaining your spiritual and physical well-being as you pursue
your career goals. There is much stress related to the practice of
law, and life certainly becomes more complicated as you grow
older. I believe that the establishment of a lifestyle that incorpo-
rates the maintenance of a healthy body and spirit are of the
utmost importance. I subscribe to such a lifestyle through regular exercise, healthy eating habits, and the maintenance of my
faith in God. Furthermore, I find that the maintenance of a solid
and supportive relationship with a very special man in my life,
as well as the strong support I receive from a network of "sister
friends" has kept me balanced and happy. These are all sources
of support critical to your professional and personal development.

Covette Rooney

Covette Rooney *has been a Federal Administrative Law Judge with the
Occupational Safety and Health Review Commission in Washington, D.C.
since 1996.*

Dear Sisters, Dear Daughters,

I am so very proud of you because you have chosen to study law and to join the ranks of the legal profession. At the end of the journey, you may sigh and utter like so many of your predecessors, that "life for me ain't been no crystal stair" (Langston Hughes). Nonetheless, I think that you will conclude, as I have, that it was worth it.

The overarching theme of this letter is, "that it is never too late to pursue your dreams if you are willing to turn stumbling blocks into stepping stones." The streets hold many people who had a "good" reason or excuse for why they could not do something. Offices across the country have many workers who lament their fate and complain about how, "if things had only worked out differently, they could have been a judge or a doctor." Households across the nation house people who cry "if only . . . then . . ." People who want to study law must decide to take and score well on the Law School Admissions Test, complete their applications, and then, enthusiastically apply themselves to their studies once they start law school.

This letter focuses on the path to the front of the classroom after law school graduation. Many people who enter teaching at a law school, first garnered clerkships with federal or state court judges and then posts with major law firms prior to entering the ivy-covered walls of the law school. While enrolled in law school, future law professors distinguish themselves by serving as staff members and then as editors of the law review or other journal. Indeed, these future members of the professoriat could easily be called the nerds among us. For latter day aspirants who did not follow the preferred route in law school, others from whom you might seek guidance may suggest that it would be futile for you to think about becoming a professor. Ignore the naysayers! While candidates who pursue the traditional path to the ranks of the academy may appeal to members of faculty recruitment committees, others who take a different route and also persist can become law professors.

If you would like to teach law, then it helps to distinguish your-self in law practice, publish articles, lecture at continuing legal education programs, and get to know the dean and members of the faculty at your local law school. Your former law school professors can serve as sources of information about vacancies and also provide references. Some people obtain a full-time faculty position after teaching as members of the adjunct facul-ty at one law school or another. Others return to graduate school to earn an LL.M. to make themselves more attractive to potential employers. Many others attend the annual faculty recruitment conference sponsored by the American Association of Law Schools.

Before going to an interview, think through the subjects you propose to teach and any ideas you have for future legal scholarship. Many faculty recruitment teams favor candidates who have identified issues drawn from their practices that need to be more fully developed in a law review article. Additionally, even though you may hope to teach a specific course or two, prepare a list of subjects, including first year or large enrollment courses that you would be willing to teach. Too often, new faculty members will only get a chance to teach their pet subjects after a senior faculty member retires or goes on sabbatical. Be patient.

Increasingly, future law professors must be willing to relocate. Oftentimes, a teaching post awaits you in a different state if you remain flexible. If the neighborhood law school just hired an evidence professor, it is unlikely that it will have a vacancy in that area for a long time. My motto is: "Have job, will travel!" Relocate if you must.

Most law professors of African descent and many women at one time or another get unflattering teaching evaluations. The most famous case involved law students at Stanford University and Dean Derrick Bell. Law students in one of Dean Bell's class-es complained and criticized the effectiveness of his teaching. Prior to his stint at Stanford, Dean Bell had gained tenure at Harvard Law School and served as the dean of the University of Oregon Law School. My best advice, if and when your awful evaluations come, is to remember the lessons of Dean Bell. Many law students think they are smarter than you are and know more precisely how the course must be taught. They hold to this notion despite the fact that you have earned your degree, gained admission to the bar, and practiced law for awhile.

My motto is: "Have job, will travel!"

After securing your teaching post, spend some time getting familiar with the subject matter that you are teaching. Then quickly get to the business of publishing law review articles. Writing law review articles means that you must spend time by yourself—alone. Avoid teaching summer school. Apply for research grants. Devote whole days to sitting at your computer churning it out. Develop a system that works for you. Tap into your colleagues and ask them how they get their articles from their heads onto the paper. Embrace the recommendations that best suit your style and personality. Then get it done. It you type one page a day, 250 words a page, by the end of the year, you will have a document that is 365 pages long.

For law professors of color, the National Bar Association has a Law Professors' Division chaired by Dean Everett Bellamy of the Georgetown University Law Center in Washington, DC. The American Association of Law Schools has two sections that focus on the concerns of women and minorities in law teaching:

the Women's Division and the Minority Law Professors' Division. The American Bar Association has the Section on Legal Education and Admissions to the Bar. All of these organizations provide seminars and programs throughout the year and can be a source for mentors to fledgling law professors. The National Bar Association, American Association of Law Schools and the ABA also provide venues for junior faculty members to present papers and thereby fulfill the professional service prong en route to tenure.

In short, law teaching gives faculty members the chance to recreate themselves. A practicing attorney can try a case to secure a victory for one client. A faculty member can teach the skills and provide the knowledge to 30, 60, or 120 students at one time and each of those students can help many more clients. Law teaching brings much gratification. To achieve your place at the front of the class turn stumbling blocks into stepping-stones.

Beverly McQueary Smith

Beverly McQueary Smith *is a Professor at Touro College: Jacob Fuchsberg Law Center in Huntington, New York and a former President of the National Bar Association.*

Dear Sisters, Dear Daughters,

Twelve years ago, I left a position in a large law firm for academia. Although I found law practice exciting, I wanted the chance to think and write full-time about social issues that concerned me. I was especially attracted to questions involving reproductive freedom. A judge's decision allowing doctors to perform a caesarian section on a dying woman against her will shocked me. As I explored the topic, I discovered that black women's reproductive decisions had been subject to regulation and abuse for centuries. Yet this injustice received little attention from scholars and mainstream civil and women's rights groups. The entire meaning of reproductive freedom seemed too narrow to fit our experiences. When I started teaching, however, feminist theory was barely recognized as a legitimate area of legal scholarship. An even newer body of scholarship by professors of color called critical race theory was just emerging. And it was common for new professors to be counseled to write about traditional topics until they got tenure. Because tenure decisions are often influenced by political considerations, many people think it is unwise to stray from the well-worn path of articles about conventional legal doctrines.

This put me in a dilemma. Shortly after I began teaching, newspaper articles about the prosecution of women who use drugs during pregnancy began to catch my eye. Women around the country were being imprisoned because they tested positive for drugs while pregnant or after giving birth. In one hospital in South Carolina, patients were hauled off to jail in handcuffs and leg shackles hours after delivering a baby. I suspected (correctly) that most of the women charged with prenatal crimes were Black, despite similar rates of substance abuse across racial lines. Yet the debate about the constitutionality and ethics of this punitive policy did not mention race. I felt compelled to explore the significance of the racial disparity in the prosecutions and how it related to black women's reproductive freedom. But I was advised by a senior colleague that this topic—the rights of poor black women addicted to drugs—was not a prudent choice. In fact, it was just about as far from a traditional topic one could imagine. It seemed to me, though, that these women's experiences had something important to add to traditional constitutional theorizing. How could we understand the constitutional principles of equality and liberty without analyzing how it applied to the least privileged citizens? And why had I become a professor if I was not willing to speak out on behalf of those whose voices were most silenced? I decided to follow my conscience. I wrote an article that argued that the prosecutions were unconstitutional, using them as a starting point to develop a more radical interpretation of constitutional liberty.

. . . there are miraculous rewards to speaking what you believe in your heart and defending the dignity of the least among us.

It was the right decision: my first article was published in *Harvard Law Review*, the leading law journal in the country. I know I would have produced something far more mediocre had I followed my colleague's advice. I could never have written as creatively and passionately about a more orthodox topic I cared less about. Since then, I have tried to pursue my conviction that theories of freedom must start with the lives of those at the bottom, not at the top. Too often, academics promote principles and policies that favor the most privileged members of our society, and hope the benefits will trickle down to others. I advocate just the opposite strategy: challenging current ideas from the perspective of the least privileged tends to produce a better conception of justice that in the end benefits everyone.

My early experience as a scholar convinced me that there are miraculous rewards to speaking what you believe in your heart and defending the dignity of the least among us. I am not advising you to be reckless: it is important to think strategically about the best way to present your views. And I am not saying it is easy to know what is right. You might strongly disagree with my positions; many others have. I spend a lot of time worrying and praying about the right way to address the tough issues that confront us in the new millennium. You may face difficult questions involving clients, employers, or family members. But I think what I learned as a young scholar applies generally to the tough issues of life. Have the faith and courage to follow your conscience and your career will be blessed in unexpected ways.

Sincerely,

Dorothy Roberts

Dorothy Roberts *is a Professor at Northwestern University School of Law, a faculty fellow of the Institute for Policy Research, and has joint appointments as a Faculty Affiliate of the Department of Sociology and the Joint Center for Poverty Research.*

Dear Sisters, Dear Daughters,

My personal story salutes the practice of law on the frontlines. I hope that it inspires you to pick up the baton of the activist, public interest, "movement" lawyer.

I was born in 1954—the year of the legendary *Brown v. Board of Education* decision. One year before Rosa Parks defied the laws of this land and was ingraciously jailed. It was also one year before the body of Chicago's 14-year-old Emmett Till was found at the bottom of Mississippi's Tallahatchie River and eight years before the indomitable Fannie Lou Hamer determined to register to vote. Each of these events involved the law, and each left deep imprints on my spirit.

Where does the love to practice public interest law come from? Is it in the blood, intrinsic and ancestral? Is it molded and shaped from conditions and circumstances? Does it occur by chance and happenstance? Perhaps it is a mosaic of all the above. For me, the spark came during the late sixties. I knew I wanted to be a lawyer. Why? Because there was a poster tacked on the bulletin board of my eighth grade black studies classroom of a black man with a black beret on his head with a gun in one hand and a spear in the other, sitting in a grand slam wicker chair. All the teenage girls in my class were talking about how *fine* he was. I, however, kept wondering why is he in jail and, even more important, why is he being represented by a white lawyer? Granted, he was a progressive lawyer, a radical lawyer, a movement lawyer—but why was the leader of the Black Panther Party being represented by white attorneys?

Thirty years ago I knew about the Panthers because they made the front page news. But I did not know about the horrific Dred Scott case, where a U.S. Supreme Court Justice stated that a black person in America had no rights that a white man was bound to respect. Thirty years ago I didn't know about the 1822 trial of freedom fighter Denmark Vesey. I didn't know about the Amistad case where in 1841, international law was applied in a domestic court in the U.S. and served as a springboard for the release of kidnapped Africans. I knew nothing about the farcical court trials of Marcus Garvey or the inflammatory case of the Scottsboro boys. So in high school and college I studied, learned, and lived through the cases of the Wilmington Ten, the RNA-11, the San Quentin Six, and Angela Davis, and immersed myself in issues involving the corporate divestiture and cultural boycott of South Africa, repressive law enforcement legislation such as "No-Knock," and the FBI's once secret counterintelligence program against black nationalists.

> *We have the choice to work against our best interests or the choice to actively promote justice.*

As I entered law school, I began to ponder the intellectual challenges—how to stimulate the ability to invent new ways by which the law can address the wide variety of substantive issues facing today's society. What was needed, I surmised, were strong, innovative lawyers who were not afraid to "think out of the box" and "push the envelope" to achieve change. I knew I would not be a lawyer who would be "chained to a desk," for I nurtured a penchant for the cutting edge. As an activist, public interest, and "movement" lawyer, I have felt the responsibility to use the research, writing, and advocacy skills I learned to challenge injustice. In the course of confronting injustice, I have been arrested three times. The first, in front of the South African Embassy in protest of continuing apartheid; the second, in front of the Longworth House Office Building in support of D.C. statehood; and the third, in Lafayette Square across from the White House, in support of restoring democracy to Haiti. Each time, the arrests were staged, the organizers having negotiated with the police and prosecuting authorities in advance of the demonstration, making sure that plastic cuffs would be used and all charges dropped. After each dismissal, I gave not a second thought about the arrest, and went on with my life, with the inconvenience of maybe several hours until processing was completed. These staged arrests and momentary deprivations of physical liberty of today, however, are a far cry from the terror, dogs, fire hoses, and nooses of yesterday. I can engage in these struggles today, because my predecessors were on the frontline battlefields of justice and sacrificed, struggled, and paid the price for a new generation to pick up the baton and struggle against new manifestations of injustice.

In picking up that baton, I have played a part in various endeavors that are dear to my heart—some of which include: helping to lead the legislative battle for statehood for the District of Columbia, which resulted in the first historic vote on that issue in Congress; advocating and organizing in support of a congressional bill to establish a commission to determine whether diasporic Africans should be granted reparations from the federal government, and getting the D.C. City Council to adopt the bill; mobilizing the successful campaign to defeat a death penalty referendum that was forced on the District of Columbia's 1992 ballot by Congress; initiating a coalition of legal service providers, city officials, and women's rights advocates who were successful in achieving a strong child support law in Washington, D.C; working on the successful campaign of the National Voter Registration Act, affectionately dubbed, "Motor Voter; " helping to fulfill the mandates of the Sixth Amendment by representing indigents accused of criminal offenses, as well as political prisoners whom the larger society has largely forgotten; assisting in the litigation of large scale class action prisoner suits against state governments; training more than 500 lawyers, law students, and legal workers to serve as legal observers for politically inspired demonstrations; and bringing the issue of the penalty disparity between crack and powder cocaine to the public eye.

In concluding this letter, I want to take a moment to embellish on a story Malcolm X often related about two types of slaves whom he described as the "House Negro" and the "Field Negro." Most of us are familiar with that speech. In sum, he told us that the House Negro lived up in the big house with massa – actually it was in the attic or the basement. He ate the same food massa ate, or at least the crumbs massa left, but he was satisfied with that. If massa got sick, he'd say, what's the matter boss, we sick? If massa's house caught fire he fought harder than massa to put it out.

Now, the field slave. Malcolm said he worked in the field, from 'can't see in the morning til' can't see at night.' He lived in a shack, if that, and wore gunny sacks for clothes. When massa got sick, the field slave prayed he wouldn't recover. When massa's house caught fire, he prayed for a strong wind.

Now Malcolm didn't mention another one who was out there on the plantation—the "yard hand." The yard hand came from the field, but succeeded in getting away from it. Now the yard hand didn't live in the big house, but she didn't live that far from it. She was close enough to look in, and sometimes got so close she could sneak right in. Now she didn't live too far from the field either. She could hear the whip of the lash and remembered its sting. The yard hand could see what was happening in the big house and she could see what was happening in the field. You see, because of this unique position, she often had a choice as to what her position was going to be. Was she going to work in the interests of her people or work against their interests?

The choice the yard hand had yesterday is the exact same choice we as lawyers of color have today. We have the choice to work against our best interests, or the choice to actively promote justice. This choice is present whether our practice takes us to the apex of the most lucrative law firm in the country or to the most modest legal service provider organization. No matter where our career paths take us, we have a responsibility to put the research, writing, and advocacy skills we have learned to struggle against injustice in society, and to reach back into the community to assist those who never made it out of the field. Perhaps the great orator Frederick Douglas put it best in 1857 when he explained:

The whole history of the progress of human liberty shows that all concessions . . . have been born of earnest struggle. If there is no struggle, there is no progress. Those who profess to favor freedom, and yet depreciate agitation, are [those] who want crops without plowing up the ground. They want rain without thunder and lightening. They want the ocean without the awful roar of its many waters . . . . Power concedes nothing without a demand. It never did, and it never will.

And that is what I feel being an activist, public interest, "movement" lawyer is all about—picking up the baton from our predecessors, and engaging in struggle for justice.

Nkechi Taifa

Nkechi Taifa *is Director of the Equal Justice Program at Howard University School of Law, where she also teaches seminars on racial disparity in the criminal justice system and public interest law.*

Dear Sisters, Dear Daughters,

A full 18 years out of law school, you would think I knew what I wanted out of a legal career. I worked for six years as a military attorney, 10 years at a large law firm (four of those years as a partner), and two years as a law professor. Each role had its advantages and drawbacks, and I could tell you what they were for me. But career decisions are so idiosyncratic: my telling you how much I loved criminal trials or how much I fretted hearing the great "unanswerable" question from the back of a law school classroom would serve you very little. On the other hand, as you may some day contemplate grabbing for the Brass Ring—a large firm career—I will share with you some observations from my decade of service to one of the best.

Mine is very much a tale of two minds. One mind wants every woman of color (hereinafter "Sister") to get in the mix and prepare herself for the most exhilarating, challenging, satisfying legal career in the whole wide world. My other—bruised, disrespected, misunderstood—mind wants no woman (or man) of color ever to set foot over the threshold of the most demoralizing, toxic work environment imaginable. "Can one place be both?" the Sister asks. Glad to answer. For a Sister to compete with the best and brightest, the typical big-city, large firm (hereinafter "Big Firm") expects a Sister to: excel at law school (what passes muster is exactly inverse to the reputation of your law school: a C at Boalt Hall is worth an A at Podunk State), which could result in Law Review membership, followed by a judicial clerkship (federal, if you can get it; Supreme Court would knock them on their butts).

The interested Sister should interview with the Big Firm in her first year of law school, preferably before the grades arrive, because, for good or ill, expectations and assumptions about a Sister's abilities tend to solidify quickly after grades arrive. Big Firms usually do not hire first-year law students as summer clerks, but a few have wised up to the competitive edge attendant to early contact. Sisters need not fret the interview process because we can usually turn on the charm long enough to end up with "thoughtful, articulate and personable" on the interviewer's sheet. The Sister will accept the offer to spend 12 weeks of the summer as clerk at the Big Firm, during which she will meet the influential partners and senior associates who influence her chances of succeeding. She receives lots of personal and professional attention, good work assignments (at which she performs brilliantly), enjoys a rich social life, and returns to school in the Fall clutching an offer to return to Big Firm and make an obscene amount of money. Sister can't believe her good fortune; her life could not be sweeter. The Sister will, of course, accept the offer after a suitably anguished period waiting and weighing other options. If the aforementioned Law Review and judicial clerkship do not materialize, fret not. Even if the Sister does not continue to excel in school, her offer to return to the Big Firm will not be rescinded; the Big Firm may sour a little on its premature offer, and lower its expectations according to the grade slide, but it will hold fast to its original assessment that Sister is worthy of its ranks. Besides, for the first two years, a Big Firm must teach new associates what they did not learn at law school (whether Boalt Hall or Podunk State).

The Sister matriculates at the Big Firm, which pays her even while she takes a Bar Review course (which the Big Firm pays for), takes the bar exam (ditto), and waits for results. (The prospect of not passing the bar exam is not even in the realm of possibility, so I won't go there.) As part of a class of 40 or so other bright, capable, well-educated, mostly white, half male freshly minted graduates of the nation's best schools (and a few legatees from elsewhere) the Sister feels welcome, and will soon become admired, respected, validated even, because of her obvious talents: she's a quick study; she cannot utter the word "No" to an assignment, no matter how grueling or menial. She works tirelessly, gets her assignments in on time (they need little editing), and always makes her monthly billable hours budget. Moreover, and to her great delight, Sister's hidden talents are lovingly nurtured by a progressive benevolent senior partner (What? A black woman with a solid "book" of exciting business? A white male partner from the same alma mater?) who makes Sister an integral part of her or his A Team.

You should suck in your tummy, hold up your chin, put your hand on your hip and charge on . . .

Sister thrives, accepts praise from all quarters, gets terrific evaluations (oh, how fair they are!), and participates on several Big Firm committees. Sister is a poster child for the Big Firm's progress since the bad old days, and she trots out to campuses to recruit others like her into the warmth and success she has experienced. Ultimately, a majority of the partners of the Big Firm anoint the Sister, and elect her to partnership. All the while Sister's stature at the Big Firm opens many other doors to her, and she is courted for civic boards and committees, but still spends quality time with her family and shares her gifts with the community. Did I mention the HUGE salary—more than she could ever really deserve—which she can put aside for great vacations, treasured gifts for loved ones and charity to boot? Ah, the Sister sighs; please don't let this fantastic dream end.

That other mind, which started to do righteous battle with my dream world after I'd been at my Big (expletive deleted) Firm for six or seven years has another tale. That mind advised me occasionally at first, then monthly, then weekly, and finally daily, that money and recognition and public stature could not cure what ails a Sister at a Big Law Firm. The things I encountered— on the bad days—made me want to dash across law campuses throughout the United States, from Howard to UCLA, warning "Don't interview here! Don't accept that offer! For God's sake, DON'T COME HERE!" That mind wants to warn you that if you thought you ran headlong into sexism, racism, tokenism at law school, then hang on girlfriend, 'cause it's going to be a bumpier ride. The Big Firm not too long ago used to be safely and intentionally their territory, and most are not eager to change. Vestiges of all of the dreaded "-isms" flower in these former bastions of stale, pale, and male. Some days you'll feel ignored, disrespected, violated, spurned or worse. And some days you will start to think you're the only one feeling that way.

You should suck in your tummy, hold up your chin, put your right hand on your hip and charge on, because the very next day could be one of those exhilarating days when a partner returns your memo with only one red mark and says he will incorporate it into the appellate brief in total. Girl, it'll make you physically warm all over. My advice, try it if you have the moxie; give it 110%, and if the great good stuff continues to outweigh the bad, you may have landed at home. Get comfy and bask in the glow.

Cunyon Gordon

J. **Cunyon Gordon** *is a member of the American Bar Association's Commission on Women in the Profession where she researches and writes about the role of women in the legal profession.*

Dear Sisters, Dear Daughters,

Seven years ago, I decided to begin my legal career as an associate at the law firm of Dorsey & Whitney LLP in Minneapolis, Minnesota. I decided to work at a law firm to receive great training and for the diversity of work opportunities. I also wanted to work with intelligent individuals who, like me, wanted to become and assist in the development of good attorneys.

I was wrong on all counts. In starting at the law firm, I realized that there was no formal training, at least of the type that would allow me to blossom into the great lawyer that I knew and imagined I would be. Regarding the diversity of work opportunities, my department had an attorney, the "work allocator," whose job was to allocate projects that would guarantee a myriad of meaningful assignments to each associate. The intent here was to develop each associate into a well-rounded and experienced attorney. I immediately discovered, however, that the only assignments that the work allocator received were assignments that other attorneys refused to work on. Some assignments had originally been given to the "prized" attorneys, but were passed on because those attorneys suddenly realized that the project had to be completed within a time frame that did not fit into the busy schedule of rising stars.

Therefore, early in my career, I found myself working on meaningless projects. I accepted some assignments because I had no other work and needed to meet my billable hours requirements. I accepted others because I was bored. It is simply no fun sitting eight hours each day with nothing to do. As a result of this lack of training, my work opportunities also became very limited. My lack of training now provided partners with an excuse to exclude me from various projects. When I asked to work on particular projects, they told me, "La Fleur, I would have loved to put you on this project but you do not have the relevant experience in that area. If you work on this file, you will have to spend more time on the project than someone else with the relevant experience." As I became more senior, they added the excuse of cost: "We cannot afford to train you at your high billable rate," they said.

The impact of the work allocation did not end there, however. During my evaluations, I received comments like, "Your billable hours are too low compared to your peers," or "You need to obtain more experience in certain areas," and "Your peers have surpassed you in expertise in a number of areas."

As a junior associate, these comments did not mean much, other than inducing unnecessary emotional stress. But as I became more senior, the comments became critical because I realized that my chances of being admitted into the partnership would be measured by those factors.

Law school did not prepare me for the experience I encountered at the firm. Before entering law school, I had worked as a tax accountant at American Express TRS Company. At American Express, I worked with a number of attorneys whose only concern was to work with individuals who were capable of getting their assignments done efficiently and correctly. I came to the law firm thinking that all lawyers held the same beliefs. I was wrong. I sadly discovered that most of the attorneys at the law firm cared little, if at all, about my professional progress. They did care about the progress of a few though. They cared about the progress of attorneys they had chosen based on personal affinity, to become "stars." The fairness of that concept still eludes me. I even once heard a white attorney say, "If I have work to give, I would much rather work with someone that looks like me."

Faced with the same lack of opportunity, a number of other attorneys of color left the firm. Partners, however, often justified their departures by "He could not cut it, you know" or "She was too lazy and could never get her work done," or "He was incapable of doing the work."

Obviously, these comments were then, and are now, untrue. I cannot believe that we all are incompetent. We went to law school and passed the bar like every other licensed attorney in the nation. All our lives, and until now, we have been good students and good sons and daughters. Why do we now suddenly have a problem? Why do we all leave? It is simple. First, as minorities, we are not given the same challenging work as our peers. Second, after trying unsuccessfully for years to get the same work, we finally give up because our self-esteem drops. At other times, we give up because we are simply burnt out mentally and emotionally from trying without results.

Based on my experience, I suggest that before you accept a position at a law firm, you consider a number of things. First, regarding training, you should ask whether the law firm has a formal training program. During your interviews, you should, therefore, ask questions that will give you the information you need to make an informed decision. One way of finding out is to attempt to speak to persons of color during your interviews. Although some of them will not be frank with you, a number of them will have no problem disclosing the facts to you.

If you find that there are no senior attorneys of color at the law firm where you interview, inquire as to why. Under no circumstances should you assume that you are "special." Some minorities think for a moment that the fact that they have been offered a position at a law firm, means that they should relax. This is a mistake. The hard work has just begun. They will soon find out that law school seems, in comparison, to be a long vacation.

Second, once you have accepted a position at a law firm, you must constantly monitor your career and determine whether you are receiving quality work. You can do this in a number of ways. You can obtain a checklist from your department, or if your department does not have such a list, you can create your own checklist after making the necessary inquiries. Additionally, you should keep an eye on the types of projects that your peers are receiving so that you can demand the same.

Another way of monitoring your career is to get a mentor. I would suggest that you get a mentor only after you have been in your department for a few months. Some firms will assign you a mentor. If the mentor assigned to you is not what you envisioned him to be, do not be afraid to ask someone else to be your mentor. There is no rule against having more than one mentor. The mentor you choose should be someone who not only has influence within the firm, but who also cares about your development. To provide you with meaningful experience, that mentor should also be a practicing attorney who has work that she can and will assign to you within your area of expertise. Do not discount the fact that mentors can be selected outside of the firm—create your own board of directors.

To monitor your career, when you receive your evaluations, also request and receive adequate information that would guide you toward your next steps. Namely, do not be afraid to ask whether you should look for another job or what experiences you need to provide you with the tools to not only become an excellent lawyer, but to also be invited into the partnership, if this is one of your goals.

Third, throughout your career, be sure that the quality of your work product is tight. I recall a conversation between a white partner and a white male associate regarding a project that the associate did. The quality of the work was less than perfect. The partner came to the associate's office and said, "Man, you really messed up that project, ha, ha, ha," and they both continued to joke about it. Had this been an associate of color, the approach would not have been the same. The associate would have heard about the poor quality of his work throughout the firm, and it certainly would have resurfaced in his evaluation.

Fourth, ask clients for whom you have worked to write letters to the partner in charge stating what a great job you had done on the project. These letters should become part of your permanent file.

The fifth tool that you should add to your toolbox after entering the firm is marketing. Marketing is critical to your survival. Learn to market yourself, both inside and outside the firm, but especially outside of the firm. Inside marketing, based on the perception that other attorneys have of you, helps you to receive meaningful work opportunities. Outside marketing takes more time but helps you to develop not only your independence through your client base, but to also develop alternative options of employment, should you choose to leave the firm. Larger firms have institutional clients who have been clients of the firm for ages. These clients are passed down to partners in the firm when the billing partner for that client retires or leaves the firm. Do not expect that these institutional clients will be passed to you. You must build your own client base if you wish to have longevity at a firm.

One final note, be vigilant—never let your guard down and never get too comfortable. This is probably the most difficult of all. You may have people whom you think are your friends, but behind closed doors, you can never determine the loyalty of law firm friends. Surviving in a law firm requires a great deal of stamina and positive thinking. In applying for a job at a large firm, you have to take responsibility for the choice you made to enter a world that is not supportive of minorities. The more prepared you are, the better you will be able to survive.

La Fleur Browne

La Fleur C. Browne *practices corporate law as an Associate at Dorsey & Whitney LLP in Minneapolis.*

Dear Sisters and Dear Daughters,

Interestingly, one of the greatest lessons that I have learned about how to succeed resulted from my own failure early in my legal career.

Directly after I graduated law school, I joined a large, all-white Boston firm. It was 1985, and I was breaking the color line as the firm's first associate of color. I was more intimidated by this environment than I was willing to admit, and felt utterly conspicuous. I attempted to blend in by playing myself down, and conforming to an ill-defined and foreign culture with unspoken rules. In the process, I lost a great deal of my confidence, buried my gifts, and lost my power. I realized that to thrive, I have to boldly draw on my unique perspective, personality, and values, and find environments that welcome and appreciate who I am.

My story, I have discovered, is like that of many other young associates of color. While there is a great deal of luck involved in excelling in the law firm culture, I found that hard work is not enough; it is a given. Most people who prosper in firms not only work long, intense hours, but they exude confidence, take an active role in directing their own careers, and look for and find ways to distinguish themselves. In other words, they never play themselves down.

I was the last person you would expect to lose herself. I had always been outspoken and my own person. I was a visible leader in school: the president of the Black Student Organization in college and the representative of my first year class in law school. I was the only sister in my law school class who did not rip the braids out of her head when interview season rolled around. My classmates were barely recognizable with their hair permed and curled!

I had never planned to go to a big firm. I was one of those people who went to law school to change the world. I had been a summer associate in a law firm in Baltimore after my first year and pretty much hated it. But, when I realized that I would be graduating with $65,000 in debt, and that I had been utterly powerless in trying to transform the ultimate fates of my indigent housing clients during my clinic experience at school, I rethought my aversion to corporate firms.

> *. . . one of the greatest lessons that I have learned about how to succeed resulted from my own failure early in my legal career.*

The firm I chose was a relatively new, venture capital firm. Of all the firms I considered, it appeared the least staid and "white shoe." The lawyers seemed to be genuinely nice and happy that I was integrating the firm. They considered themselves to be fair and open-minded people, and my presence seemed to affirm that. I was ready to commit myself to the firm, if only for a period of time.

In hindsight, I can see that the slow, unconscious, well-meaning, and self-protective process of putting my true self away started almost from the beginning. It didn't happen the first day or the first week. In fact, at one meeting early on, I spoke my mind in my customary way despite the other new associates' silence. I remember the looks on everyone's faces—a mixture of surprise, admiration, disapproval, and fear. I made a silent note to myself, "Pipe down; you're making them feel uncomfortable."

This diminishing of myself was hastened by the fact that the law firm environment was more foreign to me than any other place I had been. I knew there were rules, but no one was volunteering them. I was very conscious that my background had not prepared me to feel at ease and self-assured in this setting. I was also fascinated by this world of free coffee, marble tables, original art, and free cab rides home. My billable rate astounded me, and my first year salary was almost three times more than my father's annual salary after 25 years as a Baltimore City firefighter.

But none of the white associates seemed as awestruck as I was. I desperately wanted to compare notes with someone to see if they were feeling equally overwhelmed. If so, they did not confide in me.

I feared making even a single mistake. I knew that I stood out, and beneath all of the friendly faces, many of my colleagues and clients had racist assumptions. I tried to be and act like everyone else. I learned to laugh at jokes that I didn't understand, to make meaningless chitchat with colleagues, and to conceal what I truly thought.

Above all, I didn't want to do anything that might be construed as stupid. In retrospect, this meant I was afraid to ask questions when I didn't understand an assignment, to offer my opinion, or to take risks of any sort. When senior associates yelled at me, I said nothing, even though I disagreed. Little by little, I seemed to lose my spark. I worked diligently, but I was always checking and rechecking myself. I contributed long hours on deals that felt absolutely unconnected to who I was or what I cared about. I felt out of place, lonely, and unhappy.

Then I began to notice the strangest phenomenon. I had become two different people. Outside of work, I was vocal, alive, well-liked, energized, and confident. At work, I became small and submissive. As soon as I left the office, I reverted to my old self again. But being a rather transparent person, my sadness was palpable. My attitude was negative, and the quality of my work suffered.

Two and one-half years after joining the firm, I became pregnant, and decided not to return after my maternity leave. I worried about "letting the race down," removing the firm's only "color," and leaving my family with no big-time corporate lawyer. But having a child did a great deal to clarify the situation. I faced how much I hated my job, or at least hated who I was at my job. I was not about to take time away from my child to work at a place that robbed me of my best self.

Since then, I have seen many eager, vibrant, and talented associates of color encounter a culture that made them extremely circumspect. I have watched them move toward anonymity, losing an accurate picture of themselves and their abilities. When you combine this retrenchment of self with the isolation that is inevitable when there are so few people of color and such pervasive (although unacknowledged) racism, the result is often a person whose unhappiness speaks louder than her talents. Sadly, it is that person's unique gifts that made her attractive to the firm in the first place. As the personal erosion progresses, the firm begins to ask itself, "What did we see in her anyway?"

My first law firm experience taught me two things. First, be yourself, regardless of how you fear you will be perceived or received. This is the only way that you will be able to succeed and lend your total competence to your work. Second, work at something that speaks to your heart, and that has room for who you are.

Large law firms are usually not aware that their cultures exclude the contributions of many and reflect only one way of being. Cultures are very subtle and intangible. They are reinforced by preferences for a certain type or style that has little to do with merit.

In my current capacity as a diversity consultant to law firms and other organizations, my job is to help my clients examine the invisible cultures that discourage the development of people who differ from the majority culture. I coach attorneys of color (and women) to see when they are retreating from themselves, and to encourage them to bring the richest, most vibrant, and confident parts of themselves to work.

To be successful in a competitive environment like a law firm, you must find a way to distinguish yourself. In that way, people of color have an advantage. We already stick out, so we might as well make the best of it by taking advantage of our different perspectives and experiences.

A true sense of well-being, purpose, and fulfillment is possible when you are able to be yourself, and give the best of yourself to work that is meaningful to you. After all the sacrifices that you have made, you deserve to be happy. It is out there; don't stop until you find it.

Sincerely,

Verna Myers

Verna Myers *is the principal of Verna Myers & Associates, a diversity management consulting firm.*

Dear Sisters, Dear Daughters,

I grew up in a house full of cousins, presided over by my maternal grandmother. I was Grandma's "bright granny," and if you have any acquaintanceship with the Caribbean experience, you know that this title was as much a curse as it was a blessing. I was petted and spoiled beyond belief, and my legendary failures in the housekeeping department were usually indulged. My grades however, were always expected to be the best. Not merely the best that I could do, for my grandmother recognized no such limitation. I had to be better than anyone against whom I competed. In high school, I was captain of the science team, the math team, the debate team, and editor of the yearbook.

I moved to America when I was 15, and decided to go to Cornell University. My guidance counselor insisted that I apply to a back-up school. Cornell, it seemed, was too high a jump to attempt without a net. My classmates at Mount Vernon High School were even more nonplussed. One sad, young woman shook her head at my temerity and cautioned me to be serious. To her, the idea of attending an Ivy League university was a joke. I could not even begin to understand her attitude.

At Cornell, I began to understand. Cornell professors expected nothing of me. They seemed to think that I had accomplished some major feat by getting accepted to their school. When I showed up at their office hours, they were surprised, and instead of challenging me, they heaped praise on my head for my smallest contributions. I once received an "A" for a paper on the development of third world politics. My father took one look

148

at the paper and demanded that I redo it, this time without the historical inaccuracies. Apparently my professor had not read the paper that closely.

My awe of Cornell was soon replaced by disdain. As a part of this process, I started to figure out what was necessary to get a "B" in every class, and do it. I spent the rest of my time educating myself about being a black woman in America. The prestige of the institution afforded me the opportunity to meet and speak with many of black America's famous and indeed notorious thinkers. Despite itself, Cornell provided me with an invaluable education.

After Cornell, Howard Law School felt like going home. I loved my professors like parents. They rode us hard, demanding that we remain 40 pages ahead of them; that we write our exams as if they were motion papers; that we understand and could articulate the relevance of *Pierson v. Post* to any conceivable problem. They had high expectations for us, and in my head I can still hear them cheering when I succeed.

My professors cheered at my decision to join the law firm of Dorsey & Whitney. They thought that I would make a fine associate. Not everyone agreed. A Georgetown student, apparently shocked by the firm's decision to hire me and not her, gave a simple explanation—affirmative action—of course. I never confronted her with her ignorance. I simply packed it away in that space I reserve for hurtful things said by ignorant white people. During my time at Dorsey, that space grew crowded and tight.

A junior partner at the firm struck the second sour note. He invited all the first years to lunch a week or so before the bar exam. He greeted every one else by name, but when he came to me he seemed surprised. "Paulette," he said, inclining his head quizzically, "What are you doing here?" I was too surprised to answer him. He and I had spent a lot of time together the previous summer. I stood there looking dumb, and he stood there looking dumber, until one of my classmates rescued us. "That's

Shelly!" she announced, to his lasting embarrassment. Paulette, it turns out, was a Black associate who had been there many years before my time. I am told that she looks nothing like me. In that one moment, that partner made me feel like I wasn't a person in my own right, just the "black first year," interchangeable with the Black second year, and the black woman who left the firm five years before I came. After that, I found it difficult to accept any gestures of friendship or kindness as sincere.

I didn't trust the other partners at the firm either. It was clear that even the kindest people at the firm did not expect me to succeed there. They probably hoped that I would, but they didn't expect it. They were very liberal though. That much was apparent from their willingness to accept blame for my inevitable failure. They invited me to share with them the difficulties I faced as a black associate. They praised me for being a pioneer, i.e., a black female associate in a majority law firm in 1994.

I failed spectacularly at being an associate in a majority law firm. Or so I thought. I did not bill enough hours. I got mediocre evaluations. I got stuck on horrible tasks like four-month document reviews. I, who have always been my most honest critic, took a hard look at my life and decided that I needed to move on. And so I did. After three years, I quit my job and moved to Japan.

If my story ended there, there would be no story. I would just be another casualty of the law firm grind. Happily, it does not. I came back to the U.S. and worked as a contract attorney for a year before accepting a position as an attorney recruiter for a temporary placement agency. In the short time that I have been a recruiter, I've met many women just like me—black women in reputable law firms who are convinced that they've made a mistake. Maybe some of these highly qualified women are right, but there are too many of us. I recently joked to a colleague that half of the minority graduates of Cornell University ended up in our file of temporary candidates. Neither of us laughed.

This has prompted me to ask myself tough questions. Did I cut and run too fast? Were the white associates who stayed behind more competent than I? They were not better educated. Nor were they more intelligent. Why did they stay? In retrospect, they were on those crappy projects too. And they complained about their lack of hours as much as I did. Their evaluations might have gone better than mine, but I have no real reason to think that.

I keep coming back to this: I was never expected to stay there. It is obvious that majority law firms do not expect many of their associates to stay until they become partners. They certainly do not expect any of their minority associates to go the distance. They may cry about it, meet about it, pay consultants to write about it, but they do not expect it. And thus it does not happen often.

It is true that only a small percentage of the white associates who start with any given firm stay to make partner. Make no mistake. The ones who stay are the ones who are expected to stay. They are identified early and given work commensurate to their perceived ability. I don't quite know how this identification is made, but suffice it to say that I have never met a black associate—male or female—who has been tapped to join this elite group.

So my dear sisters and daughters, what do I propose that you do when faced with this problem? I expect you to set great expectations for yourself. I expect you to determine your course carefully, and then expect obstacles. When faced with these obstacles, I expect you to remember all of us who are rooting for you, all the sisters you know, and all of us whom you may never meet. We are all expecting you to succeed. God bless you.

Shelly Ann Panton

Shelly Ann Panton *is the Placement Director at the Offices of Special Counsel in New York and was previously an Associate at Dorsey & Whitney in Minneapolis and New York.*

Dear Sisters, Dear Daughters,

Perhaps the most rewarding experience of my professional life was my career change from education to law. After a short teaching career spanning elementary, high school, and college, I embarked on a legal career. The timing could not have been better for me. I left teaching before I became gilded, and at a time when my energy level was still high enough to tackle law school. It was a challenge. At that time, I was single, and that was a blessing. I could then devote the requisite amount of time to law school without having to concentrate on caring for a family.

Fast forward to the present. I am now in private practice, with a solo civil practice for the past 17 years. If my change in career was rewarding, running my own office has been the pinnacle of my professional experiences. By all means, it has not been easy. It is imperative to keep track of deadlines and other responsibilities, while still keeping current with the law, as well as cultivating new business. Notwithstanding these challenges, there is nothing more rewarding than beginning a case for a client from the time of a consultation and taking it through the necessary steps to a successful resolution.

If I had to note the most challenging aspect of private practice, it would be cultivating new business. At the beginning of my career I attempted to do this by affiliating with various bar associations, community organizations, and informally sending announcements to friends, associates, and business acquaintances. I do no formal advertising. Many of my attempts have been successful. In addition to representing clients in my practice, I serve as a hearing officer for several municipal agencies. This gives me an opportunity to diversify my practice.

To sisters and daughters, who have had any inclination or desire to do their own thing, my advice is DO IT. Perhaps the worst ode to one's life is to have not done something that you really wanted to do. I would advise, however, that even though you may contemplate starting your office straight out of law school, try to get some work experience first, so that you may have a point of reference when needed. With me, I worked for a large law firm for a short while, as well as held an administrative position that was law related, before opening my own office. The experiences I acquired in both positions, as well as my other work experiences, contribute greatly in running my office.

My current personal life consists of a husband, two adult stepchildren, and a four-year-old. About five years ago, my husband and I decided to become adoptive parents. Being a mommy has been the most rewarding personal experience for me, and the most tiring. It has caused me to juggle my life as I have never done before. It is also far more challenging than running a solo practice. It has forced me to complete all of my business responsibilities within the given hours of a business day. This has been a true challenge. I am still accepting suggestions as to the most successful way to do this.

Sisters and daughters, keep the torch high. You can make it. You are a survivor!

Best Wishes,

Jacqueline (Jacki) A. Walker

Jacqueline A. Walker *is a Sole Practitioner in Chicago with a general civil practice.*

Dear Sisters, Dear Daughters,

This will not be a wordy piece because writing is not one of my favorite things. I like to talk a lot, which is probably one of the reasons I became a lawyer. On my report card in elementary school the teacher always said, "Good student, she just talks too much." Oh well. Members of my family are in the legal field, and that also contributed to my decision. I have an uncle who is a retired judge and a cousin who is an administrative law judge. I know that my uncle inspired me to become an attorney early on. When I was growing up I would spend a week at his home and go to court with him. Seeing lawyers in action was a lot of fun, and I still remember going there as a little girl.

My parents encouraged me to do whatever I wanted to do in life and becoming a lawyer seemed like a good idea. I still think it was a good idea (most days). I went to Ohio State for my undergraduate degree and received a social science degree. What can you do with that? I graduated in three years because I knew I was going to law school and didn't want to be in school forever. I was accepted at Chicago Kent College of Law so I moved to Chicago. I loved Chicago, but I can't say the same about law school. I don't have anything against the school but I did not enjoy the law school experience. I had fun in college; I did not have fun in law school.

I clerked my first summer for a solo practitioner who was blind. I learned so much that summer. I would go to court with him, listen to his cases and arguments, file documents, and write briefs. We would discuss his theories, and he would listen to my opinions. It was a great experience and one that has helped me throughout my career. He always treated everyone the same whether they were the courtroom personnel or the judge. I learned so much more that summer than was in a book. I continued to clerk for him the next two summers, and we still are friends today.

After I graduated from law school, I clerked for a judge on the state appellate court. Justice Johnson and my uncle (the judge) had gone to undergraduate school together. My uncle told me to look up Judge Johnson while I was in Chicago. I did and he hired me. I certainly know that I was qualified for the job, but it helped to have my uncle as an intermediary. I clerked for the Justice for two years and then decided I really wanted to be a litigator. I went to work for the Chicago Housing Authority and was in court everyday. I loved it. After two years of that experience I worked for the City of Chicago and tried 13 cases to verdict. I couldn't have asked for better experience. I highly recommend that if you want to litigate cases the best place is a governmental agency. The exposure to big cases is wonderful, and you can't get it anywhere else. While I was there I was recruited away to a small law firm that needed a litigator. I went there for four years, became a partner, and left. Typical story these days. I tried cases, worked with partners and associates, and then decided to take the plunge and open my own place. I did think about other possibilities because that situation was not working out, but starting my own firm sounded exciting and challenging. I thought "I can do this as well as my current partners and maybe even better." I was truly idealistic at the time. Had I thought about it, I would have been scared. I had a husband and an 18-month-old son. What was I thinking?!

One of my partners at the other firm and I decided to open Greene and Letts. We did that on January 15, 1990. We had a business plan, a loan from the bank, a few clients, and a small office. One of my earliest happy times (other than getting the first check in from a client) was seeing our names painted on the door. The first two years were difficult financially. I took a substantial pay cut to have control over my own destiny. My partner and I never fought about money or how to run the business, and we still don't. After the first couple of years we began to see growth in the business and were becoming recognized as a good, small litigation firm. We have been in business for 10 years and now have 10 lawyers and eight support personnel. We have been very fortunate. We have a great client list and are happy to call many of them good friends. I couldn't imagine working for anyone else now.

> *I think if I can raise two well-rounded, honest and nice African American men I will have accomplished something great.*

If I were to do it again, I think I would still be a lawyer. I have made some good friends in the practice of law. I went to school with general counsel for the various corporations I now represent. I think that is because I always remember one of my mother's favorite lines, "You never know who your boss will be." I try to treat everyone fairly, even when it is hard to do. I know there has been business we haven't received because we are a minority firm, but then again there has been business we have received because we are a minority firm. I love what I do. I think everyone should aim for that because if you enjoy what you do then you will be happy. If you don't love what you do, then you should do something else. Practicing law is not for everyone.

I also try not to take myself too seriously. I have friends who say I am still the same person I was 25 years ago. I hope so. My best friends are those I have had for 20 years or more. They keep me grounded and help keep my life in perspective along with my husband and two sons. Practicing law is a job, not my life. It shouldn't be for anyone, that would be too limiting.

My family is my greatest joy and my inspiration. When the practice gets to me—which is almost daily—I think of them. I remember something that Jacqueline Kennedy Onassis once said about raising children. She said that was the most important thing she ever did in her life. I feel the same way. I think if I can raise two well-rounded, honest and nice African American men I will have accomplished something great.

Sincerely,

Eileen M. Letts

Eileen M. Letts *is a Partner at Greene and Letts in Chicago, where she is active in the legal community.*

Dear Sisters, Dear Daughters,

I am the Managing Counsel of the Marketing Practice Group of the Legal Department of McDonald's Corporation. My group is responsible for overseeing the legal support of the marketing and advertising activities of the 25,000 McDonald's restaurants worldwide. I recently celebrated 22 years of practice, and would like to share the five rules that I wish I had when I began my legal career. Those five rules are:

- Find new solutions;

- Think beyond the issue;

- Make the right mistakes;

- Tell your clients what you've done for them lately; and

- Do what YOU think is right.

Find new solutions.
We all must demonstrate that we are able to resolve the issues that are brought to us. We must be able to think creatively so that we are viewed as problem solvers who understand evolving business goals. All lawyers should want to be viewed as business people who have a legal background, rather than as lawyers whose first reaction is always, "No, you can't do that." Of course, this does not mean that we should approve every thing our clients propose. Rather, it means that we should constantly work with our clients as team members, not as adversaries, searching for ways that something CAN work.

This is not enough, however. To be considered for promotion to the management levels, we must always . . .

Think beyond the immediate issue.
As law students, we were trained to analyze facts, identify issues, develop alternate solutions, and articulate the corresponding risks. If we merely provide solutions to issues identified by our clients, we are not serving them well. We must continually ask ourselves, "What other issues are there?", "How will the resolution of this issue affect other aspects of the client's business?" Thinking of the bigger picture makes it possible for us to appreciate the role that the original issue plays in the context of our clients' overall business. For example, rather than focusing solely on a series of difficult negotiations regarding the allocation of liability, address the larger issue of the reasons for the difficulty. Consider obtaining insurance to solve the larger, as well as individual, negotiation issues.

If we are aggressive about thinking creatively and beyond the original issue, we all will inevitably make mistakes. In fact, if we aren't making mistakes from time to time, we are probably spending too much energy executing other people's ideas of the world at the worker bee level rather than thinking strategically at management levels. We must not be afraid to . . .

Make the right mistakes.
We all know what the wrong mistakes look like—errors resulting from poor judgment, failure to ask for clarification, inadequate knowledge of the law. Mistakes that follow thorough analysis and out-of-the-box thinking will be made by all of us from time to time if we are doing our jobs right. View these mistakes as opportunities to learn something for the next time, not as stumbling blocks to success. We learn not only from our accomplishments but also from our missteps. In fact, our clients can often learn more about their business from what didn't work than from what worked smoothly.

Make sure that your clients know what has worked and what

has not. Just as important as the time and energy you devote to the issues is the willingness to . . .

Tell your clients what you've done for them lately.
Chances are, we were told by our parents and teachers that hard work would bring us success—good grades, good schools, good jobs, and many promotions. Of course, that is simply the beginning. Sitting in our offices after hours and on weekends might get the work done, but it is not enough.

We must make certain our clients know how we are supporting them. They have a right to be informed of the resources we bring to the table. Furthermore, we have a right to earn recognition for our good work. Yes, it takes some effort, but the long-term benefits are many. Decide that no project is complete until we have communicated this last piece of information to the client.

We must use our good judgment to market our skills and to educate our clients. Not all projects call for a major wrap-up meeting. Often a memo or a short face-to-face conversation will do.

We must not be afraid to make the right mistakes.

Do what YOU think is right. There will be many times when we will feel pressured to make a decision that doesn't feel right. We must trust our training and instincts to do what makes sense. Know that whatever decision we make, there will ALWAYS be some people who will be happy and others who will disagree. Several years ago, I was elected to chair a major promotion marketing trade association. One of my first responsibilities was to appoint a number of committees. I felt a tremendous amount of pressure to make certain appointments, but I took a breath, and ultimately selected the people I thought were right for the job. Did everyone agree with my decisions? Of course not, but realizing that there would never be unanimous support regardless of what decision

I made, I knew I had to make the decision that was the result of my own analysis, not the result of someone else's judgments.

Best wishes to you as you reach for your professional goals and seek your personal dreams.

Sincerely,

Kathryn Kimura Misna

Kathryn Kimura Misna *is Managing Counsel with McDonald's Corporation and is the Group Leader of the Marketing/Advertising Practice Group.*

Dear Sisters, Dear Daughters,

As a young associate in the satellite office of a major Wall Street law firm at first I felt alone and without support. After all, I was the only female and minority sharing an office with nine white males. I was further isolated by the area of law in which I had chosen to practice—transactional finance—a world in 1981 that was dominated by white men. It was not uncommon for me to attend a meeting of 20 professionals (attorneys, investment bankers, and accountants) and be the only female and minority in the room. It became evident to me early on that if I were to be successful, I would have to seek advice from women of color who had succeeded in careers outside the practice of law. Though our careers were different, many of the issues we faced were the same. I inquired of those few women of color I did meet in corporate or political positions how they had achieved their level of success.

First and foremost, I was told to listen. Hear what your associates, senior attorneys, partners, and clients are saying. If something is unclear, ask for clarification. If you are listening, you are learning, and you can and will respond in the appropriate manner. This advice never proved more useful than when I was asked to draft a document by a then-senior associate. I remembered that this particular attorney had mentioned drafting a similar document in a different deal he had worked on a few years earlier. Though I had been given a different set of documents to work from, I went to the shelves and pulled the transcript file. I compared the attorney's work on that document to the draft I was preparing. After submitting the document for review to the supervising attorney, I was summoned to his office. He was quite surprised and upset that I had included provisions in the document that had not been in the draft I was given to mark up. He couldn't imagine where I would have gotten these inserted provisions given my level of a second-year associate. (Because I had clerked a year and received credit for that year in actual experience, I was only a first year associate.) Imagine his surprise when I walked calmly to his bookshelves, pulled the transcript down, and showed him that the very passages he was questioning had been authored by him in that earlier trans-action. What could have been a fiasco quickly turned to kudos and pats on the back.

Second only to listening is being responsive. This lesson I learned quite by accident. As a young associate in a small office, it was virtually impossible to avoid client contact. I was eager to respond to every client who called me. I was amazed at their response even when my call to them was simply to state that I did not know the answer to their question but that I would obtain it as quickly as possible. They thanked me and expressed how much they appreciated my getting back to them so promptly. Many told me that they were accustomed to wait-ing two or three days before getting a return phone call. I real-ized that I had discovered a way to distinguish myself from other attorneys even before many of the clients had the oppor-tunity to meet me face to face.

My sisters told me to take my "disadvantages" and turn them to my advantage. Because I was normally the only female of color working on a transaction, people would automatically remem-ber me. Their advice: give them something positive to associate with that memory. By nature I am an outgoing cheerful person, proud to be a woman of color. I used these traits to forge an identity. In an area of the law that is serious and often tense, as the timing of many financings is tied in large part to the actions or reactions of the financial market, I would "never let them see me sweat." I would assure persons on the deal that their transaction would close and use humor to lighten the moment for everyone. On one occasion I literally was on the phone with the cage of a major investment banking firm with less than 60 seconds to close the deal. I gave the final okay to deliver the securities and exchange the funds with nine seconds to spare. When the earthquake of 1989 hit northern California, the transaction on which I was the lead partner was the only one to close the day after the earthquake even though our office, along with most other offices in San Francisco, were closed. I used cell phones, our Los Angeles office staff and sheer determination to get the job done. My word was my bond, and the clients I worked with quickly came to this realization.

You needn't give up one ounce of your femininity or heritage to make it in your chosen field.

You needn't give up one ounce of your femininity or heritage to make it in your chosen field. You will never be a man so don't waste your time trying to pursue this approach to achieve success. The women I've seen who have chosen this road were uncomfortable in the role they had assumed and it showed. If you are not comfortable with yourself, others will not be comfortable placing their confidence in you either. The importance of being yourself cannot be stressed enough. This does not mean, however, that you should not exercise good judgment on what aspects of your character should remain outside the office environment. For example, if you love to express yourself through the clothes you wear, be sure they are office-appropriate. You can have your own style without being out of style in the professional setting where you conduct your business. It may be true that clothes don't make the person but they do make an impression, so be sure that what you wear does not overshadow the person you are: educated, confident, and about taking care of business.

Finally, do not buy into the misguided notion that having a spouse and/or children will hinder your ability to succeed to the highest level in your profession. Every male coworker at your job will have a girlfriend, significant other, or spouse. You are not only entitled to have the same types of relationships, but you need this support in your life. A loved one keeps you balanced, picks you up when you feel down, is there to share in your triumphs, and in general just makes life's obstacles seem that much more bearable and surmountable. I am a wife and mother, and I am not saying it will be easy. As with anything in life worth having, extra effort is required—but that is what the practice of law is all about—solving problems through creativity.

Do not despair sisters and daughters. If you do not have a mentor in your firm, reach out to a woman of color in another firm or profession. We have all had to face the awkward situation (the client calls you honey or wants to give you the congratulatory kiss on a job well done), the isolation of being the only one, fear of the glass ceiling, and balancing our professional and personal lives. It is for these reasons that I felt compelled to write this letter to you. You are not alone. Our numbers are small, but we are growing ever stronger!

Sincerely,

Regina Bryant-Fields

Regina L. Bryant-Fields *is a Partner with Brown & Wood in San Francisco where she became the firm's first African American partner.*

Dear Sisters, Dear Daughters,

If there is one piece of advice I can give you, it is to work toward retirement, or financial independence as early as possible, as this will open up many opportunities and options for you. Imagine being able to retire early or whenever you wish, in style. This can happen to you if you save regularly and invest wisely.

Coming from a banking background, I have always known how to manage and save money. The most important thing to do, early in life, is to pay off school loans or other debts, such as balances on credit cards, as soon as possible, and then start saving for retirement. From the beginning of my legal career, I have worked toward financial independence and a pleasant retirement. My first two positions with a title company and public defender agency had no formal retirement plans. With no retirement vehicle in place at either job, I started my own personal retirement plan with savings from my salary. My husband was working and we lived on his salary. I invested my salary in real estate and stocks, while keeping an emergency cash fund.

Usually a first investment is home ownership, whether it's the purchase of a home, condo, or a duplex. For a single, young attorney or a young married attorney, a duplex is ideal. Buy in an area with growth potential, with good schools and low crime, because the property should appreciate dramatically. You could live in one side of the duplex and rent the other side. The rental payments could cover some or all of your mortgage payment. Years later, when your mortgage payments cease, you own the property, and all rental income is cash flow to you. With homeownership, you build equity. The next step is to broaden your investments through other real estate or purchase stocks. The advantage of purchasing stocks is that stocks require less money, and the funds are more liquid.

My third job was with the Washington State Attorney General's office, and their retirement plan was a 401(k). You could defer up to 15 percent of your salary, up to $9,500 per year. I deferred the maximum salary amount.

My fourth position was with the bank, and its primary retirement vehicle was a qualified 401(k). They also had a nonqualified retirement for the top executives of the bank. As Vice President and General Counsel of the bank I qualified for this and was able to defer 25 percent of my salary into this vehicle, thus providing me with a greater retirement income.

Gone are the good old days in which the older generation of attorneys spent their entire career at one firm and were rewarded with a generous pension. The good old days may never have really existed for minority women attorneys anyway. Most attorneys thought they were always going to work and never thought about getting old until they were old. By then it was too late. Many admit they didn't give much thought to retirement while they were working.

Attorneys today are destined to spend more time moving from job to job without a retirement safety net. Baby boomers, those born between 1946 and 1964, are more financially prepared for retirement than any previous generation. An average attorney who saves and invests can be a millionaire or multimillionaire in 20 to 30 years.

For those working for corporations, the proportion of workers covered by an employer-funded retirement plan is growing, as are the types of retirement plans available to them. In addition to traditional pension plans, many companies offer profit-sharing plans, tax-deferred 401(k) plans, employee stock option plans, cash balance pension plans, and other cost-saving fringe benefits. Stock option plans for attorneys, especially if the stock soars, can be very lucrative. Pick your corporation carefully.

Most law firms, nonprofits, and government agencies have their own retirement plans. Today, legislation has accelerated vesting schedules so attorneys can qualify faster for pensions. More women attorneys will qualify for pension coverage. New types of retirement plans are more portable and flexible, allowing attorneys who move from job to job to take their 401(k) and cash balance programs with them.

> *Attorneys need to learn that they need to take care of themselves because no one else will.*

As an attorney, you need to take the initiative to contribute to a 401(k) and take a more active role in retirement planning and financial independence. As a young attorney, participating in a 401(k) or other retirement plan will give you a head start on saving for retirement, though this may not be enough. Young attorneys will need more money than their parents because they expect more out of life. They live life and enjoy themselves, and that is where a lot of the money will go. Attorneys need to learn that they need to take care of themselves because no one else will.

Timely tips:

- Learn to save a certain amount of your money from each paycheck and automatically put that amount into a savings account every month. You'll learn to live on less, and after awhile, you won't miss the money. The fun will be watching your money grow.

- Know what your monthly expenses are. Most attorneys have no idea what their monthly expenses are or where their money goes. Take control of your expenditures.

- Invest the bulk of your savings in fairly safe investments like blue chip stocks, and real estate, and invest for the long pull. Put a small amount into selected Internet stocks. If Internet stocks go up, you'll make a profit, but if they go down considerably, at least it will be a small part of your portfolio. Always keep sufficient cash in your savings account for an emergency.

- Start saving as soon as you get your first job. Due to the power of compounding (earning on earnings), the earlier you start saving, the more money you'll have later. Someone who starts saving money years later than you will never catch up to you.

Every minority woman attorney has the opportunity to be a millionaire when they retire, if she work towards financial independence.

Sincerely,

Karen Wong

Karen Wong *is Vice President and General Counsel for United Savings and Loan Bank in Seattle, Washington, where she practices banking, real estate and corporate law.*

Dear Sisters, Dear Daughters,

I began my career as a beneficiary of an antipoverty program for young, urban mothers. The government paid for my college education. I pursued a degree in elementary education as a way of giving back to my community.

After two years of teaching in the inner city, I found my students' ability to learn was being affected by their parents' problems of poor housing, abusive relationships, and drug use. I needed to address those issues to make a difference in their lives. Law seemed to be the appropriate vehicle.

I was married to a community organizer who encouraged me to go to law school. As a mother with four children (twin boys, age three, a daughter, age nine, and a son, age ten) I didn't think we could handle it. My husband assured me his support. Unfortunately, this was lip service on his part. My husband wasn't supportive. Law school gave me an independent identity that threatened him. I loved law school even as my marriage was crashing.

Law school was the hardest time of my life. Attending law school, keeping up with the constant reading, enduring the highly pressurized environment, and then coming home to mother four children was an intense struggle. Without my daughter's help, I could not have done it all.

I began my legal career when I was selected to receive a Reginald Heber Smith Fellowship. I was assigned to Union County Legal Services and represented victims of domestic violence. After a year, I was offered a permanent position with the agency. I loved the work and felt I was making positive changes in my community. My career was flourishing.

At this point the most trying period in my life occurred. My twin sister, Linda, was diagnosed with cancer and died during my second year with the agency. The futility of her death to cervical cancer because of a clinical error still haunts me. Linda's death changed my focus. I was no longer as interested in career advancement and remained with Legal Services for five years, reluctant to create more change in my life.

During this period I continued my involvement in politics, which I view as a vehicle for change. It led to a change for me. A candidate I supported was elected mayor of a major New Jersey municipality, and I was given a wonderful opportunity to develop low-income housing, which resulted in 1,000 units of affordable housing.

This work left me hungry to do more in a leadership position, but I had hit a glass ceiling. Seeing positions continually being offered to less-qualified men left me frustrated. I started seeking employment elsewhere.

I was offered a position as executive director for a federal housing agency and quickly accepted. The agency was similar to a small town with several thousand residents and staff to support their needs. It was the opportunity I wanted to direct an agency and see my ideas become reality.

Political winds changed after several years and the newly elected leadership sought the director's spot for their candidate. I held on and resisted because I simply could not believe back-room politics would control, when I was securing millions in grant funding for the agency. I misjudged the situation and remained on this sinking ship too long. I learned from this experience that you have to know when to cut your losses and move on.

The political intrigue damaged my career. I began a solo practice and found I did not like it. The isolation of the small practice was not meant for me. I needed to interact with people. I began to think of a way to get out.

As a trustee of a state college, I interacted frequently with my state senator. She seemed to respect my work and agreed to become my mentor. Through her auspices, I became an assistant prosecutor and began to rebuild my legal career.

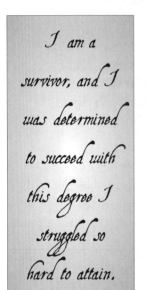

I am a survivor, and I was determined to succeed with this degree I struggled so hard to attain.

Because I have always practiced in the civil field, I had to learn criminal law. Criminal trial practice is intense, appeals are frequent, and one needs a good working knowledge of evidence rules. It was like being in law school all over again. But, I am a survivor, and I was determined to succeed with this degree I struggled so hard to attain. I was promoted to our office's prestigious trial section, and I try a broad range of cases ranging from attempted murder to robbery to narcotics distribution. I found that I enjoy criminal practice!

My wildest dream is to combine the law and television. For two years, I hosted a television show devoted to discussing African American issues. It was exciting and fun. I would have pursued this career path if there had been enough money to support my living expenses. Now that my children are grown, I am reconsidering pursuit of this dream.

I have developed some insights I would like to leave you with:

- The key to success in law is to identify your goals early and remain focused on them.

- Maintain civic and other associations that are in line with those goals.

- Look for mentors in these organizations; they are your natural allies because they share your interests.

- Try to go the traditional route for your career, because it's easier to go from corporate to nonprofit, than the other way around.

Starting out with a law firm is good preparation for any legal position. Good luck!

Patricia Weston Rivera

Patricia Weston Rivera *is Assistant Prosecutor for the County of Essex in New Jersey and is assigned to the Adult Trial Section where she litigates felonies.*

Dear Sisters, Dear Daughters,

How are you doing? I'm doing just great! I just received a monetary performance award for the successful outcome of the contract negotiations and employee strike at one of my field locations. I provided advice and counsel for this client group all summer long. Boy, was that a trying and difficult time! But, my dedication and my hard-smart work paid off monetarily and personally. I went above and beyond what the law department requires of its in-house attorneys to ensure that the actions the client took complied with the law and met their business needs.

As I reminisce, I recall numerous occasions on which I have gone above and beyond to ensure a successful outcome. Many of my female colleagues believe that we must meet a higher standard to be viewed as equals in the legal profession. When did I develop this quality of going above and beyond?

Well, my memory takes me back to my childhood in Grenada, Mississippi. When I was eight years old my mother told me to sweep the kitchen floor. I hurried through the task, leaving crumbs and dust particles here and there. She inspected the floor and made me perform the task again. I hurried through it again. She checked it again; it still was not satisfactory to her. We went through this episode about seven times until I had swept every inch of the floor and there was nary a crumb or particle to be seen. Whew! She was finally satisfied. Mom then said to me, "Always do the best that you can do at any job or task, even if it is just sweeping a floor."

Mom's advice left an indelible mark on me throughout my childhood and adult life. Little did I know that the sweeping episode and that single piece of advice would mold and shape my work ethics and values. Little did I know that it would prepare me to survive and prosper in a male-dominated profession. This single learning greatly impacted the way I achieve success both at home and at work.

How has this episode impacted my legal career? My first legal-related job was working as a judicial clerk at the Illinois Appellate Court. There, I was able to hone my research and writing skills with the assistance of the judge for whom I worked. I developed a love for writing and attempted to be artful in my drafting.

From there I landed a labor and employment law position at a large municipal corporation. At this municipal corporation the word "training" was not a part of the vocabulary. This meant that you were hired and from "day one," you were given labor arbitration files and litigation matters to handle without training. You either sank or swam! I chose to swim, as my mother had taught me to do the best I could possibly do in all circumstances.

While working there, I handled hundreds of labor arbitrations and arbitration briefs. Because of my love for writing and my desire to win, I spent the time needed to ensure a high quality product. I took my briefs home to further refine and hone— chip, chip, chipping away at this lapidary art of writing. The time I spent paid off because I was winning my cases and receiving recognition from arbitrators, coworkers, and managers. This is another example of how going above and beyond paid-off.

Notwithstanding my record of winning and the kudos I received, one of the office managers told me my briefs were too long and that I was spending entirely too much time preparing them. I told him not to worry because I wasn't wasting the company's time on these briefs; I was writing a portion of it after hours at home. And this was fine with me considering my heavy workload. Remember this key learning point: Set your own standards; do not allow anyone to influence you to compromise your standards.

The five years of going above and beyond at this municipal corporation paid-off with a coveted in-house legal position at a Fortune 500 corporation. And mind you, this position did not require private law firm experience. So this dispels the myth that it is impossible to enter the private sector after serving in the public sector. It is unorthodox, but possible.

Now the questions become: How has my above-and-beyond standard impacted my career in a major corporation? And how has my above-and-beyond standard impacted the corporation?

This standard has garnered me several promotions and the opportunity to perform nonlegal functions. In addition to handling a full-time labor and employment workload, I have been assigned responsibility in the diversity and social responsibility areas, i.e., supplier diversity and community relations.

Shortly after joining my company, the Chief Legal Officer (whom I refer to as my corporate sponsor) assigned me the function of monitoring, reviewing, and reporting the company's minority spending. Immediately, I reviewed and analyzed the current processes and results, and began working with senior management to propose a formal, corporate-wide Supplier Diversity Program. This program was fully implemented two years later. Currently, I serve as the program's compliance officer and as the Law Department's Supplier Diversity Coordinator, ensuring that the department assigns a fair share of its legal work to minority and women attorneys in small and large law firms. My company's supplier diversity efforts have been recognized or honored by the American Bar Association, Chicago Bar Association, NAACP, National Bar Association, and Chicago Minority Business Development Council. In addition to those duties, I serve as a corporate spokesperson and representative at various events throughout the U.S. Going above and beyond can create non-legal opportunities in which you can make a difference in society and your community.

My above and beyond standard has greatly impacted my client group at my company in the way of very few Equal Employment Opportunity (EEO) charges and limited employment litigation. (But some employees will file charges or sue you no matter how unmeritorious the claims.) Until a couple of months ago, I was unaware of the innovative nature of my approach to labor and employment law. At that time, I participated in a survey conducted by a large national employment law firm. The two interviewers, which included a male attorney and a female marketing consultant, inquired about my practice and current employment law trends.

I described my practice and the results of my work (one EEO charge and very limited litigation). Both were impressed with my methods and my record. They then explained that out of the 70 companies they had already interviewed, only two or three in-house attorneys were utilizing my liability prevention methods. The interviewers added that these two or three individuals had a low-volume litigation. I was amazed because I thought all in-house attorneys handled the practice similarly. Both interviewers confirmed that I was, indeed, going above and beyond the call of duty to protect my company from liability.

Have I reduced my practice to a science? Well, no, it's just plain old-fashioned hard, smart work. Have I piqued your interest in how I do it? In a nutshell, this is how:

- I gain the trust and respect of my clients by being personable, proactive, and accessible. I provide quality, timely service.

- I conduct quarterly training sessions to educate the client and assist the client in identifying issues for which legal counsel may be necessary.

- I review all recommendations for termination and draft detailed termination letters.

- I use releases. My company properly instituted the use of releases for individual terminations and reductions in force.

Utilizing this approach in the labor and employment area is as time consuming as litigation, but less costly. In this approach you are utilizing your time and resources on the front end instead of the back end; therefore, you are proactively preventing liability and reducing cost. Being proactive and innovative will prevent and limit corporate liability.

In closing, going above and beyond has paid off in both my professional life and personal life. I have climbed the corporate ladder while maintaining my personal beliefs, values, and high performance standards. In addition, I have balanced my career with the time I have to raise my two children, an eight-year-old son and a 19-year-old daughter. My daughter is currently matriculating at Harvard University in Cambridge, Massachusetts. Her acceptance at Harvard University is one of our greatest achievements. She has set the standard for her brother.

As my Mom said, if you are going to do anything, do it right, and do the best you possibly can. I must thank my Mom for instilling this quality in me because it has allowed me to make a difference at work, at home, and in this society.

I trust that I have provided some wisdom and knowledge you may use on your journey to success as a woman striving to achieve in the legal profession.

Best wishes to you in your career,

Sheila Wilson-Freelon

Sheila Wilson-Freelon *is Vice President and Senior Attorney at Morgan Stanley Dean Witter in Riverwoods, Illinois.*

Dear Sisters, Dear Daughters,

Know who you are, because they won't!

A philosopher once said, "Know thyself." When it comes to practicing criminal defense, there is no truer maxim.

In the 20 years I have defended those accused of criminal offenses, my identity as a black, female attorney was questioned by others on several occasions.

Although many in the legal profession view women attorneys in a positive light, my reflections over the past two decades are that it was fortunate I learned early in my career what being in a courtroom was all about.

For instance, I have known I was skilled at litigation ever since juries returned "not guilty" verdicts on my first two trials as I interned with the public defender's office in 1978. This accomplishment led to a job offer after I graduated from law school in 1979.

Yet, one of my best friends, who happened to be white, Jewish, and graduating from law school with me, said I was hired over her because of the office's need to fill a quota.

"Affirmative Action," I replied incredulously, "What was that in 1978?" I exclaimed that I was not admitted to law school under any special program that I knew of. I worked hard through undergraduate school, while married and with a child, to maintain a respectable 3.2 grade point average.

I told her I applied to only one law school and was accepted, I thought, on my merits. Even though my friend and I interned at the same place and time, I believe I better grasped the concept of litigation with a fierce passion and understanding that it was my job to defend a court-appointed client and not my duty to judge their actions. I simply thought that on this level, I was more qualified than she.

Yet in private practice I have learned over the years that if you intend to go into a legal arena and fight for clients such as those who are accused of first-degree murder, you had better know who you are because others in the system won't have a clue.

Years ago there were judges who suggested I not wear my hair braided to the courthouse because "they" may think I was not professional. On occasion, I was invited into chambers with a judge before trial who casually mentioned that female attorneys not wear pink, blue, or yellow suits in his courtroom. By the way, my suit was brown.

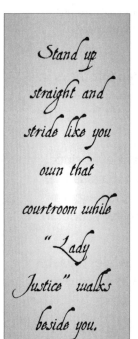

Stand up straight and stride like you own that courtroom while "Lady Justice" walks beside you.

One time I went to court and walked near the bench to better hear the judge discuss my client's codefendant's case and was asked, "Are you the defendant's mother?" I recall going to court in a small town and sitting in a row marked "Attorneys Only," just to have the bailiff ask loudly if I was seated in the wrong section. I calmly remarked that I was an attorney and yes, I had learned to read.

Through events such as these, I have come to acknowledge that you must set the tempo of who you are as a lawyer. It will not be easy, but the more you go to court, the more you learn and become comfortable with the setting. Know that the clerk of the court can be your best friend. Ask questions of court personnel when you don't know the judge's procedure. Be punctual or early, prepared to advance your clients' case as it pertains to the law, courteous to opposing counsel, and at all times representing to all asunder that it is your job, duty, and privilege to defend your client.

Stand up straight and stride like you own that courtroom while "Lady Justice" walks beside you. To thine own self be true, and you will find that your suit fits, you sleep at night, have fewer regrets over the outcome of cases, and in the process become a better lawyer. In other words, you know who you are.

Angela Langford Jacobs

Angela Langford Jacobs *has been a Solo Practitioner for 12 years and has a background in journalism and communications.*

Dear Sisters, Dear Daughters,

One of the questions I am often asked is why I decided to pursue a formal education at a time when I had one married child, one teenager in high school, and two young adults in college. I was 41 years old in 1978, when I left my job as a secretary, after working 20 years in the clerical field, to enroll as a freshman at the University of New Mexico. Going to college had been a goal of mine, and attending law school had been a dream. I was facing an opportunity to pursue my personal goals. My boss was concerned about my decision. He tried to persuade me to stay in my position as secretary to the Chief of Pathology in a military hospital laboratory. When I stood by my decision, he tried to prepare me for the reality of four years of college, without a paycheck, without credit toward a retirement plan, and without the assurance that law school would accept me. My response was that I had weighed all that against my need to find out my true potential. I had also planned to take courses that would prepare me for more meaningful employment if I didn't get into law school. Although I was afraid that I might not be law school material, I had a strong desire to learn and to work to help minorities and the underprivileged. Although I didn't particularly feel underprivileged, I had experienced the pain of discrimination many times.

In 1978 when I started my college studies, nontraditional students such as myself were definitely a minority. No counselors were available to assist us. I learned how to select courses and professors by exchanging information with other students.

Some professors were very helpful. I sensed intimidation on the part of others. I was older than they were, I was a minority, and I was determined to get meaningful information. In my first year, I was strongly attracted to sociology studies. I majored in sociology and completed a social welfare minor. I applied for law school. I was truly overjoyed and honestly surprised when I was accepted.

Once in law school I was sure that the admissions committee had made a mistake in selecting me. I really feared someone would approach me to inform me that there had been a mistake in my admission. I was one of about 120 first-year students. Most of those students were members of the legal community. I thought I was the only person in the class who felt lost. I felt the same stress I had felt when learning a foreign language. I was in real fear of not making grades that would take me beyond the first year. Thanks to some very supportive professors, I stayed in the program and I survived.

Now that I am a lawyer, I can see opportunities I could have used to familiarize myself with the work of lawyers and the language of the legal profession. I would have started clerking at the first opportunity. I didn't do it because after being in the working world so many years, I felt I had nothing to offer an employer in exchange for a paycheck. When I finally did start working as a law intern for the Albuquerque City Attorney's office, I experienced relief when I found that what I had learned in law school was very useful in the practice of law. I remember a particular young attorney in that office who invited me to join him at court hearings so that I could get more comfortable in the courtroom. Another option for me would have been volunteering my services to an agency or a project. I just didn't realize it at the time. In Albuquerque, we have a Technical Vocational Institute that teaches courses in paralegal studies. Perhaps if I had known about this before, I could have audited some courses before law school enrollment. Some of those courses are featured on cable television.

As an attorney I practiced in the area of criminal law for the first four years. I gained jury trial experience. I always had last minute jitters before trials, as well as some real fears of making a fool of myself, but I felt that trials were important to my career development. At my age I could not put off that experience. I changed direction when I applied for work with my state's department of human services. I wanted experience in civil law practice, and I thought the Department could put my sociology training to use. I accepted a position with the Child Support Enforcement Division (CSED). Again I felt a bit of apprehension as I made a change I felt was necessary.

. . . work at something you really want to do, but not at the expense of your values and integrity.

Throughout my law career, I have received remarkable help from my fellow attorneys and my mentors. I have learned to make use of all my experiences, even the unpleasant ones. I sometimes sense what I interpret as discrimination in the community. Whether I feel it is because I am a Latina, a woman, an older person, or simply not a member of the club, I keep right on striving to make a difference. I believe it is very important to work at something you really want to do, but not at the expense of your values and integrity. I advise all sisters always to deal honestly and fairly, and never to mislead the court, your opposing counsel, or your client.

CSED introduced a Native American Program last year, and I was asked to work in the program. Currently I am admitted to practice in several of the tribal courts that require admission to the tribal bar. I communicate with the staff of 21 different American Indian tribes in our state, as well as out-of-state tribes. I feel so privileged.

My advice to sisters and daughters is to explore some of your opportunities. Talk to fellow attorneys. Form a group of like-minded persons if none is available to you. Share your aspirations, your triumphs, and even your disappointments and failures if you feel comfortable doing so. Mentor a newer minority attorney of whatever age. Each of us has something valuable to offer our profession.

Sincerely,

Raquel Odila Velasquez

Raquel Odila Velasquez *works for the New Mexico Human Services Department, Child Support Enforcement Division, where she interacts with Pueblo and Apache tribes and Navajo Nation Courts.*

Dear Sisters, Dear Daughters,

I decided to attend law school after my first husband and I divorced. I found it very difficult to raise a child alone on my income and definitely needed a change in my life. Moreover, I was bored with my job as an Associate English Professor at a community college in Florida. I didn't know exactly if I wanted to be a lawyer, but I did know that I did not want to continue teaching at that point in my life. I wanted more for myself and my daughter. Having been encouraged to go to law school by a former college professor, I took the LSAT and submitted applications to five law schools. I was accepted at all five. I decided to attend UCLA in an attempt to leave Jacksonville, Florida, as far behind as possible.

Because I had done little to prepare for law school, the only area of the law about which I had any knowledge was criminal law. No one I knew encountered the law unless it resulted from an arrest or some skirmish with the police. I definitely had no idea of how difficult law school would be because I had always breezed through school effortlessly. The first person I encountered when I arrived at the law school clearly provided me with his unsolicited assessment of the obstacles I would face in law school. The very first words out of the financial aid officer's mouth to me was that there was no way that I would finish law school because my financial aid included so much work study. In his experience, no one could complete the first year of law school having to work so many hours. My first reaction was to think that he was making those comments to me because I was black.

Once I began classes, I realized that perhaps it was not racism, but realism, that had motivated the financial officer, for he knew how difficult law school might be for someone like me who grew up in one of the poorest neighborhoods in Jacksonville, Florida. I had no idea what civil law was. But a stubborn and determined young woman, I was undeterred by the comments of the financial aid officer. I have never allowed anyone or any set of circumstances to be the determining factors that set my course in life. Consequently, I made up my mind right then and there that I would finish law school no matter what.

I was very idealistic and thought that people in law school would be of the highest character. Coming from the South, I was very naive and shocked when I discovered how competitive everyone was. My first work study job was in the law library. The job provided me the opportunity to interact with many of the law students. Mostly, they were obnoxious by my standards and wholly unwilling to share information with one another. I arrived on the job just as second-year students were preparing a brief either for the annual moot court competition or for the legal research and writing course. To give themselves an advantage, students had sliced cases from books so that they would not be available to other students. Consequently, when I began my job in the library all of those books were being sent to the bindery because of the missing pages. I was appalled. With my black fundamentalist Baptist background, I had never been around such dishonest people. As a result, I became very self-righteous and disliked my fellow students intensely because all they cared about was winning at all costs.

I felt like a fish out of water because I was committed to practicing criminal law, while everyone around me was interested in a business law practice either with a big law firm or with a corporation. In my mind, to show commitment to "my people," I believed that I had to engage in criminal or poverty law. But after interning with the public defender while in law school, I realized that I could not practice criminal law because I felt that many of the individuals that we represented were guilty as charged, and I just wanted to advise them to plead guilty. And there was no way that I was going to become a prosecutor and place blacks behind bars. My next choice for a practice was poverty law. Therefore, upon graduation from law school I went to work for legal aid where I felt very frustrated because most of my clients needed money to solve their problems. I felt more comfortable working for my next employer, an advocacy group for females. Finally, I landed a trial attorney position with my current employer where I feel that I am able to assist people in addressing the issue of discrimination.

> *I had to deal with the obstacles life brought and win because I had to show my daughter how to succeed at life.*

I have been on my job for 16 years and have grown tremendously in that time. I lost my first trial and learned from that failure the need to take no facts for granted. I had my agency's first jury trial, and I won the case through some very creative lawyering; it is important to understand that lawyering can be very creative. I have worked hard to attain my current position as head of my legal unit, a position that affords me the opportunity to mentor young attorneys, both male and female. Acquiring the position did not come easy because there was a great deal of competition associated with the position. I was patient and persevered, however, until it was agreed that I was the right person for the job. During that time, I maintained a high life condition by exercising self-discipline and by not allowing myself to be distracted by the opinions of those around me. I remained completely focused on my goal.

There have always been detractors who have tried to convince me that I do not deserve to advance in the workplace. Many of you, my dear sisters and daughters, may face people who make you feel like your life has no value. Do not be swayed by such utter nonsense. When confronted with such negativity, I have always been able to muster up the strength to fight with all my life for a just result for both myself and others. And fortunately, there have always been mentors in my life to inspire me to go forward. I have also been strongly motivated by my daughter, who was six years old when I decided to go to law school. I had to deal with the obstacles life brought and win because I had to show my daughter how to succeed at life. Success at life does not come from the avoidance of the challenges life brings, but by using wisdom, courage, and confidence to deal with them.

My dear sisters and daughters, having had several positions myself and having dealt with the employment problems of thousands of employees in my job, has afforded me the chance to reflect on the relevance of the job one has. I have ultimately decided that applying personal values and principles to the job is what counts. If the job requires you to compromise on your principles, then perhaps it is a job that you do not wish to have. My best advice to you is to be passionate about what you do, be happy with what you do, believe in what you do, and have fun at it. I began my career believing that unless I was a criminal defense attorney or a poverty attorney, I would be a sell out. A more mature and wiser woman, I now know that it is necessary for people of color to be in every place where lawyers are needed. Freeing myself from that overwhelming prejudice has created great joy in my life.

Wanda Flowers

Wanda E. Flowers *is Regional Attorney for the Equal Employment Opportunity Commission in Philadelphia.*

Dear Sisters, Dear Daughters,

So you want to go to law school? Because imitation is the greatest form of flattery: Thank you. And because your decision to become a lawyer may be linked to your observations of my life, I want to share with you some lessons I have learned on my own journey. Perhaps my experiences will help light your path. Above all, I commend your motivation for undertaking such an awesome ambition.

Always follow your heart. When you feel out of place, you probably are. Spend less time trying to fit in and more time trying to create a situation in which you can flourish. Trust your inner voice; it speaks your truth and points out the path that's right for you. Be open to its guidance and confident of its counsel.

Stay grounded in all that you know to be true. In law school, it was intimidating to be among so many people who were so smart and confident. I recall one woman in particular who always spoke in class, often disagreeing with the professor. I was in awe of her self-assurance and poise. Now I realize where that confidence came from. She simply knew that her opinions were valid and her thoughts credible. She felt worthy. She knew she deserved to participate. So do you. Be open to the ideas of others, but don't look to others to validate your own.

Learn to make decisions. You have too much to contribute to fear making choices. I remember one conversation with a fellow law student about how hard it was to make choices after our parents had raised us to "keep our options open." Keeping all your options open can sometimes result in paralysis. At some point you have to foreclose some options and choose a course. If you follow your heart, the choices you make will be right for your life. In all of your decision making, pray for guidance. With every divinely inspired choice you make, you move closer to realizing your life's purpose.

Work hard. Put in the time necessary to master the material. Work smart. Exploit legitimate shortcuts. And if you are having difficulty, seek help—from guidance and career counselors, family members, friends, and fellow students. Even as you work hard, work in a way that supports those things that bring you personal satisfaction. Life is not about misery and unhappiness. The things that are right for you should bring you peace and joy.

Expect that there will be days when you feel exhausted, frustrated, or even angry. You may have to stay up all night studying. You may not do as well on an exam as you had hoped. You may not get that perfect job you want. Anticipate that there will be temporary defeats. Learn from these disappointments and move forward.

Sharpen your communication skills. Words are a lawyer's tools. You will spend a great deal of your professional time simplifying complex concepts as you advocate for the rights of others. So take advantage of opportunities to debate with others. And write; putting your thoughts down on paper helps you clarify your ideas.

Focus on today. Much about deciding to become a lawyer is very future-oriented. You may feel you need to take certain courses in high school so that you can get into a certain college, so that you can get into a certain law school, so that you can get a certain job, so that you can earn a certain income, so that you can have a certain lifestyle. It is important to prepare, to set goals, and to take the steps necessary to achieve them. You must learn, however, to balance a focus on the future with an appreciation for the present. Today is all you know. You can worry about tomorrow tomorrow.

Value and appreciate the fabric of your friendships. Stay connected to the positive people in your life. Identify role models, successful people who are doing what you want to do. Spend time with them. Talk about how they prepared for their careers. Seek advice about how they became successful. Ask them to connect you with other successful people who might be resources for you. Polish your networking skills. Be articulate. Speak with confidence. Make eye contact. Identify an area of common interest. This may take practice. Not everyone is born with these skills.

Do something to make the world a better place. Volunteer with a community organization whose mission is important to you. Be protective of the time you spend with your family. There is no job more legitimate than raising healthy, independent children. Maintain connections with spiritual communities, professional organizations and social groups. Especially value your "sister-friends." These are women who will help you to feel less alienated, support you during times of difficulty, and celebrate your successes with you.

Honor the values of honesty, respect, and integrity. Maybe it's as simple as my Mom said when I was growing up: Use your own head. Do the right thing. Don't do things that will require you to lie. After all situations, be able to face yourself in the mirror. And above all, take care of yourself. You are so deserving of the good things that will come your way. And I'm here if you need me.

Best Wishes,

Tracy Brown

Tracy R. Brown *is responsible for the Corporate Benefits function of a specialty chemicals manufacturer headquartered in Boston, Massachusetts.*

Big Picture

The letters in this section offer advice to live by

personally and professionally.

They advise taking a step back from the balancing act

and remembering why you are on the road.

The women here tend to their health and well being

and to the health and well being of their relationships

with family, friends, and community.

This group of letters is called Big Picture because they speak

to understanding one's life story and choices in the

larger context of the ones who made it possible for you

and how you make it possible for those who follow.

"We are all better women when we make the time to help each other."
—**Alpha Brady**

"If you don't enjoy what you do, it's not worth it."
—**Linda Yayoi Kelso**

"Another good lesson: If you're not taking risks, not occasionally raising eyebrows, you're probably playing it too safe. And that's no way to run a career–or a life."
—**Kathleen J. Wu**

Dear Sisters, Dear Daughters,

We thought maybe the rainbow was for us.

"Thought" is the wrong word. In the part of our souls where hope resides, we felt a yearning, as when a leaf turns toward the sun, for a connection to this symbol. I have not spoken of this to John, but I know this is as true for him. He was so excited to see it.

Rainbows are quite rare in southern California, and to see one this perfect, flung so high and wide, would have been remarkable on any day. But on this day. . .

Most women know they are pregnant before the doctor tells them the results of the blood test. They have missed their periods, they have done a home test; all they need is confirmation. In our case, we had to take the more extraordinary route of in vitro fertilization. If I became pregnant, it would have been because of $10,000 spent on a one-month regimen of 64 shots, 45 pills, 10 doctor visits, two hospital visits, and the random choice of the laboratory technician as to which sperm would fertilize which egg. A whole team of us, the accumulated knowledge of medical science, and instantaneous information on what your body has done, before your body can even begin to whisper its news.

As with the other times, I listened, I attended to the physical signs. Each sensation in my body was of interest to me, each twinge in my breasts or abdomen, even the texture of my skin, the quality of my digestion. But I could not know what anything meant, if anything at all; and soon enough, we would know for sure. Yes or no. From someone else. No gradual realization, no wondrous unfolding of a miracle. This was like those other tests we both knew, like getting bar exam results (would I be a lawyer or not?) or awaiting a jury verdict, waiting for them to tell you, did you win or lose, are you a hero or a fool? What was different was feeling so helpless to effect the outcome, except that I would learn if my minor transgressions (a hot bath, a sip of coffee one day, a mouthful of wine, a session or two of yoga, long working hours throughout) would be forgotten or would be blamed. Except for following doctor's orders, there was nothing else we could do to effect the result. It was done by now, and soon we would know: will we have a chance to be parents or not?

Will we know the expectancy of pregnancy, the drama of delivery, will I ever be able to brush back the hair from a small forehead and kiss a tear from those eyes, so like his, so like mine . . . or will it be just us, the rest of our days, just the two of us, to and from work, day after day, watching other people's children grow older while our lives remained about the same, doing our best to be a good uncle, a good aunt, would it be just us? Just us, the warmth from a small body fading too quickly from our arms as the child returns to its parents, just us in our house when the visit is over; just us? My body held a secret, even from me. Was it imbued of another life or would it all drain away, again?

I had always thought I would have children, but I also thought it could wait. Who knew this could happen? No one told us, this first generation of women to have careers first, that "first" may mean "only." The only explanation for our "unexplained infertility" is my age. Physically, we both checked out perfectly on every score, except age. The chart they showed me of childbearing statistics showed an alarming nose dive after the woman reaches the age of 35, which was exactly the age I was when John and I started trying.

If this does not work, in the years to come, when all chance is gone, and children ask why I have no children of my own, the air will hold the unspoken thought: barren. They don't use that word for men who aren't fathers. Barren. Too cruel a word for even a desert. That I would have children was something I had always assumed. In my late twenties, I purchased an encyclopedia for my future children, then stopped the subscription with a laugh at myself when I realized I could buy a more up-to-date one at the right time (which, of course, was later). Stowed away in trunks are toys and books I found and kept for that eventual day. Maybe I had assumed too much. Don't count your chickens before they hatch.

But the rainbow was stunning. "It's a good sign!" said John's mother. She had no idea what we were waiting for, that it was that very hour that we expected to receive the message, she had no idea that we expected any news at all. A good sign in my home are the trinkets of hope—the Catholic relic from John's mother, the fertility candle from my mother's friend, the African fertility doll I bought at a market, the Chinese lucky bamboo, a spray of wheat, a Kokopelli, the Shona seed sculpture—the objects into which we place the locus of chance, of luck, of faith or hope, and here, spread across the usually deserted Los Angeles sky, at this particular hour, a rainbow.

I would call in again for messages as soon as John returned from the edge of the balcony, where he was trying to get a better angle by which to photograph this rare sight, this wide arc sweeping over the deep green hills of Bel Air. Not possible to capture, he reported, it was too big, he said, his face nonetheless glowing, happy. Was the light from all the candles he has lit in so many prayers for so many years, returned now in a radiant curve of colors smiling down from the eastern sky?

John found a seat in the museum for his mother and I pretended a need to check with my office. We stood outside in the slight drizzle, the cell phone between us. Three messages this time on the home machine, where an hour before there were none. The first: from the office. The second: from John's sister. We had been huddled toward the sun in the west, but as John listened to his sister's message I turned to see the rainbow. It was gone. I turned again toward the light, which was shifting into the clouds, into a borrowed red, fiery. I knew the third message was the one, and what would the answer be?

All of the philosophizing of the past weeks and years tumbled through my head in a rush. I can live without being a parent, there are other things I'd like to accomplish, being a parent isn't everything, I can accept it, but I would love to have children. I know it is incomparable, I want to see those young eyes, I want to tell them their history, I want to see them play with their cousins, I want to search for our traces in their little faces, but I can live without it. Is it fair to one so young to be so old? We have a good life, we would have even greater financial responsibility, but I want to hear *my* baby laugh. I'll take whatever happens, is this a penance, I can take whatever happens, I'm nervous about being a parent, I'm terrified of not, I can take whatever happens, can thoughts change things, will doubts banish, will fears eclipse, will defenses prevent? Can I take whatever happens?

I'm 42. This may be my last chance. All of the hopes I had been trying to keep in a realistic box . . . did not blossom into incredulity or joy, because the news was the same as the last time. Sorry. You are not. We are not. I am certain I saw tears in John's eyes. The color was draining from the sky that we both now stared at, as if it held some other answer, but I was aware only of the echo in the vanishing place, that part of the soul where hope resides: not for us. It was not for us.

Anonymous

Dear Sisters, Dear Daughters,

As a 41-year-old mother of two young boys, ages two and four, I embrace this opportunity to write to Daughters.

My parents were divorced when I was 11 years old, and being the oldest of four younger brothers and sisters, I was thrown into the role of caretaker while my mother struggled to support us on a secretary's salary while attending night school to obtain a degree in accounting. From that early experience, I resolved at that ripe old age to be a financially independent woman. Up until my parent's divorce, I had lived in suburban Marin County, the only Asian American girl in the entire school. I remember growing up thinking that I wish I had blonde hair and blue eyes like my friends. But after the divorce, we moved to San Francisco, where I discovered for the first time other people like me and people of all different shades of color. My self-esteem and confidence soared after I took a public speaking class when I was 13 years old where I learned to argue and express my own opinions. That was probably when the seeds of lawyer-hood were planted.

I didn't have to be cajoled into studying or to get my "A"'s in high school. I was driven by ambition cultivated by watching my mother, as a single parent, struggling to support four young children working 40 hours a week for secretarial pay, and every night attending three hours of night school and burning the midnight oil studying. My mother was born in Japan, English was her second language, but this did not stop her. If she could do it, what was there to stop me?

I went on to U.C. Berkeley where I met my future husband. Having learned to be practical (based on my mother's experience), I decided to major in business administration so that I would have a solid base for getting a job in case law school didn't work out. But, I went on to law school at Hastings College of Law, and graduated in 1982.

When I finished law school, it was my dream to go into public service and to give something back to my community, but 1982 was a time when a new Republican president had decided to cut all funding to legal services. Community organizations simply did not have any positions for young new lawyers. Instead, I found a position with a small, 15-person law firm in Oakland, whose main attraction to me at the time was the hiring partner, who had worked early in his career at the Legal Aid Society in Alameda.

From 1983 until the present, I have built my practice at Wendel, Rosen, Black & Dean. In doing so, I have found ways of giving back to my community through *pro bono* efforts and through monetary contributions based on my success as a lawyer.

I have been a partner for 10 years now as an environmental litigation specialist. Because of my established expertise and client base, I have been able to build an outstanding practice that allows me to work four days a week from the office, and still have the joy of watching my two young boys grow up. My message to daughters and sisters is that even as a woman of color practicing in a traditional male job, you can "have it all." You can have a wonderful family life and an outstanding career that is self-fulfilling. You won't be able to do it the old-fashioned way, with 60-hour weeks, and weekend hours. But, if you lay a solid foundation early in your career, the payoff is tremendous.

How was I able to do this? First, as a young associate, before I was married with kids, I was able to devote the requisite billable hours a month into my work. By being a workhorse for the first seven years of my practice, I was able to make partner. By waiting a few years before having children, I was able to develop a special expertise and practice in environmental law and a solid client base. This was an area of law that no one else in my firm practiced. In effect, I was able to make myself somewhat indispensable. The firm had traditionally practiced in business, real estate, and litigation, but no one had any particular expertise in environmental law, which was expanding rapidly in the early '90s.

By the time I decided to have children, I was a partner with a comfortable book and a full-time associate who was able to handle any major issues while I was on a four-month maternity leave (twice). Computers, fax machines, and great secretaries made it possible to continue to monitor cases, edit drafts, and put in a few hours a day from home while the baby napped. I am now enjoying a satisfying career with great clients without sacrifice to my family, whom I treasure more than anything in the world.

So, while I've read that younger women may now prefer to raise a family first, and put their careers on a back burner, the personal satisfaction of knowing that my law practice is solidly established has actually given me significantly greater flexibility in taking an active part in my children's life. Of course, you can't do this alone. The support and contribution of a husband who cherishes the time with family as I do are an absolute must.

A final bit of advice, if you do go into private practice, don't forget your community or where you came from. Maintain close contact with community-based legal organizations that you can assist by either volunteering, serving on boards, or simply by making significant and consistent monetary contributions.

Christine K. Noma

Christine K. Noma *is a Partner specializing in environmental law at the firm of Wendel, Rosen, Black & Dean in Oakland, California.*

Dear Sisters, Dear Daughters,

I really appreciate the opportunity to participate in this project, because truthfully, I have not thoroughly reflected on my legal career over the years. If I had to impose a pattern or theme upon it, the recurring motif would be that if an opportunity appeared to offer the promise for personal and/or professional growth at the time, I followed it. By and large, I have not been disappointed. Another benefit is that my career path has never become stagnant, which is one common complaint about law as a profession; for that I am very grateful.

In a nutshell, that would be my advice to you—don't be afraid to pursue your dreams in this profession. Whether with brains, guts, sheer determination, or some combination of all three, we all made it through law school as women of color. The fact that we survived that academic "middle passage" should be a daily affirmation of our strength, talent, and resourcefulness.

While a law student, it was not-so-subtly impressed on me that large firm practice was "the" route to professional "success." Like many others, I followed suit for a while. As I matured professionally, other avenues presented themselves to me, and I explored them eagerly, including law school teaching and administration, municipal practice, and, at present, appellate practice at a small, but dynamic, trial defense firm.

I would be less than wholly forthright if I did not tell you that family considerations have influenced some of my career decisions. I am the proud mother of Erica (1 year old) and Fletcher

(10 years old), and I thank God for the balance and dimension they have brought to my life. I have also been blessed with an unparalleled partner in my husband, Eric. Notwithstanding the demands of the career we have chosen (or which may have chosen us), never be afraid to put **first things first** in your life. Trust me, everything else will fall into place, better empowering you to fulfill the promise that enabled us to get in and out of law school in the first instance.

I wish each of you satisfaction and happiness in your careers.

Carolyn F. Glosby

Carolyn F. Glosby *is an Appellate Attorney at Cardelli Hebert, PC in Royal Oak, Michigan, specializing in civil appeals.*

Dear Sisters, Dear Daughters,

It is my wish that you will find something contained herein useful to you as you pass through the halls of life. Upon getting
accepted into law school, my greatest ambition was to become
a world-renowned international lawyer. I set my heart and mind
on accomplishing that goal. This vision was shaped by the fact
that I had spent two and a half years in the American Foreign
Service. My tour of duty was Addis Ababa, Ethiopia.

I was so excited when I started down the international law path.
My excitement about international law began to dissipate quickly as my international law class was taught poorly. Further, during my first year of law school, I concluded that I had no interest in being a trial lawyer and certainly no interest in corporate,
financial, or securities law.

As fate would have it, however, the summer of my second year
of law school, I was selected to be one of two law clerks,
nationwide, to clerk at the newly created federal regulatory
agency—the Commodity Futures Trading Commission (CFTC).
My summer experience at the CFTC was exceptional. My first
assignment was working with several seasoned litigators with
substantial securities backgrounds. The job was really challenging. I worked diligently. My hours were long, but the experience
I received was invaluable and far greater than most of my
peers. I learned a great deal, not only about the commodity
markets, the federal commodity regulatory agency, and its role
as a regulator, but also lessons that have stood me in good
stead as an attorney, as well as an individual.

The first lesson I learned is that what you think you want most may not be the opportunity available to you. Once an opportunity presents itself, one must be open-minded, flexible, and have the necessary desire to do, whatever the task is, well. Needless to say, at the end of that summer, my attitude changed. I developed a real appetite for trial work and a desire to learn all that I could about the commodity markets in the United States. My area of practice has been in litigation with a specialty in the financial markets, including commodities, securities, over-the-counter products, and derivatives.

Because of my CFTC experience, among other jobs, I was an Executive Vice President and General Counsel for a very large, well-known, midwestern commodity brokerage firm. I worked for that brokerage firm until it was sold to another firm—almost nine years after I joined the firm. I left the brokerage firm to become a partner at McDermott, Will & Emery.

My advice to those who are embarking on a career in law or otherwise is to remember to try and maintain a balanced life. If you have a family, which I do, you must remember that they, too, need you and want to spend time with you—spouses, as well as children.

I can remember when we discovered I was pregnant with my daughter. I had been working at the brokerage firm only three months. I was petrified to inform the company that I was expecting a child. I sat down with several of my female colleagues, all of whom were lawyers, and sought advice on how to approach the subject with the President and CEO. At the end of the fretting, I decided to just be open and honest with the CEO, after all I was not going to be able to hide it and if he didn't like it, I would have to deal with his dislike. To my surprise the CEO was very complimentary. I had a long discussion with him about family, its importance, and the value of a family. The office was great. After the baby came, I was able to work a schedule that accommodated the office as well as my family. I was permitted to travel with my child and the sitter—needless to say I was a very loyal and hard-working employee.

The common thread throughout my employment history has been that I had meaningful mentors. Without my mentors, I would not have been able to accomplish all that I have achieved. Your mentor does not necessarily have to be employed at the same place you are. The role of the mentor is to be a sounding board, to provide solid, balanced guidance and direction in any area the mentee needs. The mentor should be someone who respects the mentee and that the mentee also respects. The mentor should also provide common sense advice, but at all times permitting the mentee to make her own reasoned decision.

> *Without my mentors, I would not have been able to accomplish all that I have achieved.*

Because of my career, I had only one child. If I were able to go back and redo certain portions of my life, the only thing I would change is having more than one child. I did so because I didn't think I could manage my career and home life as well as I wanted with more than one child. I regret having made that decision. I feel my daughter has been cheated out of knowing what growing up with siblings is all about—having to share, learning to cope with teasing, invasion of space, etc. I note that my daughter, at age 12, continues to ask for a sibling.

To date, my career has been one of many successes due to hard work, opportunities not lost, a supportive family, and above everything else, my belief in God.

Gloria Matthews

Gloria J. Matthews *is an Attorney with McDermott, Will & Emory, specializing in commodity, securities and commercial litigation, transactional work and regulatory matters.*

Dear Sisters, Dear Daughters,

The challenges facing the female African American lawyer is like surround sound. But, be not discouraged. With a positive outlook, proper mentoring, and luck, you can thrive in the legal profession. My experiences have not been unique.

I am the youngest of four children and the only one to go to college and do post-graduate work. I went to a high school where I was not encouraged to go to college, notwithstanding the fact that I was in the college preparatory curriculum and my grades were respectable. The focus by the guidance counselors was given to the 85 percent White population attending the school. In a sense this was good. The lack of encouragement for me to attend an Ivy League school caused me to attend a historically black college—Howard University. There, I could not have received a better all-around education. Howard University encouraged its students to be leaders and to pursue advanced degrees. They instilled a sense of self-worth that has remained with me. When I got to law school, although I was only one of eight African Americans in the first year class, I was ready and not the least bit intimidated. I did have the good sense to align myself with other African American students who were upper classmen, as well as with those who had apparent influence. The same was true with my ultimate career choices.

In 1976, men truly ruled the world, and there was little or no interest in diversity. The concept of a mentor for a woman of color, who was also a lawyer, was nonexistent. My Howard University training and my home training taught me to stand up with my head up. Ultimately, after several positions in corporate America, I found that I had to be self-reliant and in 1984, I went into business for myself. There were a whole new set of challenges, but none that could not be overcome. Too often I have been threatened with contempt of court when I objected to being treated in a disparate manner.

There was also the desire for too much quid pro quo. You do not have to succumb to this to be successful. Success comes in many forms, and you must define it for yourself. Success can also evolve, and you will continuously update your definition. My most difficult times continue to come when the judge and other court personnel obviously treat me differently than my peers. Worse than that are men of color who adopt a superior attitude with me. Most recognize that many of our interests are mutual and there has been improvement.

The world is yet unaccustomed to the woman of color, who is also an attorney. We are few in number. This is why we cannot afford to not ask questions and to not take risks. We must be involved on both sides of the fence. Participate actively in your bar of color so that you may not only be intellectually stimulated, but also get your "soul food." Participate in the majority bar because if you are not at the table, it is impossible to get into the game. You will be surprised at how your mere presence can affect outcomes.

My involvement in bar and community activities has been extensive. I look forward to you taking over for me. I have held a number of offices with the National Bar Association where ultimately, I served as its President. I have served in a number of leadership capacities with the American Bar Association. I am currently a Division Director with the Litigation Section and the immediate past chair of the Council on Racial and Ethnic Justice. On the local level, I have likewise been involved with the Garden State Bar Association and served as the President of the Association of Black Women Lawyers of New Jersey.

Be mindful of your selections. Talk to your mentor or with someone you believe you can trust before making major decisions. It is likely that she has been down that road, and you can avoid any unnecessary pitfalls. Do not be afraid to ask! If no one is available to ask, pay close attention to the subtleties.

The help you may need may be of a personal nature. Again, do not be afraid to ask. I wondered how it would be for me to become a single parent while running a law firm and having an active litigation practice. I decided, upon good advice, to go forward with the parenting. In my case, it makes my work worthwhile. My son gives me purpose. My life has been enriched because of him. He has become my number-one priority. Because he is my number-one priority, I am now facing the biggest disappointment in my career. I am relinquishing ownership of my law firm and thus dissolving an African American law firm that has existed for 15 years. It is causing much heartache for me, our employees, and for my law partner and friend of the same number of years. It was a difficult decision that I had to make. I made it so that I could better provide for my child. Perhaps one day I can come full circle.

Progress for women of color has been slower than for other groups. I am confident and ever hopeful of the progress that we will ultimately make. Always know that there is a Sister out there whom you can always call on who has "been there and done that."

Warm regards,

Paulette Brown

Paulette Brown *is a Partner in the Newark office of Duane, Morris & Heckscher, LLP.*

Dear Sisters, Dear Daughters,

Over 12 years ago, I graduated from UCLA Law School and moved to Chicago to practice at a large law firm with over 300 attorneys in the Chicago office. I was one of two Asian attorneys at the firm. Both of us were first-year associates. It was an excellent firm, but I really came to appreciate it more after I left. It was so different from law school where I ran mostly with other Asians.

Here's some advice from what I learned. When your partner—back then it was he—asks for a draft, never, never turn in a draft. Say it's a draft, but you make sure it is your best work product. If you have a midlevel associate friend, ask her or him to review your work first before you turn it in. And, of course, always do excellent work. Be confident. Your partner wants to know that whatever he or she assigns you to do, you can handle it. Firm culture may be different than what you're used to. I never used the "r" word. I found that the firm could handle being criticized as "culturally insensitive" but couldn't handle being called "racist" because they never think they are. Take time to help other associates, particularly other minorities. The retention rate for minorities in large firms is abysmal.

When I came to Chicago, I was stunned to find that there were no Asian Americans on the bench. California had over 40 judges. I got involved with the Asian American Bar Association, which had just been formed. I decided to lead a campaign to get the first Asian American on the bench in Illinois. With the help of the Asian American Bar Association, we ultimately succeeded, but it took a couple of years. I had no idea what I was doing and I did not know how difficult it would be. We started meeting with any one who could help: the mayor, supreme court justices who could appoint judges, the governor, the chief judge of Cook County, and major politicians. We wrote letters to the editors of the major newspapers. It took over two years but we finally did get one Asian American on the bench.

This campaign had some unexpected consequences both for the Asian American community and me personally. I think that the legal community in Chicago began to realize that Asian American attorneys existed and needed to be included. For me personally, I became close friends with many other Asian American community leaders. Through my work on this and other Asian American issues, I also became known to some leaders in the mainstream legal community. And, I have over the years been fortunate to be appointed to various boards and commissions. I guess I would say that if you care about issues, Asian or otherwise, get involved. Help your community. Making a difference not only helps you but also, more importantly, helps your community.

Through the friendships I made, I have some thoughts about mentoring. While there have been people more senior to me who I am proud to call friends, I don't think I have ever really had a mentor. If you are so fortunate, remember, mentoring is a two-way street. Don't just think about what they can do for you. Perhaps because I haven't really had a mentor, I think of it more as a partnership. I have dear friends who are people I love and trust. When I know about opportunities, I recommend them for jobs, awards, boards, etc. They have done the same for me. We have advanced each other's careers.

You make a real difference when you help someone else to succeed who cares about the community. I have found that, for me, the best way to network is to work on issues. I don't believe that you should work on issues to network, but rather, as a collateral result of working on issues, you build relationships. From my efforts to get the first Asian American on the bench, I worked on another campaign to get the first African American on the Illinois Supreme Court.

At my old law firm, I worked on minority recruitment and built relationships with other people of color that has lasted over the years. I worked with the gay and lesbian community to pass a county-wide antidiscrimination ordinance. At my current job, we had a poor record of hiring African American attorneys. I worked on getting an African American on the hiring committee, and we succeeded in getting more African Americans hired. As a result of working not just on "Asian" issues, I have made wonderful friendships and networked outside of my own community.

I have loved my job and my work in the community. But my greatest joy is my six-year-old son. He was unexpected. I came home from a midwest conference for Asian American attorneys some six plus years ago. That weekend, a close family member had given birth prematurely and was forced to give him up. They wanted me to adopt him and I had only four days to decide, or the state would get involved. I made the decision and became a single mom. As you can imagine, my life has radically changed. I now leave work early to take him to gymnastics. Getting him into the right school was a major decision. Homework is a constant struggle. I have cut down on my community work, but he often goes to meetings with me. My first concern now is his development, his school, his happiness—not my career or even the community. And I wouldn't change it for the world.

I wish you the best in your career and your personal life. I hope you are as blessed as I have been.

Sincerely yours,

Sandra R. Otaka

Sandra R. Otaka *is the Section Chief, U.S. Environmental Protection Agency in Chicago.*

Dear Sisters, Dear Daughters,

Like a lot of third, fourth, and fifth generation Americans of Japanese ancestry, I did not grow up feeling particularly connected to the Japanese American or the Asian American community. It wasn't until law school that I met a group of Asian Americans and discovered the joy and comfort of the companionship of other Asian Americans and my own passion for working on Asian American issues.

I grew up in Chicago and was used to being the only or one of a very few Asian Americans, much less Japanese Americans, in any group or gathering. The few that I encountered in school or church or even children of my parents' friends were, like me, fairly well acculturated. Except for a few isolated incidents, I gave very little thought to my culture. Sure, my family ate rice with almost every evening meal. New Year's traditions were more important than Christmas. Bathing was for the evening, not the morning. Didn't everyone grow up with the story of Momotaro? And musubi and teriyaki (real teriyaki, not that stuff called teriyaki that is served in hotel restaurants) remain comfort food. But those seemed to be insignificant differences. I was interested in Japanese culture enough to learn how to make sushi and mochi, but my family never attributed any importance to acquiring the trappings of Japanese culture so my knowledge of Japanese language is limited to food items and adjectives not generally appropriate for polite company. I grew up hearing about the "camp" where my mother and her family had been interned during World War II. And I took pride in the fact that my father's family was one of the earliest Japanese American families on Kauai in Hawaii. My family always emphasized a quiet pride in being Americans of Japanese ancestry.

So, when I got to law school and met these really wonderful Asian Americans who were so involved in and outspoken about being Asian American, it was surprising, alarming, radically new, and totally intoxicating. These students were unlike any Asian Americans I had ever encountered. Not only were they bright, talented, confident, and very interested in public policy and civil rights as they impacted upon Asian Americans, they were full of fire, passion, and commitment to ushering in—no, to leading a new era for Asian Americans. It was a heady experience. This was during the Vincent Chin case, the Japanese American redress movement, and the early years of the establishment of Asian American Studies at colleges and universities across the country. It was an exciting time to be an Asian American. So much was happening, and there was still so much more yet to be done.

I spent a summer clerking at a firm in Honolulu and that clinched it for me. It was invigorating to be in an environment where Asian American judges, partners, political leaders, and community activists were commonplace. The hardest and saddest decision that I ever made was to decline the offer to return to Honolulu in favor of an offer from a firm in Chicago. I loved the firm that I clerked at, I had family and friends in Honolulu, and I was so happy there. But many of the things that I loved best about Hawaii were also the very reasons why I couldn't return there. The Asian American community in Hawaii had come so far and accomplished so much while in Chicago, in the midwest, there were still so many firsts that had yet to be achieved. I felt it would be hard to enjoy and be part of all that Asian Americans had achieved in Hawaii when there was so much that hadn't even been started in Chicago.

So home to Chicago I went. There wasn't an Asian American Bar Association then but we started one. That was so much fun. At the first meeting, some 50 Asian American lawyers showed up. It was such an emotional experience to walk into a room filled with other Asian American lawyers; everyone couldn't stop talking about it. It left us feeling rather giddy with excitement and optimism for the future. I hadn't met many of the other organizers when we first began that venture, but my life has been so much richer and happier for knowing them. We have had so many good times together: defeating the retention bid of a judge with an anti-Asian attitude; organizing NAPABA; working for the selection of the first Asian American judge in Illinois; the road trips to Minneapolis and Detroit; and, even undertaking judicial evaluations.

As I got more involved in the Asian American Bar Association, I was also approached to serve on the boards of various Asian American community organizations. I joined the Japanese American Service Committee, the Japanese American Citizens League, the Asian American Institute, the Asian American Coalition, and many others. For a number of years, it was not uncommon to have to attend committee or board meetings five nights a week and Saturdays, too. In hindsight, I have to admit that perhaps we didn't accomplish all that we set out to do or all that we could have done, but I think we still did quite a bit, and we had fun doing it.

> . . . teamwork can make any task pleasurable; friendship can soften disappointment; courtesy can temper stress; and empathy can lessen sorrow and loss.

And I learned a lot, too, although I didn't always realize it at the time. I learned about leadership, about volunteerism, about business, about people skills, and about myself, too. I learned patience, compromise, perseverance, forgiveness, and humor (okay, I'm still working on that). I experienced the way teamwork can make any task pleasurable; friendship can soften disappointment; courtesy can temper stress; and empathy can lessen sorrow and loss. I found myself mentoring and being mentored by the friends I was making in these different organizations.

As I became more deeply immersed in Asian American professional and community activities, I found that I couldn't help becoming better educated about more and more of the issues of concern to my community and the underlying causes and reasons for their problems. Finally, my husband (who is not Asian) and I decided to try to address some of those concerns through education. We started a company, called Polychrome Publishing (polychrome meaning "many colors"), to create and publish children's books that would validate experiences common to children of Asian ancestry growing up in the United States as well as offer non-Asians a glimpse of life through the eyes of an Asian American. It was something that just wasn't being done. There were plenty of fables and folktales from Asia but those perpetuated the image of Asians as foreigners rather than Americans—a problem from which the Asian American community continues to suffer. Now, ten years and 13 books later (with eight more in various stages of production), our books are being sold around the world, and we're finally starting to see a small return. But the best part are the letters we receive from parents who tell us how one of our stories has made an impact on their child's life. That's a really good feeling.

I left the practice of law after 10 years. What a happy day that was! There were so many days when I used to awaken wondering if I felt ill enough to legitimately call in sick. As a recovering lawyer, I have a lot of sympathy for all the lawyers I know who wish they could do something else. Eventually, I was approached to use my experiences to help other lawyers by working to promote diversity in the legal profession. At first, I didn't feel I had enough experience, but somehow, over time, without realizing it, I found that without consciously planning it, I had acquired a wealth of contacts, knowledge, and perspective. When I was in law school, and as a new lawyer, I would never have dreamed that I would know many of the people I now have the honor to count as friends. Sometimes, I think we want instant gratification but some things just take time and patience.

As I've been working in the community all these years, somewhere along the way I have also discovered that my definition of "my community" keeps expanding. So many of the issues I enjoy working on, especially in the arena of education, go beyond just the Asian American community. My community has grown from Japanese American to Asian American to Asian Pacific American to the minority community and beyond.

Just over a year ago, I started working at the ABA. Now my sense of community includes the legal profession. It's humbling yet heartwarming, aggravating but gratifying, frustrating while thrilling, confusing and invigorating. I frequently find myself marveling at the notion that I am looking forward to going to work each day!

The smartest (or luckiest) thing I ever did in my career was to get involved in the Asian American Bar Association. It opened up so many doors for me, brought me into contact with many of the people (both lawyers and lay people) whom I now hold among my dearest and most cherished friends, and created opportunities that I had never imagined existed or that I would even want. I am so glad that I had the good fortune to find a cause in my life. Where others may question life's meaning or hunger for a purpose, I found mine in working for my community. It lets me greet each day with anticipation and enthusiasm. Life is good.

Warmest regards,

Sandra S. Yamate

Sandra S. Yamate *is the Director of the American Bar Association's Commission on Racial and Ethnic Diversity in the Profession and is a Publisher of multicultural children's books.*

Dear Sisters, Dear Daughters,

I have been an attorney licensed to practice law in the state of Hawaii for 12 years. I am so proud of our profession. Yet, I am constantly defending myself as an attorney every month.

Last month, I flew to Sacramento, California, to attend my sister's 25th anniversary party. During dinner, my niece Kristy, a senior at Santa Clara University, was telling a male relative that she decided not to go to law school. I was disappointed because Kristy has always exhibited such superior intelligence from the time she was a year old. This relative was happy about her decision and went on and on about negative things about lawyers. Finally, I said, "I'm an attorney and I'm proud to be one." When I shared this episode with my Asian American relatives, their comment was that he was "hakujin" (Caucasian). Then I thought, what was an attack on my profession was viewed by my Asian American relatives as a racial stereotype based on the person being white.

Living in Hawaii, the degree of racial tension is different from the mainland. I sometimes feel my gender is more a barrier than my ethnicity.

When I applied to be a family court judge in 1994, I remember being asked by the judicial selection commission how I would take care of my family with the busy schedule. When I shared what happened during my interview with an older Caucasian applicant, he was shocked they asked me that question. Yet, another person told me the question may have been asked because of my normal work schedule and what two female colleagues said about me.

Today, I am applying for the same position. I feel confident that I can be on the list again (of six finalists). Yet, I analyze every facet of my life to see where the commission can amplify my weaknesses. Only time will tell. There will always be people who encourage you and people who talk behind your back or are lukewarm.

Our daily stride to succeed may be dampened by people who seem to be knocking you down. You will ask yourself, "Why?" "Is it because I'm a woman attorney? Is it because I am Japanese American? Is it because I grew up in the mainland? (Even though I've lived here for over 20 years!) Is it because I live on a neighbor island? (Not in Honolulu.) Is it the way I'm dressed?"

Associate with positive people. They will support you and help you with your goals. They will not plant doubts in your mind, but will mentor you and believe in you and guide you.

The ABA has been my favorite professional organization since becoming involved in the Young Lawyers Division (YLD). I encourage minority attorneys to get involved in the ABA. The people you meet will be lifelong friends. The YLD is colorblind. They want you to succeed. They help you to succeed. They support your goals. But always remember your roots.

I want to share with you something I wrote when I was a law student. I wrote it for the Asian American Law Student Association (AALSA). Today, I think it can apply to my situation as I strive to achieve my goal to become a judge, and bring with me, my life experiences as a minority woman.

Although I should be studying for my final right now, I felt compelled to express some of my personal views in this newsletter.

What is the purpose of the Asian American Law Student Association? Is it just another "social" club? I submit to you that it is not. AALSA is a club on the surface, but the significance of the organization goes much deeper.

The club is not limited to Asians at McGeorge. Non-Asian law students, faculty, administration, and alumni who share our goals should be part of AALSA as well. But if you are Asian and do not make time to attend AALSA meetings and AALSA banquets nor contribute to this newsletter, then you should reevaluate your priorities and your commitment to the Asian community.

Sometimes, it is hard to remember the injustices that have occurred in America to minority groups. Sometimes, we want to forget those humiliating and painful episodes. We block out those experiences as a means of survival.

As Asians and future Asian attorneys, we must NEVER forget the history of Asians in America. Why? Because we are entering a profession that can protect the constitutional rights of citizens, particularly when those citizens are in the minority. Although the U S. Constitution did not protect American citizens of Japanese ancestry during World War II, our profession can lend a helping hand to people who may need our assistance in the future. We can prevent future violations of our constitutional rights.

Those of us who will be graduating should not lose sight of the experiences of our ancestors. I, myself, am guilty of getting caught up in the excitement of becoming a full-fledged lawyer. I daydream about my job in Hawaii, the material things I want to purchase, the prestige of the law firm, and the future.

Then, I come back down to reality. This is when I stop and think about what really matters in my life. The people who have done so much for me. My family and friends who have made sacrifices for me so I could achieve my goal. . . .

My struggle has been different than the struggle of my parents and other Nisei (second generation Japanese Americans). They paved the way for me. They sheltered me from the pain they endured. In many ways, I live for them.

The benefits I enjoy were not available to Japanese Americans in the 1940s. Back then, for example, Niseis were not welcomed at public swimming pools and derogatory names were painted on mailboxes belonging to Japanese Americans.

*I feel humiliated and sad just thinking about the concentration camps that the Japanese Americans were put in during World War II. These American citizens were imprisoned in camps surrounded by barbed wire and armed guards for committing **no crime**. This was a blatant violation of the constitution, but the U.S. government justified its action under the guise of military necessity (translate: wartime hysteria).*

The pain I feel cannot be compared to what Nisei and Issei (first generation Japanese Americans) actually experienced. I believe the experience of my parents, grandparents, and other Japanese Americans will live through me. Their struggle is my struggle; their pride is my pride; their success is my success; their happiness is my happiness.

So . . . remember the significance of AALSA. It is a vehicle for Asian Awareness, education and advocacy, and for alleviating racial prejudice.

This letter is for you, my sisters and daughters. It is also for my sisters Sharon, Diane, and Donna, my daughter Colette, my husband Gail, my brother Robert, and especially my wonderful parents, Shig and Lillian Kuroda, who have been the pillar of support in my life, and who have been married for 51 years.

With much love and aloha,

Margaret Kuroda Masunaga

Margaret Kuroda Masunaga *is an Attorney practicing in Hawaii in the Kona Branch of the Office of the Corporation Counsel for the County of Hawaii.*

Dear Sisters, Dear Daughters,

I spent approximately 13 years as a law professor who specialized in antitrust, torts, and women and the law. Without a
doubt, this was a wonderful experience overall. I enjoyed working with and teaching students, handling the personal intellectual challenges presented by those students and colleagues,
developing topics that became articles, and working, in many
different ways, to make a meaningful and positive difference
within the law school and surrounding community. I love learning, being in a place dedicated to learning, and with others who
are inspired, excited about, even jazzed about learning. But,
there was at least one aspect of my experience in legal education that was completely trying, and that was being a law
professor who was also a woman and a person of color in
predominately white male institutions. More importantly, it was
being a woman of color who refused to assimilate even as she
attempted to construct her professional identity as professor.

It would have been easier to just melt into the institution and let
it define me completely. But, I could not allow that to happen.
Consider the following analogy.

Diversity means more than adding a different color or type of
flower to the arrangement of flowers presently occupying the
center of the institutional table.

> A flower arrangement made up of white daisies may
> survive and prosper quite well with one type of flower
> in the vase. When a red rose is added to that flower
> arrangement, however, some adjustments in the vase

may be necessary. If the red rose is thoughtlessly placed in the daisy arrangement, then that rose will always seem out of place. Indeed the rose may not be able to survive in the daisy vase or may be removed [the equivalent of being asked to leave]. Altering the rose by cutting its stem, spray painting it white, or otherwise forcing it into the daisy arrangement, is similarly unsatisfactory. The rose will always be a distraction in the arrangement; never quite fitting in and eventually, perhaps, dying. Meaningful diversity means changing the vase so that the daisies and rose can all prosper collectively as well as individually. The vase represents the institutional grounding—norms, values, ethos. The daisies will have to make substantial and meaningful changes in order to accommodate the roses. These changes include listening and perhaps even valuing the rose. Eventually, blue tulips, pink orchids, and other exotic flowers can join a vase that is capable of adjusting and changing so that all the flowers can thrive. (10 Harv.Blackletter J. 37).

Being able to thrive fully within the law school environment was no small task. Everyone is challenged, but it was those special challenges that I encountered often enough that made me wonder, at times, am I crazy?

In my eighth year of teaching torts, I received the following note from one of my first-year first semester students (no name of course). The note said: Professor Dark—I would also suggest that to keep us focused on your question so that we do not wander back and forth, you might make the statement, "Mr./Ms._____, make a case for plaintiff/defendant." First-year students often feel that discussions in law school classrooms are disjointed because a form of the Socratic method is typically employed in the classroom. But I am sure that this student did not give any of my white male colleagues this advice. I am willing to bet that he thought that "they" knew what they were doing and had everything under control. At the time that I received this particular note, I had already received one teaching award from the University of Richmond.

There was another time when a first-year student (again in Torts) told me in a class of approximately 75—80 students that a point that I was making was wrong because "Prosser said otherwise." He had the *Prosser on Torts* hornbook open (instead of the assigned casebook) on his desk. Fair enough, I said, perhaps I was mistaken (I believe that I was in my tenth year of teaching Torts at that time). I asked him to read the statement from Prosser. He read it and indeed it seemed contrary to my very words. But wait! I asked him if there was a footnote to the statement (in Prosser there are always footnotes to every word) and asked him to read the footnote. I interpreted those symbols and abbreviations for him and the class thusly: The citations that you have read indicate that the cases are Canadian. The rule, therefore, that he read previously is one in Canada (specifically British Columbia) and not the American rule of law. In this class, we would learn American tort law and I encouraged him to consult his casebook with the same level of zeal that he tackled a hornbook. The class was extremely quiet.

I took no pleasure in having to put a student in his place because he is seeking to challenge me personally. These kinds of challenges by students (and dare I say colleagues within and outside of the institution) usually occurred in ways that made it difficult for someone who is not the target to see the racism or sexism inherent in the act, request, statement, etc. This is what is called new racism by some psychologists.

"New racism has grown in the place where the old racism used to be . . . [T]he old-fashioned racism of Jim Crow, used explicit biological theories of White superiority to support legal segregation and discrimination is gone." (Mark Feinberg, *Racism and Psychology*, American Psychological Association.) Today, a more elusive, subtle form avoids the blatantly negative racist statements in favor of political codewords and symbols. This form of racism is still fueled by negative stereotypes and negative emotions toward African Americans and other ethnic minority groups and it is still premised on a belief that, "white is superior to black." Someone who is a target can see it and experience it, but it is increasingly difficult to prove it is real to someone who is not a target.

Often, I would get tired of trying to describe, explain, justify, and explain again these special challenges that I encountered whether from students, colleagues within and outside of the institution, or other staff. To make it through the days, weeks, and months in a way that permitted this red rose to flourish to some extent, I simply had to develop and employ strategies to respond when necessary and otherwise, "detox" myself. For example, I maintained a file that I titled "incidents." This was kind of like a personal journal of special challenges. Once I committed the incident to paper, then I could put the memory of the incident, along with the pain, behind me. After all, I told someone (myself) about the incident and that person (myself) believed and valued that experience. Eventually, this incident file became the basis for an article appearing in the *Harvard BlackLetter Journal.*

Another survival strategy that I used was to find other women of color who were employed by the university. In the law school, the only other African American women employees worked in housekeeping. They were wonderful to me! They often gave me words of encouragement or sometimes they would just let me stand near them (just for a few minutes) and bask in the renewing power of the sisterhood. This red rose was not going to die or leave (except on my own terms).

But there was yet another way that I managed to survive and even sometimes thrive in an institution full of daisies. One must learn to recognize and accept support from allies—white men and white women who were working to change the institutional ethos so that it can be a welcoming, nurturing and productive work and learning environment for all. My dear sisters and dear daughters, be careful about considering everyone the enemy because they are not.

I recall that in my second year of teaching, I was struggling to complete an article. I went to the Dean and told him that I would not be able to teach during the summer months because I wanted to complete my article. He told me that I had no choice but the Dean did make the following offer. He said that he would let me out of the teaching assignment for the summer if I could locate someone on the faculty who would be willing to give up his summer research project and teach in my place. Of course, this was not a real offer and I didn't think that anyone would agree. I happened to mention this conversation to a colleague, who was a white male, and his response was immediate. My colleague told me that it was very important that I complete my article so that I could be successful at the law school. His next words were quite surprising—he told me that he would take the summer teaching assignment.

Allies can be found within the places where we live, work and learn. I would not have obtained tenure without the support of the ladies in housekeeping, many of my students, colleagues of color at other law schools throughout the country and allies within my own institution. On being a thankful red rose . . .

Okianer Christian Dark

Okianer Christian Dark *is an Assistant U.S. Attorney who is developing a civil rights component in the Affirmative Civil Enforcement Unit of the U.S. Attorney's Office.*

Dear Sisters, Dear Daughters,

I think the most difficult part of being an African American lawyer has been dealing with the lack of respect afforded to me than that afforded to non African American law professors and lawyers. In most environments, I am treated differently solely on the basis of my race. Outside the legal arena—where I am known only as an African American—the lack of equal treatment and respect is a given. My momma prepared me well for that environment. So this part of my experience is no surprise and is not new. As a general matter, whenever I find myself in an environment where a person is unaware that I am either a law professor or a lawyer, I am immediately given certain presumptive characteristics: low income, unintelligent, a liberal, and an apathetic Democrat who rarely votes, lacks political savvy or economic power, and who plays the "race card" at every opportunity. Although the actual person is quite dissimilar to many of these presumptions, there seems to be no way to break out of this forced molding. And even though I stopped being surprised by disparate treatment in this environment since my early teens, it still hurts today to walk past a car and watch the person inside hurry to check that the door is locked and the windows closed, or to see the faces of people who look at me with disgust when I enter an environment. But this is no surprise.

In the other environment in which I live—the legal one—people know not only what I am (an African American woman) but who I am (a lawyer and a law professor). Accepting and dealing with disparity has been much more difficult. Here was the real surprise for me. Back in 1985, when I graduated from law school (and after performing exceptionally well there), I almost immediately forgot the lessons learned early on in my life. I naively assumed that my achievements in law school would lead to instant recognition, equality, and acceptance by all. Not true: my badges of accomplishments have failed to overcome certain stereotypes and assumptions about African Americans. So, I am sad to say that my experience is that even as we approach the new millennium, black attorneys continue to have tough times in white firms. Tough because some clients don't want black attorneys handling their affairs. Tough because there normally are not many mentors for us in those environments. Tough because mistakes, absences, and omissions by us not only seem more noticeable, but also seem to have a lower tolerance threshold. Tough because even if you can tease out racism, bigotry, and discrimination, there is still the reality that most people feel comfortable with and are more accepting of people like themselves. The African American female (or the African American male for that matter) may not immediately come to the mind of the white male golf-loving law partner looking for someone at the firm with whom to work.

Having been reacquainted with these forgotten lessons while in private practice, you'd think I would have learned, once and for all, what to expect; that I would be ready for anything. Well, as my momma always said, I have a very hard head! After the firm life, I entered academia expecting people to treat me differently because of my race. I was certain that any surprise factor on my part would be reduced to a minimum—the lessons having finally been learned. But guess what? The people I expected to treat me differently on the basis of my race did not. To my surprise, my colleagues were not the challenge for me. It was my students! A few examples along these lines will suffice. When I first taught legal research and writing as an adjunct professor, I set up meetings with each student to critique the student's work at my home. Despite the beautiful home and culturally-fascinating neighborhood I then lived in, my assistant called me a couple of days before the critiques to tell me that the women in the class were concerned about coming because of rumors that I probably lived in a "real bad" neighborhood. Several years later during my first semester teaching as a full-time professor, I'll never forget how I was criticized in my student evaluations for: being pregnant; canceling class for the ten days immediately after the baby was born (our school had no maternity leave policy for faculty at that time); and making up the three cancelled classes in a 10-day period. Contrast the male professor on the faculty at that same time, who taught the same class I did, and who canceled class for approximately two weeks to go to either India or China without one complaint. More disturbing was an incident I experienced a few years ago. I hung an 11" by 13" photograph of my then three children (I now have a fourth) immediately outside my office on my bulletin board. During a time when only the law school community had access to the facility, someone wrote "kids got no daddy," "on welfare," etc., on the picture. Deep stuff.

Today, although tenured, I continue to experience students who look me in my face and simply refuse to speak, students who feel very comfortable calling me "Kim" while calling all of my colleagues "Professor," and students who constantly challenge my intellect in ways I know my colleagues aren't being challenged. I am called to defend my reading of the case, my determination of what is important, my assessments and conclusions, and my practical experience. True, there has been a decrease in these experiences since making tenure—part of the reason for this may relate to the tenure status itself, but I think a lot of it also has to do with my developed ability to establish early in the course the boundary line between professor and student. More importantly, while these kinds of experiences have decreased, they have far from disappeared.

Validation must come from within.

Well, my message to you, I guess, is the message I was given as a child, the message my grandmother gave me, the message my mother gave me, and the message I somehow didn't think I needed in the legal world of intelligent, logical, reasonable thinkers: the first thing most people see is my "blackness." Well, I think I got it now. At almost 40 years old, I think that I am finally coming to terms with this reality. That brings me to the second lesson momma taught me that remains loaded with relevance today: validation must come from within.

Kimberly Jade Norwood

Kimberly Jade Norwood *is a Professor at the Washington University School of Law. She was the first black Professor to receive tenure there.*

Dear Sisters, Dear Daughters,

As a child growing up in the deep south, I learned from my parents to live my whole self, and my mother and grandmother were the best examples of that edict. I pass it along to you now: Live your whole self. It is advice that is susceptible to many interpretations, but in the context of your entry into the world of law, legalities, legalese, and litigation, I will focus upon two interpretations. First, it is not necessary to become a man to be treated equally to a man. Second, as my own mother said recently, it takes both the black and the white keys to play "The Star-Spangled Banner."

Creatures of logic that we are, too often we are tempted to assume that movement toward one landscape necessarily implies the abandonment of one's former environs. Consequently, house slaves preferred sleeping on the floor of the big house to sleeping on makeshift, but more comfortable, mattresses in the shanties; African American schoolgirls responded to Kenneth Clark's questions by choosing the white dolls over the darker ones; the big promotion of last year's first Black administrative assistant is quickly followed by her relocation to Meadowlake and her husband's purchase of a set of irons; and when Adams, Jefferson, Madison, Monroe and Adams called to extend her an offer in its real estate division, Bernice Johnson surrendered her brilliantly-colored dresses in favor of an impressive array of power suits in midnight, charcoal, and taupe.

Just think of all the identities you had before "lawyer" became one of them. You were a child, filled with wonderment about this amazing universe, curious about each new day, and capable of being genuinely moved by little things. You were a student, eager to learn and to integrate every new fact or function into your bank of understanding. You were a female, complementing—not matching—the masculine take on life and its experiences. And you were a card-carrying member of an ethnicity or culture—not White or European—that is replete with distinctive folkways, language, music, food, and dress. All before you became a lawyer. Your new identity should augment your other selves, not displace them.

I want you to think about a revolutionary idea—maybe the road to success in the still male-dominated business of lawyering is a circle, instead of a straight line. If you accept that, then you can also accept the fact that the farther you move from your starting point, the closer you come to it. Thus, work should not be a separate, untouchable sphere of being that requires you to force the "Jill-in-the-Box" into its packaged darkness. Give Jill the same latitude in decision-making, and in the quality of the decisions themselves, as men routinely give Jack. And do it with pride, not apology.

> *Just think of all the identities you had before "lawyer" became one of them.*

Obvious compassion, appropriate irritation, measured maternity (applied to clients or cases), and expressed sensitivity are not demerits at the bar. It takes a healthy portion of each to serve the law. Experience has also taught me that acknowledged, though not brandished, femininity is also useful and helpful. Even on those rare occasions when it makes no difference at all, being feminine is still easier for a woman than being otherwise—and it's a lot more fun!

Twenty-five years after taking the oath of admission, I have also learned that men are not nearly as immune to the influence of estrogen from within themselves as we think they are. They disguise it well though, and even when it emerges, they have a different name for it (aggressive or pushy, and demanding or irritable, etc.). So why should you suppress useful qualities that are already in the functional domain of lawyers anyway? And because your progesterone is in permanently limited quantity, why not compete on your own hormonal field?

For several reasons, I believe even more strongly in allegiance to culture. First, external judgments based on cultural or racial differences are often more harsh, more historically grounded, and more difficult to overcome than those based on gender. Second, the truth is that the only kind of chocolate tolerated in many corporate, governmental, and law firm environments is white chocolate. In the face of these pressures, my advice to you is to savor your cultural heritage, and through your preparedness and energy for work, leave your coworkers, whether subordinate or superior, no choice except respect for what W.E.B. DuBois so aptly called your "two-ness."

I offer the same advice to you about your cultural heritage that I offered about your femininity: It is more comfortable to adhere to it than it is to dodge it, and your adherence provides a much stronger and more enduring pivot (commonly known as "being yourself") for productivity and upward mobility. But it isn't just about your personal advancement. By expressing and reinforcing the validity of your cultural origins and by integrating your culture into the workplace, whether as art on the wall or as the choice of or venue for office functions, you actually perform a service. That service is the edification, and thus the betterment, of your colleagues, the broadening of their perspectives on issues, on people, and on the history and future of our great country.

As you traverse the often rocky plains of your legal career, I hope you will remember that, even though it may be cloaked with jurisprudence, your core is distaff. It is better, and ultimately easier, to learn to manage, rather than to suppress, its inevitable emergence. Remember also that after all our cloaks are removed, or snatched away by wind, rain, or foe, that core is still there.

I can also assure you that your new professional environment welcomes, or should welcome, your singularity, and that one of your responsibilities is to introduce an alternative human dynamic. The new setting won't be multicultural if you abandon yours. And it won't be diverse if you erase all the differences.

Welcome to this wonderful and immensely fulfilling service. May you enjoy during your whole life all of the joy of living your whole self.

Vanzetta Mc Pherson

Vanzetta Penn McPherson *is a U.S. Magistrate Judge for the Middle District of Alabama in Montgomery, Alabama.*

Dear Sisters, Dear Daughters,

There's something humbling about being asked to impart your wisdom on those who will follow. Part of me wants to take you all by the hand and guide you, gently, down the path you have chosen, helping you avoid all the boulders and potholes I encountered. Another part of me feels silly and foolish, as if the mere thought that I have something worthwhile to say is ridiculous beyond reason.

For the time being, I'll ignore those latter voices in my head and offer up whatever advice I can.

Because you have chosen the law as your calling, you are in for an interesting career, no matter what happens. I chose to practice in a large law firm because I was looking for the stability a large firm typically offers, as well as for the diversity of practice.

But a large firm environment isn't for everyone. To some, being one of 20 incoming associates in a 200- or 300-lawyer firm is a bit daunting. For those people, a small firm is probably better. It's important to know what's important to you when deciding which course to take. And don't be afraid to reevaluate those decisions in midcourse, in case your priorities change. Age and children have a way of doing that.

I wish I could tell you that I had some grand plan for my life or my career. But I didn't. In fact, the more I think about it, the more I attribute much of my success to my relative aimlessness. I know many lawyers who spent a fair amount of time in law school and in their first jobs calculating what they needed to do to get ahead, to make law review, to get an offer at a Wall Street firm, to make partner, etc.

I did none of that. My focus was always on the task at hand. It was unacceptable for me to make anything less than an "A+" on any given project. Not because I wanted to be on law review, but because there was a little voice inside me that would berate me if I didn't make "A"s. Healthy? Perhaps not. But it got the job done. That little voice, more than anything, earned me good grades in law school, plentiful job offers, partnership, clients, the respect of my peers, and, most recently, the job of managing partner of my firm's Dallas office.

Do I ever feel like my gender has been an issue? Not really. That doesn't mean I haven't encountered sexist behavior. I did early in my career, and I continue to encounter it today in some of the most unlikely places. I never felt like I was being held back because I was a woman, however.

Nor have I ever felt like being an Asian American has held me back. If anything, the mere notion that somebody might hold my ethnicity or my gender against me has driven me to prove them wrong before they even had a chance to let such thoughts enter their mind.

What motivates me is closing a big transaction and knowing that I got my client the best deal he could have possibly gotten. There's something about having a client rely on you for protection that inspires you to be the best you can be. And when I'm able to deliver on that promise, it makes my day.

That being said, there's also something very humbling about being part of a major, multimillion dollar transaction. The knowledge that, even at several hundred dollars an hour, I'm a mere cog in the wheel keeps me grounded and prevents me from getting a big head.

Practicing law is definitely a craft, and it takes a long time to master. I say that not to discourage you, but to give you permission to panic in the early years. I don't know how many times I confidently accepted an assignment from a partner only to wither once I closed my office door. The only thing that kept me from getting fired was, I hate to tell you, long hours at the office.

Long hours notwithstanding, it is absolutely crucial that you maintain a life outside the office. Four and a half years ago, my life took on new meaning when I had a son. It was an adjustment for both me and my husband, who is also a lawyer. My son has forced me to put a bit more balance into my life, and that's been a good thing. I absolutely cannot "phone it in" with him. If he wants me to play dinosaurs, I can't be mentally reviewing a client's lease. It just doesn't work.

My last bit of advice is that you occasionally stick your neck out. A few years ago, I started writing a monthly column on issues affecting women in the legal profession for a local legal publication. It hasn't always been popular, and I've had my share of critics—both male and female. But it's been cathartic and fun.

I've also helped institute a recurring women's retreat at my firm. It's expensive and not every partner believes it's worth the expense. But, in my eyes, it's absolutely crucial to the development of our firm's women lawyers. If I've expended a bit of political capital in the process, that's okay. I'm not trying to be popular, just effective.

Another good lesson: If you're not taking risks, not occasionally raising eyebrows, you're probably playing it too safe. And that's no way to run a career—or a life.

Kathleen Wu

Kathleen J. Wu *is the Managing Partner of the Dallas office of Andrews & Kurth where she practices real estate law.*

Dear Sisters, Dear Daughters,

It gives me great joy to write this letter to you. It allows me the perspective of writing in a sense to my own daughter, Camille, who is only eight years old, but clearly will face the same struggles that I faced and continue to face today.

I listened to Reverend Tutu speak of the Truth Commission held in South Africa and his feelings about the American experience. He said that the lie we live as Americans is our belief that we have transcended the ravages of slavery and subordination. This thought left me shaking my head and completely agreeing with him. He went on to speak about the feelings of most African Americans in this country who continue to live with the pain of racist seeds planted long ago in the American psyche. The seeds perennially manifest their fruit—Be it in the dismantling of affirmative action programs, increased hate crime activity, denial of health benefits to the poor and needy, or the continued increase in the Black male population in jail rather than in college. Reverend Tutu suggested a need for Americans to have their own Truth Commission to open the long-dormant discussion about race relations.

The notion in this country that everything is all right must continue to be challenged. The efforts to maintain consciousness raising needs to be kept in the forefront of American race relations. Until there is an honest discussion and acknowledgment about the realities of racism, significant change will never occur. America needs its own truth commission to open the wounds and wash away the ever-present racist aggression, which is presented in a more sophisticated form than ever before.

I grew up in house where I was told that I could be anything I wanted to be. Then I would go to school and be the only one in a class and be treated differently because I spoke another language and my parents were immigrants. Some of my teachers felt that maybe I wasn't like the "others." Sometimes the immigrant status was more of a disadvantage than an advantage. My parents, however, held steadfast to their dream that their children would succeed in this country. By providing love, protection, and a continuous presence at the schools, my parents shielded me and permitted an environment where I grew and flourished. The constant support I had received in my early years provided a strong base for me to navigate and negotiate the educational community.

It wasn't until I reached law school at Howard University, where for the first time in my life the race issue was not evident, that I felt I could "drop my shoulders'" and relax. When I re-entered the white world as a graduate law student at Temple University, I had to deal with the "society of one," which continues today where I remain the only person of color at my law school and one of only five at the university where I teach. The most important advice I can give you in this time of retrenchment and destruction of the affirmative action policy is to maintain mental health through mentors and connections with others of like minds. The isolation on campuses, corporate offices, and law firms is daunting. I never accepted that there would be a glass ceiling for me until I was told that it would be politically unwise

It is imperative for women of color to forge other relationships outside of the job and to understand what is truly important in this world . . . family and friends.

for a person of color to be elevated to an executive position where I toil everyday.

The reality is it doesn't matter how much you do, how committed you are, or how well you play the game, there is always the color rafter that prevents advancement, which is steadfastly maintained by those in power. It is imperative for women of color to forge other relationships outside of the job and to understand what is truly important in this world, which comes down to the immensely personal—family and friends. Always understand that you must create your own agenda outside of the institution. You must find support and compassion in venues where you are cherished and can be safe, both emotionally and spiritually.

It is very disquieting when women of color and people of color generally feel that the yeoman effort never seems to be enough. The ability of those in power to constantly move the bar leaves frustration and depression in its wake. We must understand that it is necessary for both mental health and sheer survival not to give up our souls in the pursuit. We must work more efficiently and effectively not to burn ourselves out for the sake of an illusive goal that oftentimes is not worth the work associated with the journey. Learn to manage this world you have decided to place yourself in rather than be managed by it. Audre Lorde said many years ago:

> Those of us who stand outside the circle of this society's definition of acceptable women; those of us who have been forged in the crucible of difference—those of us who are poor, who are lesbians, who are Black, who are older—know that *survival is not an academic skill.* It is learning how to stand alone, unpopular and sometimes reviled, and how to make common cause with those others identified as outside the structures in order to define and seek a world in which we can all flourish. It is learning how to take our differences and make them strengths. *For the master's tools will never*

dismantle the master's house. They may allow us temporarily to beat him at his own game, but they will never enable us to bring about genuine change.

(From *Sister Outsider* "The Master's Tools Will Never Dismantle the Master's House " pg. 112 (1984))

I am not saddened by Audre's words. I am, however, disappointed that I did not heed them earlier in my life. But that's all right, for it is more important to understand them at some point rather than never understanding them at all. I have learned that it is important to create your own "real" rather than permitting someone else to dictate your existence. Understanding and placing value on the truly important parts of your life and understanding that this career is simply a means.

Barbara L. Bernier is a Founding Faculty Member and Tenured Professor at the Roger Williams University School of Law in Rhode Island.

Dear Sisters, Dear Daughters,

> Life for me ain't been no crystal stair.
> It's had tacks in it,
> And splinters,
> And boards torn up,
> And places with no carpet on the floor—-
> Bare.
>
> —*Mother to Son*, Langston Hughes

As a child, I remember when my mother would read poetry to me, including *Mother to Son*, by Langston Hughes. The poem has taken on different meanings for me over the course of my life, and its message remains relevant and a continual source of inspiration to me as an attorney, both in practice and in my personal life, although it was written many years ago.

As a child, I remember vividly imagining the "splinters" in the stairs of the poem. Our house had wood floors, and I knew that splinters could hurt and that torn up boards were not pretty—both were to be avoided at all costs. The "crystal stair" was surely the preferred path—something much better—pretty as it reflected light, smooth to the touch and cool. . .

I wanted the crystal stair.

Over the years, even through law school, my mother often reminded me of the poem during those times when there were "splinters" and "boards torn up" in my life. At these times, the poem became a kind of emotional salve she would apply to the intangible wounds I suffered growing up: the inexplicable first-place loss during a national speech contest (I still recall the audible gasp in the room, when my name was not called) and the rejection letter from a top law firm when others (often the sons and daughters of industry leaders) who seemed less qualified were invited to join their summer programs. During these times, the splinters represented racial injustice, sexual inequality, and the unfairness of society—a bitter reminder that not much had changed since Langston Hughes lived during the Harlem Renaissance of the 1920s. The poem became a taunting challenge, tempered by the reassurances of my mother, to continue up the steps, past the splinters, and around the torn up boards.

> But all the time
> I'se been a-climbin' on,...
> ....And sometimes goin' in the dark
> Where there ain't been no light...

As I grew older, I began to realize that these splinters and torn up boards were not necessarily racial or sexual injustices. Yes, such prejudices still exist as they did when the poem was written, but I began to understand that sometimes these splinters are the challenges of life faced by everyone. This realization and acceptance that sometimes people and circumstances can be unfair and unjust to anyone, irrespective of race or sex, commenced a mental healing process for me. Believe me when I say, dear sisters and daughters, that it can be a full-time preoccupation to distinguish accurately when a particular slight or injustice is racially motivated or just the happenstance of life. In fact, the exclusive pursuit of such distinctions can be maddening, unfulfilling, and a diversion from our path up the stairs. To release myself from the bondage borne of the constant analysis of these injustices has now allowed me to devote more time to developing my practice and my personal sense of accomplishment and self worth. This is not to say that I don't realize that racial and sexual injustice continues. I have no doubt that it does, but I began to view the words of the poem as inspiration to continue to strive despite whatever obstacles are thrown in my path by the "splinters" and "boards" that are the challenges of life.

I now see the poem, as I try to see life, not just from a racial perspective. Langston Hughes did not speak of racial injustice in the poem (although it is implied from the circumstances of the time and the likely perspective of the author). He wrote of challenges in general and the need to continue to strive upward of continuing up a path that might not be as smooth as glass, of the need to persevere past obstacles and most fundamentally, of the need of a mother to equip her child with the inspiration and determination to continue on a path unfairly strewn with obstacles that others are not challenged with and which are in addition to the everyday challenges of life. As I began to appreciate the differences in my perception of these challenges in life, I became empowered and freed to identify solutions to these challenges. Viewing a setback as a racial or sexual injustice has a sense of finality to it. I cannot change my race or sex, nor the injustices meted out if a particular obstacle arises as a result of either. When I view a challenge as simply an obstacle to be overcome, however, I am able to set about developing a resolution. I find this viewpoint to be freeing and full of hope.

> *When I view a challenge as simply an obstacle to be overcome . . . I am able to set about developing a resolution.*

When I transitioned into partnership at my law firm, the poem took on still new meaning for me. Surely, I thought that in 1997, my invitation to join the partnership of a large firm could not possibly be viewed by others as a journey into a place where there "ain't been no light." To my surprise, however, I marveled at how few women of color had preceded me in law firms of similar size. It was difficult to find role models and mentors, and sometimes as I stumble alone and in the dark, I am reminded still again of the poem. . .

> Don't you set down on the steps
> 'Cause you finds its kinder hard.
> Don't you fall now—
> For I'se still goin honey,
> I'se still climbin',
> And life for me ain't been no crystal stair.

I still seek the crystal stair, but now not just for me, but as part of a legacy I leave for you—one more step up the stair, one more board made smooth.

I imagine that Langston Hughes could not have dreamed, and could only hope, that an African American woman could join in partnership in a large law firm practice in the years that have passed since he wrote his poem. I am excited by this thought, because I have great hopes and expectations of those who follow me up these stairs. Perhaps my lesson, as stated in these words, will smooth the journey for you. Perhaps my words will equip you with the determination you need to focus on your accomplishments and side-step the time and energy-consuming diversions that racial splinters create on your climb up the stairs. That is my hope for you and one of the sincerest offerings that I can share with you as I pause to reflect upon my climb up the stairs.

...don't you fall now...for I'se still goin'...I'se still climbin'...

With love, admiration (and always hope),

Cynthia F. Reaves

Cynthia F. Reaves *is a Member of the firm and Shareholder of Epstein Becker Green, P.C., in Washington, D.C. where she specializes in corporate transactional, tax-exempt organization, and managed care law.*

Dear Sisters, Dear Daughters,

I write to you as a person who entered the law with a firm belief that as a part of the system I could do good. I was first told that I could not succeed because of my race in law school. I didn't believe it, and I went on to practice as a legal services attorney, a prosecutor, and a law professor. In each job, I was the first woman of color. I have encountered success, and I have endured battles of self-doubt prompted by the hostility that confronted me. I have held leadership positions in state and national bar organizations, and I have been alone in new environments where no one knew me.

In my journey, I have sometimes felt like a motherless daughter. Lost, adrift, and alone. The most important thing I have discovered is that even when I feel that I am alone, I know that I am not alone. There are others who have come before me or after me who will understand. It has become my personal goal to reach out to others and remind them that they are not alone. This is the challenge we all face. This too will be your challenge. At the present time there is talk about the growing numbers of us in the legal profession, and although it is not as bleak as it once was, what I fear is the emergence of places where we are shut out. All around me I see places where others gather and speak without us. Our voices and presence scare these people who do not know how to address us or the concerns of our community.

Your challenge is to build on that which has been done and to speak with clarity and a new vision. When you share your reality with others they can begin to understand that there are many different ways that people experience life and law. In speaking we share not only our experiences but also the experiences of those who do not make it. Because there are so many who do not have the opportunities that you or I do, we must not forget them. We each must carry others who are lost and alone with us. In this way, the gifts and talents we have can be used to shape the future.

Even when we bring others and ourselves, some people may remain unable to learn, and many may simply deny our existence. By acting as if we are not present, those who hold power in this society can maintain their institutions without opening the door to us. But my sisters and daughters, the gift that we have learned is that we cannot be ignored or silenced. We scare them because we speak truth and force changes in the structures that conspire to silence us.

Truth always has a cost. Remember that there are those who have gone before you who have paid the price for you. When some of us spoke, we were silenced. But when we did not succumb to the desire of those who did not want us, we found our voices and spoke—not only against the injustices exacted against us, but also those against our communities and against you. So do not forget that you have many of the opportunities that you have because others fought to open the doors for you and fought to change the dialogue. I wish you well and hope your vision opens doors for those who will come after you.

Cecelia M. Espenoza

Cecelia M. Espenoza *is an Associate Professor of Law at St. Mary's University.*

Dear Sisters, Dear Daughters,

You enter law school and legal practice at a very different time from the time I entered them. When I entered UCLA Law School in 1979, the *Bakke* case had just been decided. While the case caused a restructuring of many affirmative action programs, it affirmed that law schools could legally seek to diversify their student bodies. UCLA had an affirmative action program. Thus, I was (and am) an affirmative action baby. UCLA, because of a state mandate, has now virtually dismantled its affirmative action program. While I benefited from affirmative action and was privileged to attend UCLA, I might not be so privileged today. That fact has very important implications for you who are entering law schools and legal practice today. The following story illustrates a bit of the complexities of being an affirmative action baby.

I remember my first day of law school at orientation. A white male, son of a prominent Los Angeles attorney asked me what my LSAT score was. I proudly (but naively) told him. He responded, "What do you think got you into UCLA, your LSAT or your last name?" While I admit he did upset me, somehow I had the presence of mind to say, "I don't know what political movement got me in here, but you can be damn sure I am going to stay." As it turns out, he may have done me a favor. I worked very hard and did well in my first year. I wrote onto the *UCLA Law Review* and served on the *Chicano Law Review*. My grades attracted the notice of very generous professors at UCLA, such as Steve Yeazell, Alison Anderson, Gary Schwartz, and

Richard Delgado. They helped me find a summer clerkship, encouraged me to try out for the law review, helped me apply for a federal judicial clerkship, and encouraged me as a law teacher. Their mentoring started me on a path that eventually led to a very rewarding law teaching career. I am very grateful to them and to the political movement that opened the doors of UCLA to me. I must say that persistence in the face of negativity has paid off for me. I urge you to persist in your chosen path, no matter what obstacles may face you.

Despite the apparent shift in affirmative action policies in this country, I know that you will have tremendous opportunities. I believe that those of us who were allowed to enter those doors in the 70s and 80s will continue to keep those doors open for you. Your responsibility is to work as hard as you can so you can be ready when you go through the doors of opportunity.

The most important piece of advice I can give to you is to remember your family and your community as you travel a path of opportunity that may lead away from your home and community. As you get older and begin to realize success in your chosen professions, it will be very lonely if that success is at the cost of a loving family and a connection with your community. Many of you come from communities that have not shared in the current economic and social prosperity. You must work with and for your community to make life better for those with fewer opportunities. Just as you will benefit from scholarships, mentoring, and the privileges of education, you must return that favor to your community.

Sometimes, the craziness of the meaning of merit affects successful people of color. I wrote the following poem after observing a Latina who did not think a Native American woman job applicant was "authentic" enough. I think it speaks to some of the challenges you will face as someone seeking to open the doors of opportunity and as someone who will have power to determine whether others will be given those opportunities. I share the poem with you in a spirit of love and support. Good luck with your chosen endeavors.

> "Gatekeepers"
> They let us in
> because of
> or despite the
> color of our skin
> now we have keys to doors
> slammed shut to our parents
> what to do about the color of skin?
> it was about access then
> it is about access now
> close the gates
> because those with the color of our skin
> have chosen a slightly different path
> than ours?
> let them find their path
> the pain of
> society's response to
> the color of skin
> led them down a different road.
> They will find their way
> back home
> because all winding paths of the hear lead to home
> and home
> will give them peace.

May your choices ultimately bring you peace.

Sincerely,

Antoinette Sedillo López

Antoinette Sedillo López *is a Professor at the University of New Mexico Law School where she teaches a variety of courses and practices in the clinical law program.*

Dear Sisters, Dear Daughters,

Congratulations. You have acquired the key to true freedom for yourself and your family and your community: a law license! Whether you practice law in the traditional sense or not, there is nothing sweeter than knowing that option is always open to you. Sweeter still is the awareness that, financially, you are always able to take care of yourself and your family by merely hanging out an "Open for Business" sign at any time, start your own law practice, and claim your acquired right to control your own future. This realization is never nicer than when you are unhappily employed. The mere thought that you could choose to exercise the options your law license affords you may be just enough to get you through the day. There is no better feeling, and it's what I now think of as "true freedom"! Protect it fiercely. Never surrender it, and never do anything that could result in its revocation. You remember the most basic definition of a license don't you? It is a privilege, not a right. Revocable at any time by the licenser. This may seem obvious; and, of course, after working so hard to receive your law license you certainly would never deliberately do anything to risk losing it. Nevertheless, you cannot afford to be naïve about the many dangers that lurk in what may now seem to you to be the most unlikely places. Dangers that can easily place your law license in jeopardy. Most of them involve money. Follow this simple advice and you should be okay. Be very wary of opportunities to make fast money. If it sounds confusing and you can't connect the dots between all of the players (including your own role in the scheme) and the money, it is probably better just to say no.

Never co-mingle clients' funds, especially not with your own. Develop systems to help you to easily maintain files and records of clients' matters. Always require documentation. Follow these rules even if you work for someone else who doesn't. Maintain a file of all of your accomplishments. Keep your c.v. current. Remember that you have nothing but your reputation for protection. Develop a good support system in your personal life.

As a young attorney you have many attractive career and lifestyle options to consider and to pursue. My strong advice is that you should take an active part in planning and pursuing the career you imagine in your work-related fantasies. During 10 years of teaching law and 18 years since law school, I have been dismayed by the fact that so many young lawyers take a decidedly passive role in this process. Don't make the same mistake. The best career choices for you are waiting for you to claim them. They already belong to you. They are waiting for you to reach your point of readiness. To reach your point of readiness, you must first identify the choices—you must know what you want; you must develop a picture of yourself enjoying the work you imagine yourself doing under the most ideal conditions (if you are not happy in your vision, then you should rethink your choices); you must get good at doing what you need to be able to do in order to demand access and to be successful; you must do whatever is necessary to become physically and mentally strong enough to go the distance; and you must demand entry into the ranks from those who control access to them. I repeat, stay strong and demand entry from those who control access to them! Adopt this as your mantra.

As for your community. You've already been places and done things too, so I need not speak to you about childish things. There are serious threats to your community. Your minority community needs young attorneys to join the struggle to preserve its rights. Ask yourself this question: What will you want to be remembered for at the end of your career? It will come sooner than you think.

As I write this letter to you, I am at the mid-point of my own sojourn in my life and in the law. The longer I live and observe the people around me the more I understand the truth of the *new age* sound bite: "If you are not a part of the solution, you are part of the problem." Consequently, I can only justify writing to you about what is currently on my mind.

As I rapidly approach my 20th year as an African American female attorney, I see evidence all around me that we are in a national period of retrenchment away from the civil rights gains of the all too recent past. There is an article in the November 1999, issue of *Vanity Fair* magazine entitled, "Damsels in Dissent" that features five prominent young white women who are the leading arch-conservatives in their respective fields (actually there are only four named in the caption of the article, but upon reading the article you are introduced to the fifth subject, an Asian American—go figure!). The point of the article is that these women are "leading a counterrevolution" . . . [and that they are] . . . "the coming thing, heralds, or sirens, of a genuine conservative chic." At the same time, Bill Lann Lee, the head of the Civil Rights Division of the U.S. Justice Department, gave a speech during an ABA meeting in Los Angeles in October of 1999 about the alarming increase in the number of hate crimes that are under investigation by his office. Yes, I too am alarmed. And you should be too. Alarm is not paralysis, however, so look for ways to become an activist. Otherwise the only momentum will continue to occur in conservative circles that feel no allegiance to the "old" commitment to your civil rights. My new favorite saying is, "just because you're paranoid doesn't mean they're not out to get you."

I am particularly alarmed by the fact that so many young lawyers are uneducated about the importance of and oblivious to the attacks on affirmative action programs. Although I don't expect everyone to devote as much energy to this particular issue as I have, I believe that there is no more important issue in the African American community. Other problems such as poverty and police brutality and poor services and poor education are all destined to worsen if we lose the right to access opportunities to prevent them. I feel strongly that the reason why more minority attorneys have failed to speak out on affirmative action is because they are too busy enjoying its benefits. They are complacent. The sad consequence of the silence of minority attorneys is that the rest of the minority community remains unaware of the threats it faces—believing, erroneously, that the attorneys in the community would have sounded an alarm if there were a problem. The minority lawyers and bar associations are in woeful neglect of their implicit duty to sound such an alarm.

Younger attorneys and law students are justifiably proud of their achievements, but go too far when they ignore the role that affirmative action programs continue to play in their success. Without affirmative action programs, access to opportunities for education, wealth, and status will be limited to those who kept it all to themselves before affirmative action. It is really very simple. Most non-minorities who have the power to confer access to important opportunities can be reasonably expected to follow the human impulse to help those who are more like, as opposed to less like, themselves.

Yes, you are smart. Yes, you work hard. So was I. And so were your ancestors and all of the legions of descendants of former slaves in this country who came before you and who will come after you, but who will not be successful unless access is assured for them the way that it was made possible for us. Your actual success, however, has probably been the result of the existence of a certain amount of pressure to allow your meritorious attributes to be given the full credit they would not have received without that pressure.

I will end by sharing some legal information about affirmative action that you may not know. The term itself has a long history, but its modern usage began when it was included in Executive Order Number 10925 that was signed by President

Kennedy in 1961, mandating "affirmative (as opposed to merely passive) action" to provide access for the descendants of former slaves. President Johnson backed off of it for a period of time and then Nixon re-instituted it upon issuing Executive Order Number 11246. Executive Order Number 11246 has remained in effect under every chief executive since Nixon.

Of course, it is crucial to understand this history of the current use of the term "affirmative action" in order to reject the noise being emitted from every corner that insists that we no longer call it by that name. We are encouraged to spend precious time and energy developing a strategy that will result in us calling it something else. In fact, the majority of the supporters of affirmative action – those who don't think that it is dead and/or unimportant—are now engrossed in many such efforts. Their time would be better spent educating themselves and their communities about what affirmative action really is and why it is important.

I have never spoken to a critic of affirmative action who wasn't silenced (at least briefly) upon being informed "affirmative action" is an official term from language in a Presidential executive order that has been renewed by every president for more that 30 years. It is not something common and offensive that we should suddenly be ashamed of. Consequently, changing the term is not within our power. It is not an option, and we should stop allowing this strand of illogic to divert our attention into efforts to figure out what to call it now. Affirmative action means that pressure to recognize your merit will continue long enough to see you through this brilliant start to your dream career.

Linda R. Crane

Linda R. Crane *is a Professor of Law at the John Marshall Law School in Chicago where she teaches courses in property law, commercial law and federal securities regulation.*

Dear Sisters, Dear Daughters,

More than ten years ago, I was asked to submit my thoughts to the *New York Law Journal* regarding the theme for Law Day—"Access to Justice." The thoughts and ideas that were embodied in that article have changed very little and remain valid today. These comments are excerpted from my article entitled "Black Women Lawyers Are Outside the Power Structure."

When called upon to think about access to justice, my thoughts naturally turned to Honore Daumier's satirical comments on lawyers and justice. By portraying lawyers, the servants of justice, through his lithographs, as unworthy, Daumier causes us to be introspective. More than a century later, his works bid us to confront the question of whether and how much we have changed.

Daumier lived at a time when few spoke for minorities. In his France of 1824-1847, the increasing and ever-spreading poverty kept pace with those amassing huge private fortunes. The times spawned Victor Hugo's *Les Miseres*, which was almost finished by 1847, and later became *Les Miserables*. Daumier viewed lawyers and judges as insensitive to poverty. In one of his lithographs, the accused, who might be Jean Valjean, is pushed toward the judge by the gendarme. The judge, almost reclining in his armchair, says, "You were hungry . . . you were hungry . . . that's no excuse. I am hungry practically every day, yet I don't go out stealing."

The unfortunate soul in that lithograph has a kind of access to justice. It is the kind and quality, however, that is the subject of this statement. To the extent that lawyers and judges remain insensitive in the manner of Valjean's judge, we will have failed to learn from our past.

For blacks and more acutely for black women, time has taken us from bondage. Enslaved, disenfranchised, and segregated by law, we have finally begun to win equality by law. Winning equality by law is not the functional equivalent, however, of winning equality in fact. Among minority practitioners, access to justice has neither been truly accessible, nor has it been a distinct reality. Access to justice may be viewed as something more than the rule of law by statute, regulation, or order. It is the "old boy's network" that continues to elude most of us. It is that vague sense of discomfort, almost sensed rather than felt, when one enters a room and conversation stops; it is the refusal to meet one's gaze during conservation; it is being advised of that important meeting an hour before it occurs, when one's white colleagues had been advised days in advance; it is those shared lunches among the group to which the lone black is not invited; it is the male practitioner before a black female jurist who refuses to accept her ruling as final, who is more belligerent and clearly less respectful . . . When the informal mentoring so critical to one's success in any firm or corporation is lacking, something else is operating. These subconscious impediments have more to do with how high one is permitted to advance in the hierarchy and not whether one is permitted entry. The greatest hurdle to our advancement is this simple matter of comfort, not competence.

In the private sector, lawyers and some judges are looking for someone like themselves, someone they can "relate to," someone they can trust. This is very subtle territory. It does no less violence than the slap in the face. Civilized society has cultivated more genteel maneuvers to accomplish the same goals that the "Black Codes" (laws passed post 1877 to erode gains for blacks) achieved—it is the "violence of the mind."

Lawyers, as the guardians of society, are obliged to exert some influence to preserve society. Nothing prevents that exertion from being an ethical realization that more is required than merely following the strict letter of the law

To the extent that black women lawyers continue outside of the power structure, access to justice continues to elude us. This is less a phenomena in government than in the private sector. Although more hospitable, our numbers in government and public interest have not yet spelled the demise of an organization like the Association of Black Women Attorneys (ABWA). ABWA has been a backbone of support for many of us who have felt isolated in the struggle. In much the same way that selected individuals have reached out to assist many in the trenches, ABWA has provided an added strength in the knowledge that one does not go it alone. When the merger movement in New York City advocated that ABWA should become a part of one organization, it was opposed. It was opposed for the very reasons that there is still a need to address the ways in which we do not have access. We will have reached a truly advanced stage in society when all so-called minority bar associations can be eliminated. If that stage of development continues to be postponed, we will have failed to learn from the lessons of history. Daumier's lithographs will continue to taunt us, and Cervantes' writings in the 17th century will continue to have a place in modern times. Cervantes satirizing men's follies wrote, "in the streets of by and by, we arrive at the house of never."

The 20 years that I have been in practice has seen some change, if in no other arena than numbers. Nonetheless, Daumier and Cervantes still resonate with me.

Sincerely,

Eileen D. Millett

Eileen D. Millett *is General Counsel of the Interstate Sanitation Commission in New York.*

Dear Sisters, Dear Daughters,

I had worked for the American Bar Association for a total of 10 years, and I thought that I had seen and done all there was to do in the Association, but I was about to initiate a journey that I never experienced before in life: Multicultural Women Attorneys Network (MWAN).

MWAN was a small committee comprised of deeply committed and well-seasoned women of the law who desperately wanted to make a difference in the lives of minority women lawyers. We were a rich mixture of women from different racial and ethnic backgrounds, and we represented the spectrum of the rainbow—African American, Asian, Caucasian, Latina, and Native American. Our backgrounds and experiences were similar, yet different. We met for hours on end and still we did not know how to reach the core problems of minority women lawyers. Do we start with a national conference? Should we do surveys or questionnaires? Would one-on-one interviews be more effective? Will the women open up and share their experiences?

Finally, the idea of small, intimate roundtable discussions hit us like a rock in the face. We would hold as many of these roundtable discussions as possible and work to attract women of different racial and ethnic backgrounds. We would listen and provide support and guidance when possible. I knew the stories well; I had lived some of these stories and suffered through the pain and agony. So had many of the members of MWAN. We intuitively knew the stories were sad, emotional, and yet full of richness.

You cannot imagine how surprised I was when we initially held the roundtable discussions. The minority women lawyers who attended came from every area of the legal profession, including corporate America, large majority law firms, legal services, and governmental agencies; some were judges, prosecutors, law professors, students, and a number owned their own law firms. It did not matter what level they had reached in their careers; their experiences had been very similar.

Like me, the women talked about their naiveness, dedication to making positive changes, and working to make the legal profession a better place for all women. They spoke about how they were treated by people in the profession and how that saddened their dreams about equality and justice for all. They spoke of inequities, denied opportunities, damaged careers, and severe barriers and disadvantages. The tears were profuse and heart wrenching. We all cried together during these sessions. The double-edged sword of sexism and racism was devastating, and in many instances, there was no one to share experiences. I also knew the feeling of isolation and having nowhere to turn. It was so comforting and reassuring to all of us to know that MWAN was there to listen, share, and care.

After the roundtable discussions, when we attempted to analyze and decipher what had happened, we relived our experiences in the legal profession and cried again for both the brave women and ourselves. I can remember that some sessions left me so completely drained that I was mesmerized and unable to respond or move. I just cried. I could see the scars that these women were carrying, and I felt the heavy weight of my own scars. The challenge for us was in determining what to do with this emotion-filled package of knowledge and experiences.

Here we were nearly a year and a dozen roundtables later. We learned and accumulated an immense wealth of knowledge, but we were not sure what to do with this fortune we had amassed. We spent hours, days, and months discussing and debating what we should do with this powerful information. As the staff person, I always felt an additional burden of needing to come up with a solution that was practical and would have an impact. I carried the emotional package around my shoulders like it was an albatross. I was desperately looking for solutions, and at the same time I needed a place to unleash the package.

I was acutely aware of my vulnerabilities, emotionalism, and powerlessness while I was carrying the package around. My perceptions of the legal profession were changing. I saw clearly that the problems I experienced were not personality disorders or flaws in my character, but instead the problems stemmed from the fact that I was a black woman who had entered a white, male-dominated profession. I could clearly see the clashing of two cultures, and it was quite tumultuous.

In 1990 and 1991, we held two phenomenal national conferences on the east and west coasts. Through the conferences, roundtables and meetings, MWAN touched the lives of thousands of women lawyers of color. I felt so proud of being a part of this historic movement. It was not until 1994, that *The Burdens of Both, The Privileges of Neither* was completed. It was truly a labor of love that contained the many jewels of wisdom that had been accumulated. The revelations in Burdens were stepping-stones for those who followed.

Dear Sisters and Daughters, I hope as you read this letter today, that your lives and experiences in the profession are different from the ones we confronted in the past. Battles were fought to ensure that you would have a more positive experience in the legal arena. We knew you were coming and we never stopped fighting.

Rachel Patrick

Rachel Patrick *is the Staff Director of the American Bar Association's Council on Racial and Ethnic Justice in Chicago.*

Dear Sisters, Dear Daughters,

What an adventure and accomplishment to choose to become a lawyer and to actually succeed. I write to you to talk about how being an African American woman in this profession brings a special responsibility and an extraordinary opportunity.

We, as African Americans, have been shaped by the history of African Americans in this country. The motivations that drive me were shaped by the social injustices experienced along the way. Therefore, I have a special perspective to bring to the practice of law and my work as a judge.

Many in the predominantly non-minority power structure, have had few occasions, if any, to encounter the likes of you or me. Even with the advances of African Americans in this country, we still remain the few in many circles, such that many infrequently encounter someone like us. Therefore, as I practiced law within the power structures, I have had to "teach" them about me.

How has this teaching been accomplished? At the least, through personal example. We show ourselves through our knowledge of the law, our ability to articulate our clients' positions, and our ability to handle the human dynamics of the cases. We show ourselves in every interaction with our clients and in our advocacy of their positions. Our personal example also includes the dignity, grace, courtesy and, yes, humility we show when we are challenged by a difficult situation. And we also teach when situations draw us beyond passive example and compel us to be more pointed and aggressive in responding to unfairness.

Even then I have tried to remain dignified.

Yes, I, along with many others, have said, "I am tired of having to carry the burden of teaching this every day." But with the advantage of hindsight and the perspective that comes from years as a lawyer and judge, I know that even if we are tired, we must continue teaching this every day. We must persevere because I realize we have the power to make a difference. By being so public and ever aware, we, as lawyers, can ensure that conversations continue about whether our society is being fair to the "others" like ourselves.

There were times when I have felt frustrated by the difficulty of breaching the barriers of insensitivity and lack of understanding. But I had to get over it, and you must too, because those who view the dignity of our efforts, may yet be learning. Persons, whom we may not hear, will praise our excellence and will store our image as an exception to their stereotype of our group. And bit by bit, the entire wall of their stereotypes may fall, letting in the light of reality and humanity. It is a goal worth reaching for, and we, who embody the progress African Americans have made in this country, must ensure progress continues.

By teaching through personal example and encouraging conversations about fairness, we as African American lawyers can help to shape the law and the court's response to the nettlesome issues of discrimination in our increasingly multicultural world. We have a special responsibility and role to play. I hope these insights strengthen you in accepting that responsibility.

Very truly yours,

Sophia H. Hall

Sophia H. Hall *is the Administrative Presiding Judge of the Resource Section of the Juvenile Justice and Child Protection Department of the Circuit Court of Cook County, Illinois.*

Dear Sisters, Dear Daughters,

I once had a dream that I met God walking in a garden. We sat down at a bench to talk. He saw that I had an intense look on my face and he said, "What's the matter my child? You look troubled."

I looked at him and replied, "My Lord, I have often wondered what I have done to displease you so. My life and career as a black woman lawyer have not been easy." God replied, "You have not displeased me. In fact, I am very proud of you and what you have accomplished."

I thought for a moment and then asked, "Then can I ask you a couple of questions?" God replied, "Sure my child, what would you like to know."

"God, why did you make me smart enough to go to Harvard Law School and get a job at a Wall Street firm, only to leave me without a significant person in my life? My uncle told me that by going to law school, no man would want me because I would intimidate them. My father said I walk to the beat of a different drummer. Who was right? I am still single, and some people are intrigued with my mind, but test me just to see how I will respond. I am not like other women, and men often think of me as a novelty."

"My child, your father was right. I have a special plan for you to be a role model for generations to come, inspiring young men and women around the world and helping them prepare for the challenges of information technology in the new millennium. I sent you to Harvard to get the best education and exposure so that you could create and develop your own vision. I know you want to be loved, but I don't want you to define yourself by the standard set or imposed by a prospective mate. Marriage may happen for you; but I want you to embrace a larger family of men and women and reach out to them when they need you."

I thought for a moment and then said, "God, may I ask you one more question? Why did you select opportunities for me that often left me feeling isolated and alone—being the first, only black, or female, or both. Whether it was the only black of 197 lawyers at a Wall Street firm; the only black and woman interning at an all-male labor firm; the first non-scientist faculty member and black at NASA; or the first black tenured professor at the law school where I am teaching; I always felt like I was an outcast, apart and never fully accepted by my peers."

Have faith that you are special in His eyes and you shall prevail.

God replied, "My child, you were never alone, for I was always with you and never let you fall. Remember when you felt desperation that others were setting you up to fail, I gave you the wisdom to develop a plan and strategy to protect yourself? You ended up leaving that situation and getting your first client from your former employer. Or remember when you were afraid because the politics of your job forced you to make tough decisions that left you struggling to find your way out, I gave you the courage, support, and resources to start your own business? And when you realized that the business you had selected had made you become someone that you did not like, remember I helped you realize that by walking away, you had not failed, but merely been given the chance to see a new window of opportunity open up for you around the corner?"

"Yes, I know you often felt alone and isolated, but that was necessary so that you would learn to feel comfortable being on the cutting edge, outside of the box. I wanted to build a strength of character in you that would enable you to feel confident navigating in unchartered waters. Now, taking the less traveled path is second nature to you."

As I listened to the Lord's words, I realized that I was not a victim, but one of his chosen few, filled with God's blessings. It has not been easy but I have always prevailed and excelled in my endeavors. I felt ashamed for feeling sorry for myself, and I realized the virtue of looking at the glass half full, not half empty.

Today, I am at peace with my life choices. I have no regrets and enjoy the freedom and fulfillment that comes from doing something about which I can feel good. My challenge has not been unlike the challenges of other professional women; that is, coming to terms and finding some balance between the myth, the expectation, and the reality of what it means to be a minority female professional. Hopefully, in the process, we can grab a bit of happiness, however we choose to define it.

So, if you feel estranged and out of sorts as a black woman lawyer, take heart. It simply means that God has a special plan for you. Have faith that you are special in His eyes and you shall prevail. May God bless you and keep you in his care....

Andrea L. Johnson

Andrea L. Johnson *is a Visiting Professor at Chicago-Kent College of Law and a Full Professor at California Western School of Law.*

Dear Sisters, Dear Daughters,

I will open by saying that I consider it a great honor to have been asked to share my experiences in the profession with you. I hope that this letter will be of some assistance as you start your journey.

Upon completing law school, I began my career in the area of civil rights with the Georgia Commission on Equal Opportunity (CEO). This agency's focus is on the regulation of fair housing and employment practices pursuant to Georgia statutory law and Title VIII of the Civil Rights Act of 1964.

Although I never had a strong interest in the criminal process, an opportunity to work with the Fulton County Solicitor General's Office as a prosecutor soon presented itself, and I accepted. This choice turned out to be a good one, as I was almost immediately in court trying cases. Specifically, I success-fully tried my first jury trial after being with the office for only three months, and I was given my own courtroom assignment in a record four months.

Although the caseload was astronomical, the trial experience and skills I acquired as a prosecutor have proven invaluable. Such experiences included preparing witnesses, marshalling evi-dence, preparing and arguing pre-trial motions, conducting voir dire, presenting jury instructions, conducting direct and cross-examination, and drafting appellant briefs.

More importantly, as a prosecutor, I was not only able to ensure that the state was adequately represented, but I was also able to ensure that defendants were fairly treated. For example, I made great use of the First Offenders Act and numerous diversion programs for young adults and first-time offenders who may have just temporarily gone astray.

This experience also gave me a reality check as I saw first hand some of the atrocities that one human being was capable of exerting upon another—it was truly a revelation. I can honestly say that I was naïve to the fact that such things were going on in Atlanta. I was further appalled by the realization that most (I'll venture to say 90%) of the defendants were young, African American males. Sadly, most of their victims were also African American. What a disturbing commentary on the state of our community.

My experience at the Solicitor's Office laid the foundation for my career. I was blessed with a very good teacher. Then-Solicitor General and now-Fulton County District Attorney Paul Howard was a great mentor. He always made himself available and implemented what was fondly referred to as "boot camp," an intense training program for new prosecutors whereby we were required to meet after hours everyday to engage in thought-provoking legal research and writing and trial preparation exercises.

Although I was not seeking other employment, I left the Solicitor's Office after being courted for several months by the Georgia Secretary of State's Office—Securities and Business Regulations Division. This office is charged with the regulation of all stock market activities in the State of Georgia, basically functioning as the state equivalent to the U.S. Securities and Exchange Commission. I have been with the agency for nearly six years and have worked in many capacities, including Staff Attorney, Investigations Supervisor, Director of Securities Registration, and now as Chief Counsel.

I am not in court as much as I was as a prosecutor (something I must say I still miss from time to time). I find my job quite rewarding, however. This position has opened new horizons for me, as the securities practice is a very specialized area of the law. I have had the opportunity to learn the very sophisticated and often complex intricacies of financial markets and securities transactions.

Most of my day is spent drafting numerous legal documents (legislation, orders, rules and regulations, correspondence, declaratory rulings, No Action letters, etc.) and providing legal advice on securities related issues to all members of the staff, the legal community, and the general public. I'm also responsible for the supervision of the legal staff; I give strategic direction on cases and assist in the development of appropriate legal theories. At the same time, I manage an extensive caseload.

I'll reiterate the importance of finding a mentor early in your career. I was fortunate enough to clerk on the North Carolina Court of Appeals under the tutelage of the Honorable James A. Wynn, Jr. Judge Wynn was a great mentor. He taught me too many things to enumerate here; however, one thing in particular has stayed with me and I think it is worthy of mention. As a judicial clerk, my primary responsibility was the (rough) drafting of opinions of the court. Although I have always been an avid reader, Judge Wynn advised me that the best way for one to increase his or her writing skills was to constantly read. Throughout my career as well as in my personal dealings, I have found this lesson to be profoundly true, and I am forever grateful for Judge Wynn's instruction.

I come from a family of four children consisting of two boys and two girls. I am the "knee baby," as Southerners fondly refer to the child next to the youngest in the birth order. Although my immediate family is very close, I'm also blessed with a tight-knit extended family of aunts, uncles, and cousins. My sister and I are only eleven months apart. This closeness in age helped to solidify our ironclad bond. Without doubt, she is my best friend and dearest confidant. I can't express enough the importance of keeping your families close to you.

I am inspired most by my unwavering faith in God and the examples of virtue my late maternal grandmother bestowed upon me as a child. My grandmother was a strong, God-fearing woman who taught me to stick to those things in which I believed and to have respect for my elders, lessons that serve a lifetime well.

It's quite easy for me to stay centered and grounded. I often hear the following phrase from individuals not in the profession, "You don't act like an attorney. You're so down to earth." I don't know how people expect attorneys to act, maybe with some grandiose air about themselves...I'm truly not sure. I take the aforementioned comment as a compliment, however. I think that it's so important always to remember from whence we came, to remember those who we represent (family and community), and to remain humble.

I've been asked to share my greatest disappointments with you. I'll have to honestly say that my law school experience was not one of my most memorable adventures. I won't even mention the rigors of all-night study jams; instead, I'll touch on something that a lot of minority law students experience. Because I attended a predominately white, private institution, the feelings of isolation were almost paralyzing. There were only twelve blacks out of a class of 150. Without doubt, if I had it to do over, I would certainly make another law school choice. Although Wake Forest University offered the highest of academic standards, the cultural and social trade-off for this African American female was not worth it.

One of my greatest joys in life was actually seeing the tears in my grandfather's eyes and the love in his heart as he witnessed me receiving my law degree. Knowing that I had brought such pride to my family was priceless. Needless to say, it made all the struggles and challenges well worth it.

I was also greatly moved a couple of years ago when I was asked to be the keynote Women's Day speaker for one of the more prominent churches in my relatively small hometown. It seemed as though the whole town turned out to hear the native daughter who had made good. My whole extended family was there, including first cousins, thrice removed. The jitters of first-year law school case-recitals were no match for the case of nerves I had on that day. I shared my experiences and God's blessings in my life with my very captive audience and received the most thunderous ovation. What a homecoming! I will forever cherish that "warm fuzzy," which was more precious to me than anything money can buy. My sisters, these are the things that enrich a life, not partnerships, material possessions, or fair-weather acquaintances. Always remember to go back to and give back to your schools, churches, and communities.

On a more personal note, I think it is so important to have a meaningful hobby outside of the profession…some outlet that gives you an opportunity to develop your artistic side and allows you to fully express yourself. I've found such an outlet through a part-time professional modeling career.

I receive great pleasure as well as financial reward from doing elaborate runway shows and print assignments. I just shot a few scenes in the soon-to-be-released Disney feature film starring Denzel Washington entitled *Remember the Titans*. Getting away from the grind of practicing law and participating in the more artistic arena of modeling has made for a much more colorful life. I encourage you to seek such balance in your lives.

Money management is one of the most important things an individual can master. Early on, I made a conscious effort to set aside a certain percentage of my earnings for my savings. I called this commitment to savings "paying myself." This money is earmarked and comes right off the top of my net earnings. It's amazing how the funds start to accumulate once you get into the routine of saving and with the accrual of interest.

In my current position, I have the responsibility of hiring and firing attorneys. I've found the interviewing process to be just as challenging when you're sitting on the other side of the table conducting the interview as when you are the interviewee. I've had the tedious experience of deciphering through hundreds of resumes and writing samples and having to put many hours into preparing for interviews as well as the uncomfortable duty of rejecting applicants. Trust me, it's a lot harder than it seems.

Finally, I leave you with a word about our deepest obligation, which is to our community. I can't stress enough the importance of community service. I know that you've heard it all before, so I won't belabor the point. I will say, however, that there are many little black girls and boys who would benefit greatly by just a few hours of your time. Oh, I realize there are the demanding work schedules and the social engagements, but giving just a little would make such a huge difference in the lives of so many needy children. I am a strong advocate for the betterment of our youth. Throughout college and law school and even today, I've always made an effort in earnest to affiliate with those programs and organizations that strive to uplift our children. Such organizations have included Big Brothers/Big Sisters, The Urban League Reading Olympiad Program, United Way Cool Girls, Inc., The Boys and Girls Club, and Our House, Inc.

My sisters, I wish you the best as you step boldly into the new millennium with dignity, strength, and determination. Remember those seekers of justice who came before us...Harriett Tubman, Sojourner Truth, Ida B. Wells, Rosa Parks, Mary Bethune Cookman, Barbara Jordan, Constance Baker Motley, Patricia Roberts Harris, Shirley Chilsom (I could go on, but the most important things is for you to add your name to the roll call).

Very truly yours,

Debbie Thompson

Debbie D. Thompson *is a Staff Attorney with the U.S. Securities and Exchange Commission—Atlanta District Office.*

Dear Sisters, Dear Daughters,

Welcome to the profession. Your contributions to the profession, society and your community will be noteworthy in the differences they will make.

I would like to share a couple of thoughts with you to aid you on the road to success—however you may define it.

Know yourself. There are those detractors who are only too willing to explain why you cannot go to law school, and if you manage to gain admission and graduate, you will never pass the bar, and if you happen to pass the bar examination, you will never successfully practice law. And once you enter the practice of law, there is often another set of detractors who will try to pigeonhole you into the type of practice they believe is best for you. I knew that I did not want to use my law degree in the traditional way—practice at a law firm, so it was up to me to do some deep searching within myself and some research to determine what else was out there for me. I found my niche in the not-for-profit sector and have been happily (most days) using the skills honed in law school to develop programs and support projects. And in my most recent position, I provide support to the leadership of the organization.

You, better than anyone else, know what you are capable of, and that you have the drive and ambition to achieve. You know what motivates you to do well. You know what, if any, barriers you have overcome to arrive at your present place. You have a good idea of where you would be most comfortable. You know better than anyone else what it is like to be an African American, Asian American, Latina, and Native American woman in America.

And because you know this, you know when to receive comments meant to be constructive criticism as just that—words to help you improve. You also know when to ignore comments meant to be denigrating. There are those who want to help you and those who want to hinder you. You have a responsibility to yourself to learn and know the difference.

Take Care of Yourself. While we know ourselves, it is also necessary to regularly come away from the hustle and bustle of the day to refresh and reinvigorate our spirits. Take an hour, a day, and a week to spend time restoring your energy, spirit, and humor. No one can take better care of ourselves than we can.

We are all better women when we make the time to help each other.

Network. A part of taking care of yourself is being surrounded by supportive, caring people. In the professional realm, this means people who can empathize with your concerns about professional development, barriers to success, and other issues. In other words, network. I mean network in the positive sense. We all have something to contribute to another sister's efforts to reach her goal. I consider networking an opportunity to make that contribution. The same way you have something to contribute, someone else has something to contribute to your efforts. We are all better women when we make the time to help each other. Let that sister know of the job opportunity or the promotion possibility. Send a note of "just thinking about you" on an occasion "just because." We have an obligation to support and help each other – so have a little fun while doing it.

Mentor. And finally, remember that someone said a kind word to you that helped you along the path to becoming a lawyer. Return the favor by spending time with another young lady—become a mentor. Studies show that individual time spent with a young person can make the difference in that person becoming a productive member of society or a drain on society's resources. Young people are bombarded with messages that often are not positive, so they need someone to counteract those negative messages with words and acts of encouragement.

You made it, and now you can help someone make it. Congratulations and again welcome to the profession.

With best wishes for a bright future.

Your sister,

Alpha M. Brady

Alpha M. Brady *is the Director of the American Bar Association's Division for Policy Administration in Chicago.*

Dear Sisters, Dear Daughters,

I am a 1979 graduate and can tell you that the road ahead of you will be filled with a lot of joy and a lot of challenge. Most importantly, I can tell you that the career path you have chosen is one of promise. You are our future, and I feel it an honor to be able to share some thoughts with you which have aided me over the years.

First and foremost, follow your dream. When I entered the profession in the late seventies, there were many who tried to discourage me because the practice of law was not a field occupied by women, let alone women of color. Instead, I was urged to become a legal secretary. I would hope that today you are not experiencing these words of discouragement. Sometimes, the "friends" or "men" in our lives have a hard time with professional women and will try to dissuade you due to their own insecurities. Do not listen. Those who are truly your friends or the man who is truly worthy of you will understand and embrace your passion to pursue a career in the law and will be there for you when you need them most.

Believe in yourself! I remember an occasion when a client with whom I had been working for some time, came to my office to review a file. What was most memorable about that experience was the fact that he literally stood in my doorway in shock and disbelief because he had not realized before then that I was a woman of color. There have also been instances when the careers of my white colleagues have moved much more quickly. It is quite easy during these times to doubt yourself. My advice to you is to stay focused, to believe in yourself, and do not allow these events to discourage you. Instead, I have let my work speak for itself and my career has progressed.

Find balance in your life. The practice of law can be very demanding. You will also encounter peaks and valleys over the course of your career. I would not have made it over the years without my girlfriends. If you don't do anything else, make sure you have a strong support base to get you through those difficult periods. Having hobbies and other interests also helps. At one time, I was a workaholic with no outside interests. When I had difficulties at work, I internalized everything and sometimes read more into situations than really existed because I was too close to the situation. Once I started to power walk, collect art, travel, and expand my interests, I found I was also better able to put the challenges at work into a proper perspective, and I was better equipped on an emotional level to handle them. As you weather life's challenges, your self-confidence will also grow and you will surely be stronger and better prepared for the challenges that will surely come.

Find a mentor. There are many who believe that a mentor, to be of any value, should be someone in a senior position within your workplace. I have not found that to be the case. If you do not have a mentor where you work, find one, if possible, from another corporation or law firm. Oftentimes, you need not come from the same workplace to provide guidance on the politics of surviving in a corporation or law firm. Also, keep in mind that you can obtain a wealth of information about your own organization or boss, for that matter, from some of the support staff. In many instances, you can learn a lot through an executive secretary. I have also had situations when people in the mailroom have alerted me to things going on in the organization because they have access to the mail being distributed throughout the organization that covers any number of things. Your peers can also be of some assistance to you. As an example, I met one of my current mentors through a peer.

Assume an active role in bar association activities. I have found bar association activities very rewarding from a professional standpoint. If you do not have an opportunity to take on visible assignments at work, another avenue to pursue can be to take on a visible, leadership role in the bar association. I have found that most firms and corporations look favorably upon their attorney participation in bar association activities, particularly where you have a leadership role in the organization. In fact, some younger attorneys invite their bosses to participate on panels. This can be a "win win" opportunity for you to spend more time with your boss, have your boss observe your role in the bar association and provide some visibility for your boss as well.

As you weather life's challenges, your self-confidence will also grow and you will surely be stronger and better prepared for the challenges that will surely come.

Being a person of color can enhance your value in the workplace. I recall a situation some years ago when my clients decided not to invite me to a meeting with high-ranking officials from Africa and invited my boss instead. To my boss's credit, he declined the invitation and sent me. The client only came to realize the value of my participation when a representative for the African delegation commenced the meeting by expressing his joy at seeing his African American sister at the meeting and how after several years of doing business with our organization, this was the first time a person of color had been present. In today's climate, attorneys of color offer value to an organization through a variety of avenues. On another occasion, I happened to attend a black-tie dinner in Washington, DC, and sat next to a person from South Africa. The dinner I attended was not work-related, however, the contact made at that dinner became useful in the work context.

Finally, never underestimate the power of prayer. I have found that my belief in God and the power of prayer have aided me over the years. In fact, I have a Bible in my office and have had many an occasion at work when passages from the Bible have helped me to face the challenge I was dealing with at the time.

Best of luck to you in your careers!

Your Sister,

Sharon D. Hatchett

Sharon D. Hatchett *is an Attorney with the General Motors Corporation Legal Staff in Detroit, Michigan.*

Dear Sisters, Dear Daughters,

Somehow, more than 20 years have gone by since I first sat terrorized in a law school class. I wish there had been sisters of color in the law that I could have turned to with all my doubts and frustrations, but back then they were few and far between. I am glad to have this opportunity to contribute a few words to the next generation of minority women in our profession. While the law can be a rough taskmaster and there have been many ups and downs, I would choose it all over again. Although I may always be part of a disenfranchised group as a black woman, the law has given me much ability to maneuver in a racist and sexist society. As an international lawyer, I realize that it is only in the United States that I, as a minority group female, could be a tenured full professor of law. While I may never make as much money as a white male partner in a big law firm like the one I once worked in, I have a lifestyle that puts me in a privileged position as compared to most African Americans, not to mention women of color around the world!

I decided to offer you Ten Tips for survival, success, and transcendence:

REACHING IN. Make actual appointments in your date book for yourself, whether it is to meditate, pray, leisure read, exercise, have a health checkup, go to the hairdresser, watch a movie, have a massage, pedicure, take a real vacation etc. When I feel bad mentally, my slipped disks start acting up as well. Once, I was in the emergency room for my back, while my baby was a patient in the pediatric ward.

BEING HUMBLE. Remember that everything you value can be taken away or destroyed in a minute. It could come in the form of a car accident, front page headlines, or the IRS!! A few days of negative publicity many years ago affected my entire life.

FREAKING OUT. Give yourself a break and remember Superwoman is in a comic book. I struggle with this one every day as I juggle the balls of professor, mother, partner, grand-mother, activist, mentor, mentee, friend, daughter. Sometimes I have to laugh when the house is a wreck, I'm yelling at the kids, my clothes need mending, the cat ripped up the steps, I missed the article deadline, I lost your phone message, and I forgot to call back my mother.

REACHING OUT. Make actual appointments in your date book to have quality time to see your loved ones, significant others, spouses, friends, children etc. Don't cancel them!! I might have saved my marriage if I had followed this tip.

RAISING UP. It does take the village to raise a child. There are a lot of needy children of color out there. Whether you have a partner or not, please consider being a foster or adoptive par-ent, informally or formally. In addition to my two biological sons, my life has forever been enriched by my three sons that I didn't give birth to! If you are not ready for all the responsibility, become a Big Sister. Help with your nieces and nephews or the neighbor's child.

GIVING BACK. In the words of Marian Wright Edelman, "service is the rent we pay for living on the planet." Due to our relatively privileged positions, we must not forget those who will never have the luxury of spending nearly twenty years in school or the potential for earning six figure incomes. Working with Bloods and Crips helped keep me real!

MENTORING. Whether you want to be one or not, you will be regarded as a role model for many people. Be proactive and mentor colleagues, students, and family members. On the other end, recognize that you need mentors yourself and seek them out. Be aware that mentors come in many colors and both genders. My most unlikely mentor was a conservative Republican partner, who had never worked with a woman, and we stayed in touch until his death many years after I left the firm.

POLITICKING. Racism and sexism are alive and well, so it's even more important that we become savvy at office politics. Don't assume because someone is the same race or gender that they are your buddy! I think I didn't get a job once because of this error. Don't assume that someone with a different race or gender cannot be your friend. Master the art of small talk, but be careful it doesn't descend into gossip.

HARASSING. I have been sexually harassed at every job I ever held, and I would never sue because of the personal toll it would take on my psyche and my family. Remember, harassing behavior can come from superiors or peers, but I have found that it can also come from subordinates as well!! I have been scared at times of some of my younger male students!!!

NETWORKING. While we don't all have access to the "good old boy" network, we have alternatives. I found that jobs that many women and minorities hold in a workplace can be great sources of support as well as information. Don't ignore or neglect the janitors, secretaries, file clerks, bookkeepers, word processors, mail persons, and copy center staff. My best tip came from the shoe shine man and it saved me thousands of dollars.

Please feel free to contact me and I wish you every success.

Yours in the struggle,

Adrien Katherine Wing

Adrien Katherine Wing is a Professor at the University of Iowa College of Law where she teaches constitutional law, critical race theory, human rights and comparative law.

Dear Sisters, Dear Daughters,

I'm delighted that women and minorities are no longer rarities in the legal profession. This measure of progress is one of many that allows me to write this letter with confidence about the future of women and minorities in our craft.

If I can share one important truth, it is that each of us must develop a set of deeply held principles to guide us on our way. The key is to identify and retain values and priorities that work for you and the people around you. Here's what has worked for me:

We must be willing to work very, very hard to learn our craft. Outstanding achievers have credibility, exude self-confidence, and are able to perform well in a variety of settings. Successful people also take on the tough jobs, work the extra hours, consistently exceed expectations, ask for challenging assignments, and are committed.

We should define ourselves by setting personal and professional goals. We should not allow others to fit us into their picture of what our lives should be. Setting priorities also gives us more control over our lives because decision making becomes easier.

We must communicate effectively — speak and write clearly. The best communicators are those who keep things simple and understandable in both their oral and written communication. Many people overlook the importance of clear communication because it's not a primary function of their jobs. But if we can't communicate our ideas simply and clearly, they will be lost.

We must be willing to take risks. We should stay open to new challenges. Career opportunities are mind-boggling if we're flexible, if we're open to change, but most of all if we're *willing* to change. I've had 10 jobs during my career and, at age 40, I seized an opportunity to switch entirely from labor law to communications. It was a scary move, but one I've never regretted.

We should learn the politics of our organization. This skill is as important as talent, ambition, and hard work. We must know who the key players are and how the game is played. We should be willing to ask for help when we need it, and we should learn how to best use others' talents and expertise.

Network! We should take the time to build relationships inside and outside our organization—at all levels and in all disciplines. Networking increases our visibility, and it enables us to establish contacts before we need assistance.

We must consider our education an on-going process. Today, one formal education does *not* last a lifetime. In a high-tech global environment, the best opportunities go to the most highly skilled and the best educated. We can't allow our skills to become outdated, and we should not too narrowly focus our formal education. Specialties are useful and often necessary, of course, but global businesses need people who also understand different cultures, world history, politics, and religion.

We should be nice — which does not mean being soft. The saying is true that we are hired for what we know and fired for who we are. If we aren't nice to people, our behavior will come back to haunt us.

We should take our job seriously — not ourselves. Woodrow Wilson once said there are those who come to Washington and grow in their jobs, and then there are those who come and just swell up. In my jobs in and out of government, I've always tried to remember that humor keeps your feet firmly planted on the ground, so you have less far to fall. A sense of humor also helps us keep a positive attitude and develop a thick skin.

Having a chip on our shoulder is ultimately self defeating.

We should never compromise our personal integrity. We must always do what we commit to do. People see through insincerity faster than anything else. We should all strive to be known as people who are honest and trustworthy. Candor is disarming.

We should try to lead a balanced life and keep our priorities straight. As hard as some people may try, I don't believe it's possible, or healthy, to attempt to keep our professional and personal lives entirely separate. Several years ago, I was in an important meeting in my office with some CEOs when my hot-line rang. It was my daughter calling in tears to tell me her third goldfish had died. Not wanting to sound unprofessional, I replied, "You should analyze the facts, and then let me know your options." At first my daughter couldn't believe what she was hearing judging by her stunned silence, so I repeated, "Analyze the facts, assess your options, and then get back to me." Finally, she said, "Mom, is someone in your office?" Later, when I shared this story with a male colleague, he said I should not have tried to disguise the nature of the call. He pointed out that when women show that personal problems sometimes must take precedence over work, this acknowledgment liberates men, as well.

My personal credo. Here's the abbreviated version, based on words that an Austin songwriter, Lisa Rogers, wrote:

> Work like you don't need the money.
> Love like your heart's never been broken.
> And dance like nobody's watching!

Patricia Diaz Dennis

Patricia Diaz Dennis *is Senior Vice President and Assistant General Counsel for Regulation and Law at SBC Communications, Inc.*

Dear Sisters, Dear Daughters,

I graduated from law school in 1993, and started my legal career at a large law firm. After spending a few years in the private sector, I made the switch to public interest and now work in state government. While I think I obtained great litigation experience in the law firm setting, I find my work today much more gratifying.

In some ways it seems like I just graduated from law school, in other ways it seems like light years ago. I remember when I first joined the legal profession, it was somewhat of a shock not to see very many women in the courtrooms or at depositions. There were times when my opposing counsel or co-counsel, upon meeting me, would confuse me for the receptionist or paralegal—anyone except the attorney of record. I even remember waiting in a conference room packed with lawyers, for a deposition to begin, when an attorney entered the room and asked me to label exhibits. He assumed I had to be the court reporter—even though the court reporter was sitting at the table with her equipment in front of her. Not that there is anything wrong with being a court reporter, receptionist or paralegal, but it is frustrating when people create a "profile" for you. I have found that being underestimated can work to your advantage, however, especially when your opponent realizes that not only are you an attorney, but that you actually know what you're doing.

I don't know if there is one single piece of advice that I would have for young multicultural women attorneys. But there are several things that I would recommend. First, I am sure all my contemporaries would agree that it is imperative to identify a mentor early on in your career. Whether it is someone within your office or outside of it, the kind of invaluable advice and insight they can provide is absolutely critical to succeeding in any area. Second, work extremely hard toward obtaining your goals. I have often heard it said, and unfortunately I agree, that we have to work twice as hard to get half as far. Third, make sure that you remain involved in community activities, if nothing else to keep you grounded. Fourth, after you have been practicing for a few years, make an effort to identify someone younger to whom you can be a mentor.

Warmest personal regards,

Amalia S. Rioja

Amalia S. Rioja *works in Chicago as Deputy General Counsel to Illinois State Comptroller Daniel W. Hynes.*

Dear Sisters, Dear Daughters,

Congratulations on your decision to pursue a career in law! I welcome you to the profession and trust that you will find it as challenging and rewarding as I have. As you embark upon your legal career, I want to share a few words of wisdom with you.

First, be honest and trustworthy. Your reputation means everything in this profession, and you will gain the respect of clients and peers if you are known as a person of integrity.

Second, make sure you are thoroughly prepared for all tasks. Conduct proper research, rehearse presentations, and perfect writing skills. Take no short-cuts and always prepare a quality product.

Third, be proud that you are a black person in this profession. I do not believe that you have to abandon who you are and your cultural experiences in order to achieve success. If you are good at what you do, then doors will open. I do acknowledge that opportunities are not always as readily available as they might be to others. If you lose sight of your heritage, however, then there really is no reward in obtaining compromised success.

Fourth, do not be afraid to ask questions (this is something I was guilty of early in my career). If you do not quite understand an assignment or issue, ask for clarification/explanation so that you can provide an accurate response.

Fifth, maintain and/or establish a community presence. Get involved in civic and charitable causes. This is a great way to make contacts that can result in client development. Also, community involvement provides an opportunity to reach out to others. Our youth need role models and as a lawyer, you have the ability to provide positive influence.

I wish you the best in your legal endeavors and hope you will serve the profession well.

Donna M. Wilson

Donna M. Wilson *is an Attorney with Polsinelli, White, Vardeman & Shalton, P.C. in Kansas City, Missouri, and concentrates her practice in land use and public law.*

Dear Sisters, Dear Daughters,

I have five simple pieces of advice. As you will see, they do not necessarily apply only to multicultural women. But I offer them here nonetheless.

First, if possible, all other things being equal, choose your niche by who is available as a mentor. When I started practicing, I expressed an interest in a practice group headed by a person who I believed would be a good teacher. He turned out to be a wonderful mentor, and I can't thank him enough for everything he did for me. While I love the specialty in which I practice, I am sure there are others that would have been equally interesting. I thought it was more important to have a mentor.

Second, use your distinctiveness to your advantage. I'm not talking simply about networking with your own affinity groups as a potential source of business. If your ethnicity makes you stand out as different, capitalize on it. I am frequently surprised by clients and others I have met in the practice of law who remember my name, often years after we have worked together. Well, of course, it's because, as an Asian American woman practicing law in Jacksonville, Florida, I look different from my peers. So keep in mind that as a multicultural woman, you will have a leg up in being noticed. If you excel at what you do, people will not forget you.

I also believe that in transactional work, being a woman has its own advantages, even if you have a non-confrontational personality, as I do. I often suspect that people try to be on their best behavior when dealing with a woman. However "sexist" that might be, use it to your advantage. It's easier to move a deal forward if people aren't screaming and shouting. Similarly, I have been surprised in my dealings with individuals with reputations for being "difficult." I can only surmise that they are reluctant to be rude to a woman.

Third, and most importantly, always strive to excel. Always ask what you can do better the next time. There are lessons to be learned everyday, even after you have been practicing law for many years. The best lawyers tend to be the ones who worry the most about what they may overlook or what they could improve on the next time.

If you don't enjoy what you do, it's not worth it.

Fourth, don't sweat the slights. So what if someone didn't realize that you're the lawyer, not the court reporter. So what if someone didn't realize that you're the partner, not the associate. Look at it as *their* problem, not yours. Laugh at it, if you can. As more women and minorities enter the legal profession and the business world, people will eventually stop making these gaffes.

Finally, always try to keep a sense of humor. If you don't enjoy what you do, it's not worth it.

Sincerely,

Linda Yayoi Kelso

Linda Yayoi Kelso *is a Partner with the Jacksonville office of Foley & Lardner and head of the office's securities practice.*

Dear Sisters, Dear Daughters,

As you embark upon your careers as attorneys, I want to impress upon you one simple, yet important, message— remember to give back to the community. This message was ingrained in me many years ago and the impact of putting it into action has given me wealth beyond compare.

It began in middle school when I worked for my sixth grade teacher, Mrs. Sheppard, during my sixth and eighth grade school years (I skipped the seventh grade due to my academic performance). During this time, I graded papers and acted as an assistant earning $10 per week. About a month before my 8th grade graduation, Mrs. Sheppard stopped me in the hallway to ask whether I had been told the good news that I was selected as class valedictorian. I told her yes. Then she asked whether I had everything I needed for graduation. Well, I already had an outfit, but I didn't have any shoes. I hesitated in responding because I was embarrassed. Then I shyly stated that I didn't have any shoes. Well, one day during graduation practice, I returned to my seat after giving my valedictorian address to find a card on my chair. When I opened the card, it read as follows: "there is a law of compensation that keeps working all life through, when you give your best to something, the best comes back to you." My teacher had enclosed some money in the card along with the following note: "buy yourself some graduation shoes." What an effect this act of love and giving has had on me throughout my career. Her care and concern gave me the confidence to climb to higher heights. It also prompted me to remember to give back. This is why I feel so strongly about delivering this message to you as you begin your careers.

As you probably already know, you have been blessed to attain a level of success and skill that can be utilized to help those less fortunate than you. Whether it's mentoring students, providing legal assistance to poor and battered women, or feeding the hungry, you need to maintain a sense of giving back. None of us have attained our level of success in a vacuum; we've all stood on the shoulders of others. Whether it was a parent, teacher, aunt, friend, or stranger who gave us that added boost, we didn't do it alone. As a result, we should be motivated to reach back and help someone else. As it has been said many times before, "to whom much is given, much is expected." You will know that you have made an impact, when your blessings begin to overflow to others.

There is a law of compensation . . . when you give your best to something, the best comes back to you.

As a practicing attorney, I realize that many times our workload puts us in the position of saying, "how can I give time to the community when I barely have enough time to give to myself?" Well, there are ways if you decide this is something you truly want to do. For example, speaking at a school during career day, donating money to a women's shelter, or filing a restraining order in a domestic violence matter doesn't take an inordinate amount of time. You will have to decide what fits into your schedule. I have had the opportunity to file divorces for poor and battered women, speak at inner-city and suburban schools, reinforce the message of the D.A.R.E. (Drug Abuse Resistance Education) Program in grammar schools, sponsor the valedictorian award at my middle school and much more. Giving back has operated to make me a well-rounded attorney and has given me a sense of satisfaction that matches my greatest accomplishment on my career side. I am constantly reminded of how my giving has affected the lives of others. I have received many letters from students who are appreciative and motivated by my simple act of giving. Whether it's a speech encouraging them to stay in school and to do their best or a savings bond that tells them that they should be congratulated for their hard work, these students will be impacted for life by your giving. I know that if I can touch the life of another and motivate them to reach back and help someone else, I have succeeded. As the card stated, "there is a law of compensation that keeps working all life through, when you give your best to something, the best comes back to you." It has been twenty-plus years since I first read this message, and I can attest to its reality.

I hope that you will feel the emotion I want to convey regarding the notion of giving back. I feel the need to impart this message to you so that you won't get blinded by income and position and forget about what our true duty is as attorneys—service. I wish you well in your career and know that you will be a success in whatever area you decide to pursue.

Fondly,

Donna Bunch Coaxum

Donna Bunch Coaxum *is Business Counsel for Kraft Foods, Inc., in Northfield, Illinois.*

Dear Sisters, Dear Daughters,

Someone, not me, once said, "If you can get 15 minutes of sunshine on the back of your knees, it's been a good day." To me, the notion of sun on the back of my knees is uplifting: it makes me think of freedom, and of "wind-at-your-back" sort of encouragement. More literally, it invokes images of laying face down on a beach somewhere, making no pretense whatsoever of doing anything productive.

I suspect that you will get lots of letters full of sage advice about the components of success and about the need to pursue excellence at every turn. Meeting high standards of achievement and integrity is critical. I write about something different—about perspective and balance—and the need to ensure their presence in your life. I am particularly drawn to write about these things, because while these are values that I march towards, they are not goals I have reached.

Despite the numerical gains in our numbers, there are still not enough of us. There are not enough of us in charge of things, there are not enough of us to ensure a collegial soulmate in our places of employment, and there are not enough of us to fill all the spaces where some (often well-meaning) person thinks one of us should be. Into this latter category, I put the times when we do all the counseling, all the mentoring, all the outreach. I also include the times when we're forced to cheerfully appear as the entity's minority representative. And I include the times we're asked to be a spokesperson for every non-white everywhere.

As you will likely soon discover, your most profound lack will be a lack of time. Oh, you'll wish you had more money; everyone does. But whatever your pay scale, you'll adjust. And for most, the transition from student to attorney is at least a favorable one in financial terms. What you will find, however, as you define your new self as a lawyer is that opportunities exceed your ability to avail yourself of them. You can become involved in the local bar, the state bar, or a national bar, though you will quickly discover that at most levels there is more than just one. There are women's bars and minority bars. There are associations based on professional specialties or on areas of interest. And there remain community and civic organizations in which you used to participate and where your expertise and status as an attorney might be of valuable assistance. And this list does not include your most important asset: your support structure, be it family or friends.

> I want to give back—to the community that raised me, to the profession that is sustaining me . . . but this desire must be balanced . . .

My advice is this. Keep tabs on your self. I quite purposely did not say, "Keep tabs on yourself" because we often use that phrase casually to mean, "Make sure you check the external signs." Is my career on target? Did I accomplish all that was on last yesterday's "to do" list? Instead, I mean, keep tabs on how your inner self is holding up. Are you happy? Are you content? Are you fulfilling your spiritual needs? Are you giving to your support network as much as you take? Do you laugh regularly? Can you still enjoy doing something utterly frivolous? When you look in a mirror, do you like not what you see, but who you see?

If allowed, the legal profession will take from us as much as we can give. Many days, I feel like I'm in a race, running harder and faster, only to fall farther behind. My motivation is, I tell myself, pure. I want to give back—to the community that raised me, to the profession that is sustaining me, to the many coming behind me who might be helped by hearing some of what I've learned. But this desire must be balanced. It must be put in its proper perspective. If the cost to me is greater than the benefits I gain, then I have made an unwise choice.

By almost any measure, I've been blessed with a successful career. I've had numerous stimulating and rewarding experiences and have met people who have become important and enduring parts of my life. But if I had it to do over again, I would do a little less. I'd say "no, thank you" a bit more. And I would try to have a few more days where the sun shined on the back of my knees.

JoAnne Epps

JoAnne A. Epps *is a Professor of Law and Associate Dean for Academic Affairs at Temple Law School.*

Dear Sisters, Dear Daughters,

Sixty years ago, walking into a tiny office in Washington D.C., I heard the words that set me on my path, that told me I must be about something, whatever I chose to do. The speaker was the great black educator and activist, Dr. Mary McLeod Bethune, whom I'd first met as a child in Charlotte, North Carolina. As I came to her doorstep for counsel and guidance in the early days of 1942, she said, "If you aren't going anywhere, don't come through my door. And if you come in, come to work and to serve others."

To work and to serve; those are the watchwords I hold out to you today, in this 2000th year, my sisters, my daughters in the legal profession. It's easy to think that merely becoming a lawyer is enough. But that is not enough. Nor is it enough to amass a great fortune. Becoming a millionaire requires nothing more than the ability to count your money. No, that is not nearly enough. You haven't made it until you have tried in your endeavor to help somebody else. I learned that from Dr. Bethune. And from her I learned that the people I must help are everywhere, in high stations and in low. To Dr. Bethune, everybody counted. She lifted up children everywhere, as she lifted me up that day, letting me know that I must be about something. As she sat talking with Mrs. Eleanor Roosevelt about women, both black and white, entering the Army, she kept looking at me—saying nothing, but simply looking. Dr. Bethune scoured your face when she looked at you. And I knew that from that moment, I was branded, chosen by her for something important.

I knew then that I wanted to help the whole person, to have a broad influence in the fight for justice. That day was the beginning of my walk toward the law. Because of Dr. Bethune, I became part of the first group of black women to integrate the Women's Auxiliary Army Corps, as it was called then. Having served in the Army for three years, I attended Howard Law School on the GI Bill, had the opportunity to be schooled in the law by the giants of the civil rights movement, had the chance to become the person Dr. Bethune believed I could be.

I visited her grave not long ago at the school she founded, Bethune-Cookman College in Daytona Beach, Florida. I plucked yellow flowers—she loved yellow—and laid them at her grave, and I thought, "What a little grave." I thought of the grave of another woman of righteousness as great as Dr. Bethune, my grandmother, Rachel Graham. Her grave, too was small, great though she was. Indeed, all graves are small. It is life that is large—life, and what you are able to do for others in the course of your life.

Today, we women live in a time of enormous opportunity. The world is open to us as it has never been before. I believe that Dr. Bethune knew this day was coming. And I believe, as I speak of her now, that she was a forever person. I attached myself to her, modeled my life on hers, tried to walk as she walked, working and serving.

I urge you, sisters and daughters to attach yourselves to some of the marvelous women on the scene today, of all ages and stations—women like Joan Higgenbotham, the first black woman to become an astronaut, a brilliant young mathematician who has broken the proverbial glass ceiling. Look to women of greatness like Dr. Dorothy Irene Height, who succeeded Dr. Bethune as president of the National Council of Negro Women. Dr. Height has won so many awards she could be blinded by them. But awards should not blind us. They should open the way, as they have for great women like Dr. Height, to serve others better. It is service that the professions—all the professions—are truly about.

If Dr. Bethune and Mrs. Roosevelt were alive today, I believe that they would be about the business that lies heaviest on my heart in the year 2000. That is the business of saving our little children. We live in a world where children murder each other. Last week, we lost a six-year-old to gunfire, at the hands of another six-year-old. This week, unless God Himself intervenes, we will lose more. I say to you: "Help me!" I'm putting out a sigh and a call because of my little grandson, James Andrew, and all the James Andrews coming of age in this violent world. For the sake of our children, I say to you, "Help me!"

We say, "We've got social workers!" Where are they? Do we have what we need to help our children? What do they learn in the schools? What medicine suits this ailment of indifference? We must dedicate ourselves to finding that answer.

That is my challenge to you today, my sisters, my daughters, who have chosen to enter the legal profession. I challenge you to lead the way, not to settle for merely being a lawyer, but instead to be about the business of seeking justice in the truest sense, of building a better world for our children.

Dovey J. Roundtree

Dovey J. Roundtree is a pioneering civil rights lawyer, Army veteran and ordained minister who is the winner of the 2000 Margaret Brent Women Lawyers of Achievement Award.

Editor Biography

Karen Clanton is an attorney in the Business and Finance Group of CCH Incorporated. As an Acquisitions Editor on the group's Business Development team, she is responsible for developing new products, which include *Securities Disclosure in Plain English, Journal of Global Financial Markets,* and *Managing Marketeers: Supervisory Responsibilities of Broker-Dealers* and *Investment Advisers.* While at CCH, Ms. Clanton has also written for and edited securities law reporters and newsletters. Committed to working on issues facing women attorneys, Ms. Clanton chairs the American Bar Association's Multicultural Women Attorneys Network and is co-vice-chair of the Chicago Bar Association's Alliance for Women. She also serves on the editorial boards for two magazines: *Business Law Today,* a publication of the ABA Business Law Section, and the *CBA Record,* the flagship publication of the Chicago Bar Association. Ms. Clanton tutors with Partners in Education, a program that provides educational support for children and teens from Chicago's Cabrini Green and Henry Horner developments. In addition, Ms. Clanton interviews Chicago-area students who have applied for admission to Georgetown University through the University's Alumni Admissions Program. A native of Rochester, New York, Ms. Clanton received her B.A. from Georgetown University, studied Literature for one year at King's College, University of London, and received her J.D. from Northwestern University School of Law.

Author Biographies

Penelope E. Andrews is an Associate Professor of Law at the City University of New York School of Law where she teaches torts, international human rights law, and critical perspectives on race and the law. She obtained her B.A. and LL.B from the University of Natal in Durban, South Africa, and her LL.M. from Columbia Law School. She started her legal career at a public interest law firm in Johannesburg, South Africa, and has also taught law in Melbourne, Australia. She has written extensively on issues of law and race, gender equality, and human rights in America, Australia, and South Africa and has lectured on human rights on all three continents. She is active in a number of international organizations.

Crystal Elizabeth Ashby is originally from Detroit, Michigan. She came to Chicago, Illinois, to attend law school 16 years ago and stayed. She received her B. A. in 1983 from the University of Michigan. She has a double major in English and Psychology. She received her J. D. from DePaul University College of Law in 1986. Ms. Ashby clerked for Judge Odas Nicholson in the Motion Courts. Before entering private practice she was an Associate at the law firms of Jones, Ware & Grenard and Hinshaw & Culbertson before joining Amoco Corporation, now BP, as an In-house Counsel. She is 38 years old and divorced with no children.

Ruthe C. Ashley, R.N., M.S.N., J.D., is a Nurse-Attorney and Consultant on medical/legal and risk management issues to health care facilities across the nation. She is nationally known as a dynamic speaker for health care and legal professionals. Ms. Ashley's previous legal experience includes trial work in both large and small law firms, specializing in medical malpractice and health care law. Her nursing career included public health nursing and as Assistant Professor of nursing in a baccalaureate nursing program. Ms. Ashley was nominated as an Outstanding Woman in the Area of Law by the

YWCA, was named a Woman in Business by *Sacramento Magazine*, and serves on numerous boards and committees. She is listed in *Who's Who in American Nursing*.

Barbara Bernier is a first-generation American whose parents hailed from the islands of Haiti and Martinique. She is a graduate of Howard University School of Law and has a Masters in Law from Temple University School of Law. Before entering law school, she received a Masters in Social Work from Adelphi University. Ms. Bernier practiced law in Washington, D.C., doing real estate and trust work with a small firm before moving into the academic arena. She has taught at Temple University, Howard University, the District of Columbia School of Law, and most recently she was a Founding Faculty Member at the Roger Williams University School of Law, the only law school in the state of Rhode Island. She has since received tenure and continues to work for human rights and writes in the area of international human rights of women. She is currently a visiting scholar at the Harvard University School of Divinity where she is researching and writing a book on international witchcraft and the law.

Paula K. Bouldon was raised in Maywood, Illinois. She is a graduate of Proviso East High School and Purdue University in West Lafayette, Indiana. She received a J.D. from the University of Missouri-Columbia and an LL.M. from Chicago Kent College of Law. After serving nine years with the Illinois Department of Human Rights as a Senior Staff Sttorney, Ms. Bouldon joined the Cook County Recorder of Deeds Office where she currently serves as Counsel to the Recorder. Additionally, she serves as an Adjunct Professor at Chicago Kent College of Law. Ms. Bouldon served as Chair of the Administrative Law Section/Council and the Committee on Law Related Education of the Illinois State Bar Association. She is also a member of the Cook County Bar Association and the Alpha Kappa Alpha Sorority. She is a tutor for Minority Legal Education Resources and a Fellow for the Council on Legal Education Opportunities. Ms. Bouldon has published several articles.

Alpha Brady is the Director of the Division for Policy Administration at the American Bar Association (ABA) in Chicago, where she was previously Special Assistant to the President. Ms. Brady has also served as the Associate Director of the ABA's Commission on Racial and Ethnic Diversity in the Profession. Before joining the ABA, Ms. Brady worked as Assistant Corporation Counsel for the city of Chicago. Ms. Brady received her B.S. in History and Business Administration from Elmhurst College in 1983 and her J.D. from Northwestern University School of Law in 1986. She is the Co-editor of *Burdens of Both, Privileges of Neither*, a Report of the Multicultural Women Attorneys Network. Ms. Brady is a Board Member with the Center for Re-creation and Family Training , Inc. in Hopkins Park, Illinois.

June Brown is a licensed attorney in Chicago and a native of Bessemer, Alabama. She completed her undergraduate degree at the University of Southern California. While at U.S.C., she studied political science at the London School of Economics. She completed her legal studies at the John Marshall Law School in Chicago, Illinois. Ms. Brown's Life is one of dedication to the service to others. She has long been a volunteer for youth civic and social action issues. She has taught and consulted at the community college and university levels. During her law career, she has represented underserved and battered and abused persons. She is a member of several organizations and boards, including the League of Black Women, the Chicago Bar Association, and the National Council of Negro Women, Inc. Ms. Brown is a past National Chief Operating Officer/Deputy Director of Rainbow-PUSH Coalition (Formerly Operation PUSH), where she represented the organization locally, nationally, and internationally. Currently, she works in private practice and as a Consultant on technology and strategic development issues.

Paulette Brown is a Partner in the Newark office of Duane, Morris & Heckscher, LLP and practices in the area of civil defense litigation, with an emphasis on product liability and employment matters pertaining to sexual harassment and race and gender discrimination. Before joining Duane, Morris & Heckscher, LLP, Ms. Brown was a Founding Partner with the law firm of Brown & Childress, LLC for 15 years. Ms. Brown served as Judge of the Municipal Court of the City of Plainfield, New Jersey, and was Corporate Counsel for several Fortune 500 companies. A former President of the National Bar Association and the Association of Black Women Lawyers of New Jersey, Ms. Brown served as chair of the American Bar Association's Council on Racial and Ethnic Justice and is currently a Division Director for the ABA Section of Litigation. She is a frequent lecturer and panelist for national and international legal education programs and has received numerous awards in recognition of her commitment and contributions to the legal community, including the Equal Justice Award from the National Bar Association. Ms. Brown is a 1976 graduate of Seton Hall University School of Law and a graduate of Howard University.

Tracy R. Brown received her B.A. in Economics from Tufts University and her J.D. from Harvard Law School. She has practiced law with private firms and corporations and, currently, is responsible for the Corporate Benefits function of a specialty chemicals manufacturer headquartered in Boston, Massachusetts.

La Fleur C. Browne has been an associate at Dorsey & Whitney LLP in Minneapolis, Minnesota since 1992, and practices in the areas of securities regulation, underwritten public offerings (debt and equity), mergers and acquisitions, and general corporate transactions. Ms. Browne graduated from Howard University School of Law in 1992, and is a member of the following organizations: American Bar Association, National Bar Association, Minnesota State Bar Association, Minnesota Association of Black Lawyers, Twin Cities Committee on Minority Lawyers in Large Law Firms, and the National Association of Securities Professionals. Ms. Browne is currently a Member of the Board of Directors for Resources, Inc. and MELD, and a Vice Chair for the American Bar Association Commission on Racial and Ethnic Diversity in the Profession—Minority Counsel Program.

Regina L. Bryant-Fields considers herself to be primarily from the East Coast, as her schooling since the seventh grade took place there. She attended Bowdoin College in Brunswick, Maine, graduating *cum laude* and proceeded directly to the University of Columbia School of Law where she served as Editor-In-Chief of the *Human Rights Law Review*. She moved to the west coast to clerk for the Honorable Cecil F. Poole of the Ninth Circuit Court of Appeals. After her clerkship ended, she joined the firm of Brown & Wood, LLP. Seven years after joining Brown & Wood, at the age of 33, she was voted in as the first African American Partner, male or female, a feat that would have been much more difficult to accomplish without the love and support of her husband. Together, they have a beautiful daughter. She has served as President of Black Women Lawyers of Northern California, and sat on the Boards of the Oakland Youth Chorus, the Court Appointed Special Advocates, and the ABA's Conference on Minority Partners in Majority Owned Law Firms. Currently, she is on leave from her firm on long-term disability.

Clarissa Cerda is Vice President and General Counsel for Open Port Technologies, Inc., in Chicago and was formerly a Partner in the Corporate and Securities Group of Sonnenschein Nath & Rosenthal in Chicago. She also served as Assistant Counsel to the President of the United States. Ms. Cerda's practice involves a wide variety of corporate, securities and commercial matters, including mergers and acquisitions, initial public offerings, private placements, corporate reorganizations, acquisition financing, and general corporate governance matters. Ms. Cerda is currently a Commissioner of the American Bar Association's Commission for Racial and Ethnic Diversity in the Profession, a member of the Board of Governors of the Hispanic National Bar Association, and a member of the Board of Directors and the Corporate Secretary of the Chicago Committee on Minorities in Large Law Firms. In addition, she currently sits on the Board of Directors of the Chicago Central Club of ZONTA International, a service organization dedicated to the advancement of the status of women worldwide, and provides *pro bono* counsel to the Women's Business Development Center, a not-for-profit corporation.

Violet M. Clark became a Staff Attorney with the Legal Assistance Foundation of Chicago upon graduation from Cornell University School of Law in 1982. She attended her final year of law school at the University of Chicago as a student-at-large. Ms. Clark received her B.A. from Brown University in 1979. In December 1984, Ms. Clark began practicing as a Trial Attorney with the United States Equal Employment Opportunity Commission where she was responsible for litigating corporate employment discrimination cases. Ms. Clark served in that capacity until January 1988, when she joined the firm of Laner, Muchin, Dornbrow, Becker, Levin and Torninberg, Ltd. In January 1994, Ms. Clark became a Partner of the firm. Ms. Clark serves as a Hearing Officer for the City of Chicago Commission on Human Relations and the Cook County Human Rights Commission.

In addition, she has lectured extensively in the areas of affirmative action and employment discrimination. Ms. Clark is a member of the Black Women Lawyers Association and the Cook County Bar Association. Ms. Clark is also a member of the Board of Directors of Leadership Illinois and a member of the Leadership America Class of 1998. She serves as Secretary to the Board of Directors of the Chicago District Tennis Association and of the Love to Service Tennis Academy, Inc. She was born in New Bern, North Carolina, in 1957, She is married and has three children.

Donna Bunch Coaxum was born in England, Arkansas, and currently resides in Naperville, Illinois, with her husband Harry and daughter Maya. She is Business Counsel for Kraft Foods, Inc. in Northfield, Illinois, providing corporate legal support to the manufacturing, comanufacturing, sales, customer development, and state government affairs groups. Before that, she worked as an Attorney/Assistant Secretary for the Oscar Mayer Foods Division of Kraft. She received her Bachelors Degree in Accounting from Purdue University and is a Certified Public Accountant. She received her law degree from the University of Wisconsin. She is a member of the American Bar Association, Wisconsin State Bar, Illinois State Bar, Alpha Kappa Alpha Sorority, the Links, Inc., Junior League, and a member of the 2nd Leadership Greater Madison Class of Madison, Wisconsin. Ms. Bunch Coaxum is a past board member of the Madison Civic Center Foundation and freely volunteers in the community. She began a five-year sponsorship of the valedictorian award at Gladstone Elementary School where she graduated as class valedictorian.

Linda R. Crane is a 1977 graduate of the University of Illinois at Urbana, Illinois, and a 1981 graduate of Northwestern University's School of Law and the J.L. Kellogg Graduate School of Management. Since 1989, she has been a Professor at the John Marshall Law School in Chicago, Illinois, where she teaches courses in property law, commercial law, and federal securities regulation. She has authored numerous articles for law journals on various subjects, including: rights of unwed fathers, mortgage lending discrimination, discrimination against Haitian refugees (with Joyce Hughes), legal education, and affirmative action. Ms. Crane is a member of numerous non-profit boards, including: MacCormac College and Little

Company of Mary Hospital Foundation. She is the past President of the Cabrini-Green Tutoring Program and Legal Elections in All Precincts Research and Educational Fund boards. She is currently the President of the Central States Law Schools Association, an officer of the Midwestern People of Color Legal Scholarship Conference, Inc., and Chair of the Affirmative Action Committee of the Cook County Bar Association. She is Co-chair of the Women in Legal Education Committee of the Women's Alliance of the Chicago Bar Association and a member of the Audit Committee of the Association of American Law Schools. Ms. Crane is married to Associate Judge William Stewart Boyd of Cook County Circuit Court. They live in Chicago with their red Doberman, Hamlet.

Roni Michele Crichton is a 43-year-old woman who has been a lawyer for 17 years and worked at Xerox Corporation for 14 of those years. She received her J.D. from Hastings College of Law, University of California at San Francisco, and her B.A. from Stanford University. Ms. Crichton is a mother of three in all permutations of mother-hood—foster mom, stepmom, and mom. She is married to a man she loves and likes enormously. She works hard to make time for interests outside of family and career. She plays tennis, piano, and meditates in fits and starts.

Okianer Christian Dark joined the United States Attorney's Office (USAO) in May 1995 as an Assistant U. S. Attorney to develop a civil rights component in the Affirmative Civil Enforcement Unit. She is also responsible for the community relations unit in USAO for the district of Oregon. Before joining the USAO, Ms. Dark was on the faculty of the University of Richmond in Richmond, Virginia, with specialties in antitrust, torts, and women and the law. Ms. Dark has published articles on race, gender, and the legal academy. She received her B.A. *magna cum laude* from Upsala College in East Orange, New Jersey, and her J. D. from Rutgers University School of Law in Newark, New Jersey, where she was the recipient of the Alumni Senior Prize (graduating senior exhibiting highest achievement in law school and potential for success in the legal profession).

Pamela Moran Dashiell serves as Legal Counsel to the Attorney General of the Commonwealth of Massachusetts. In this position, she advises and represents the Attorney General and his staff on a variety of legal and policy issues. She has also worked in municipal government and practiced corporate law in the private sector. A native of Chicago, Illinois, Ms. Dashiell is a graduate of Simmons College and Northwestern University School of Law. She has served on various boards and commissions, including the Boston Human Rights Commission and is currently the President-elect of the Codman Square Health Center in Boston. She is a member of the American Bar Association, Section of Business Law, serving on the Section Council and several committees. She is a member of the Massachusetts Black Women Attorneys Association and the Boston and Massachusetts Bar Associations. In 1994, she was a recipient of the Boston YMCA Black Achievers Award. Ms. Dashiell resides in Boston with her husband and two children.

Patricia Díaz Dennis joined SBC Communications, Inc., in 1995, as Senior Vice President and Assistant General Counsel for regulation and law, representing and advising SBC in the areas of state, federal, and international law and regulatory policy. In her present position, she is responsible for SBC Communications national constituency relations and regulatory, legislative, governmental, external affairs, and industry relations activities for SBC Telecom. Before joining SBC, Ms. Dennis was appointed to the Federal Communications Commission by President Reagan and served as a Commissioner from 1986 to 1989. She was also appointed by President Reagan to serve on the National Labor Relations Board. President Bush appointed her Assistant Secretary of State for Human Rights and Humanitarian Affairs in 1992. Her experience in the telephone industry includes her legal practice as Special Counsel for Communications Matters in Sullivan & Cromwell's Washington, D.C. office, as well as Partner and Head of the Communications Law Section for the D.C. law firm of Jones, Day, Reavis & Pogue. Ms. Dennis was also Vice President for Government Affairs for Sprint from 1991 to 1992.

Susani N. H. Dixon graduated from the University of Denver, College of Law in 1984 and immediately joined Holland & Hart's Natural Resources Department. She earned her B.A. in English from the University of Colorado (Colorado Springs) and her M.A. in Scientific Linguistics from the University of Arizona (Tucson). After concluding a long tenure as Director of Attorney Recruitment and Development and as Chair of Holland & Hart's Recruitment Committee, Ms. Dixon is now beginning a newly created position at her firm—Director of Diversity and Professional Development. She is also available through her firm as an Executive Diversity Coach to business executives and law firm leaders.

Joanne A. Epps received her J.D. from Yale law school in 1976. She is a former Deputy City Attorney for the City of Los Angeles (1976–1980) and a former Assistant U.S. Attorney for the Eastern District of Pennsylvania (1980–1985). Ms. Epps has been a member of the Temple Law School faculty since 1985, where she is a Professor of Law and also serves as Associate Dean for Academic Affairs. Ms. Epps's teaching areas include criminal law, criminal procedure, evidence and interviewing, counseling and negotiation. Ms. Epps is a member of the American Law Institute and in 1997 was appointed as the ABA's representative to the ALI-ABA Committee on Continuing Professional Education. She is currently President of the Board of Directors of the Defender Association of Philadelphia. From 1995–98, Ms. Epps served as Co-chair of the ABA Section of Litigation's Committee on Training the Advocate and, in 1997, was appointed to the Board of Editors of *Litigation Ethics*. In 1998, she was appointed Codirector of the ABA Litigation Section's Division III (programs). She also served as a member of the Third Circuit Task Force on Equal Treatment in the Courts, a member of the task force's Commission on Race and Ethnicity, and as Co-chair of the Commission's Committee on Special Issues in Criminal Justice. Ms. Epps is a frequent faculty member for the National Institute for Trial Advocacy in trial, deposition, and motion practice programs, and is a frequent teacher in ethics and professionalism training programs. Since 1994, Ms. Epps has served as Temple University's Faculty Representative to the NCAA. In 1995, she was also appointed as the Atlantic 10 Conference's NCAA Faculty Representative. From 1988 to 1994, Ms. Epps served as a member of the Board of Trustees of her college, Trinity College, in Hartford, Connecticut.

Cecelia M. Espenoza is an Associate Professor of Law at St. Mary's University where she supervises students in the criminal justice and immigration clinics and teaches trial advocacy and immigration law.

Previously, she taught at the University of Denver, where she supervised students in the Criminal Law Clinic and Immigration Internships and Placements, and taught immigration law, evidence and criminal law. Before teaching law, Ms. Espenoza was a prosecutor and a Legal Services Attorney in her native state of Utah. She has numerous publications in the areas of immigration law and crime including *Administrative Federal Practice: Immigration*, West, Spring 1999.

Wanda E. Flowers now lives in Voorhees, New Jersey, but grew up in Jacksonville, Florida, where she attended the public schools. She graduated with a B.A. in English from Bethune-Cookman College. A *summa cum laude* graduate, Ms. Flowers received a fellowship to study at Florida State University from which she received a M.A. in English. After teaching English for four years, she went to U.C.L.A. Law School. She is currently Regional Attorney for the Equal Employment Opportunity Commission, Philadelphia District Office. Her first job out of law school was as a Staff Attorney for Jacksonville Area Legal Aid where she worked on many paternity cases. Committed to the community, she is active in the Philadelphia and New Jersey legal communities. She devotes a great deal of time to community advocacy groups including the Delaware Valley Chapter of the Bethune-Cookman College Alumni Association, Progressive Women's Investment Club, UNCF, the Opportunities Industrialization Corporation, and the NAACP.

Paula J. Frederick is Deputy General Counsel for the State Bar of Georgia. Ms. Frederick came to the State Bar in 1988, after working for six years as a lawyer with the Atlanta Legal Aid Society. A native of Riverside, California, Ms. Frederick attended Duke University in Durham, NC, and earned her B.A. in political science in May 1979. She is a 1982 graduate of Vanderbilt University School of Law. Ms. Frederick is the President of the Atlanta Bar Association. She is a past President of the Georgia Association of Black Women Attorneys and is also an active member of the Gate City Bar Association and the Georgia Association for Women Lawyers. Ms. Frederick has been actively involved in the American Bar Association since 1987. She holds a seat on the ABA Nominating Committee as Minority Member-at-Large. She has been a member of the House of Delegates since 1994. Currently, she serves on the Standing Committee on

Professional Discipline and the Council of the Fund for Justice and Education. In the past, she served as a Commissioner for the Commission on Racial and Ethnic Diversity in the Profession and as Chair of the Multicultural Women Attorneys Network. Within the General Practice, Solo, and Small Firm Section of the ABA, Ms. Frederick is Chair of the Minorities in the Profession Committee, a member of the Section Council, and a member of the Long-range Planning Committee. Ms. Frederick is a member of the Boards of Directors of the Atlanta Volunteer Lawyers Foundation, the Georgia Legal Services Foundation, and the American Civil Liberties Union of Georgia. She is a member of the Emory Law School Child Advocacy Project Advisory Committee, and a Barrister of the Lamar Inn of the American Inns of Court. Ms. Frederick recently received a community service award from the Black American Law Students Association at the Georgia State University School of Law.

Kalyn Cherie Free is an enrolled member of the Choctaw Nation of Oklahoma and grew up in Red Oak, Oklahoma, a town of 600 in the heart of the Choctaw Nation. Ms. Free has a B.A. in Communications and History from Southeastern Oklahoma State University and a J.D. from the University of Oklahoma. In law school, Ms. Free served as the National President for the Native American Law Students Association. She lives in McAlester, Oklahoma, where she is completing her first year of a four-year term as the elected District Attorney for two counties in southeastern Oklahoma. Ms. Free is the first woman ever elected to this position. Before returning to Oklahoma to seek public office, she served as a trial attorney in the Environmental Enforcement Section and Senior Counsel in the Indian Resources Section at the U. S. Department of Justice for more than 10 years. Ms. Free is a member of and/or on the board for numerous organizations, including the American Bar Association, Federal Bar Association, Oklahoma Bar Association, Oklahoma Indian Bar Association, Native American Bar Association, National Congress of American Indians, American Trial Lawyers Association, National Association for the Advancement of Colored People, Oklahoma Coalition Against Domestic Violence and Sexual Assault, Children's Advocacy Center, National District Attorney's Association, Oklahoma Public Employees Association, Parents of Murdered Children, Democratic National Committee, Pittsburgh County Democrats, and Stigler Chamber of Commerce.

Rita Aliese Fry was reappointed to a second six-year term as Public Defender in June 1998, having been previously appointed and confirmed by the Cook County Board of Commissioners March 1992. In this capacity, she is the Chief Executive of the Office of the Cook County Public Defender. Ms. Fry has been an instructor, lecturer, guest speaker, and panelist for numerous institutions and organizations such as Harvard Law School, The University of Chicago Law School, Operation PUSH, and the Council for Court Excellence's 1996 Public Forum. In June 1994, Ms. Fry was selected by the President of the Supreme Court of Ethiopia to assist in establishing a long-term administrative structure for Ethiopia's first public defender system. She is the 1995 recipient of the Anne O'Brien Stevens Award and the 1992 recipient of The Ida Platt Award, the Kizzy Award, and the Sixth Amendment Award. Ms. Fry graduated from Northwestern University College of Law (J.D., 1979), Loyola University (B.A., 1973) and Prairie State College (A.A., 1968).

Carolyn F. Glosby is a 1985 graduate of the University of Virginia School of Law. Currently, she is an Appellate Attorney at the law firm of Cardelli Hebert, PC, of Royal Oak, MI, specializing in civil appeals in state and federal courts. She has served as Assistant Dean at the University of Detroit Mercy School of Law, as a Visiting Professor at the Detroit College of Law, and also as a Visiting Professor at the University of Michigan School of Business Administration. She is a past board member of the Walter Ridley Scholarship Fund at the University of Virginia, which extends financial assistance to deserving African American students attending the University of Virginia.

J. Cunyon Gordon was the first black woman Partner at Chicago's Jenner & Block, where she practiced complex general litigation. She also served as a Military Attorney in the United States Navy. As a Law Professor at Boston University and Boston College, Ms. Gordon taught criminal procedure, evidence and trial skills. At present, she is a member of the ABA Commission on Women in the Profession where she researches and writes about the role of women in the legal profession, and serves on the boards of numerous professional and service organizations.

Sophia H. Hall is the Administrative Presiding Judge of the Resource Section of the Juvenile Justice and Child Protection Department of the

Circuit Court of Cook County. As the newly created section's first head, Ms. Hall brings broad knowledge to this position, as she served as the Presiding Judge of the Juvenile Division for three years before it was divided into two divisions and the resource section in 1995. Ms. Hall was elected a Judge of the Circuit Court of Cook County in 1980. She served in the criminal division for four years, and thereafter in the chancery division for five years. Both assignments made her the first woman to serve in either division for over 20 years. When assigned as the Presiding Judge of the Juvenile Division in 1992, she was the first woman ever to serve as the Presiding Judge of any division or district of the Circuit Court of Cook County. Ms. Hall was appointed by President Clinton to the Board of the State Justice Institute and served a three-year term. Ms. Hall is a past President of the National Association of Women Judges and a past President of the Illinois Judges Association. She is the region 7 representative to the Executive Committee of the National Conference of State Trial Judges of the Judicial Division of the American Bar Association. She is a past member of the board of directors of the National Center for State Courts. Ms. Hall was an Adjunct Faculty Member of Loyola University of Chicago School of Law. She received her J.D. from Northwestern University School of Law and her B.S. from the University of Wisconsin at Madison, Wisconsin.

Connye Harper was born and raised in Detroit, Michigan, where she attended Detroit public schools. At age 19, she dropped out of the University of Michigan to get married. The next year her son was born. She returned to University of Michigan and graduated with a degree in Journalism. She began the University of Michigan Law School the next week. She and her husband were law students together until he graduated and they divorced. Ms. Harper graduated from law school in 1975, and returned to Detroit to practice law. Her first job was in the legal department of an insurance company where her major responsibility was to bring the employee retirement plan into compliance with ERISA. Six months later, she began to work for a law firm that specialized in plaintiff's product liability and personal injury work. Five years later, she left to start an all women's law practice that specialized in employment discrimination and women's rights law. In 1986, she joined the legal department of the International Union, UAW where she litigates labor law issues on behalf of the union. She holds several leadership positions in the American Bar Association's Section of Labor and Employment Law.

Sharon D. Hatchett was born in Mayfield, Kentucky, but grew up in the Chicago area. Currently, she lives in Bloomfield Hills, Michigan. She is a 1976 graduate of Illinois State University with a B.A. in Political Science and Spanish. Ms. Hatchett obtained her J.D. in 1979, from DePaul University College of Law, where she was also a member of Law Review. She has been an Attorney with the General Motors Corporation legal staff since 1981. Currently, she is Counsel to the GM truck group and for GM's health care initiatives. Before this assignment, she was General Counsel of the Electro-Motive Division of GM. She has also served as Regional Counsel to the Latin American Operations for General Motors Acceptance Corporation, GM's finance subsidiary. Following graduation from law school, she worked for a year in Washington, D.C., with the National Labor Relations Board, Office of Appeals. From there, she worked a year at the U.S. Department of Justice, in the Office of the U.S. Trustee, with responsibility for supervising the administration of Chapter 11 business reorganization cases. She is a member of the Council Group of the ABA Section of Public Utility, Communications, and Transportation and Vice Chair of the Railroad Committee and the Membership Committee.

Antonia Hernández is President and General Counsel of the Mexican American Legal Defense and Educational Fund, a national litigation and advocacy organization that uses the law, community education, and research to protect the civil rights of the nation's 29 million Latinos. She directs all litigation and advocacy programs, manages a $5.2 million budget, and a 75-person staff. Ms. Hernández earned her B.A. at U.C.L.A. in 1970, and her J.D. at the U.C.L.A. School of Law in 1974. She began her professional career as a Staff Attorney with the Los Angeles Center for Law and Justice in 1974. In 1977, she became the Directing Attorney for the Lincoln Heights office of the Legal Aid Foundation of Los Angeles where she administered a six-attorney staff. An expert in civil rights and immigration issues, Ms. Hernández worked in the U.S. Senate Committee on the Judiciary. She formerly served as a member of the Board of Directors for the Federal Reserve Bank of San Francisco, Los Angeles branch. Currently, she serves as a member of the Board of Directors for the Automobile Club of Southern California; National Endowment for Democracy; Golden West Financial Corporation, and America's Charities. Active in community affairs, Ms. Hernández also serves on various panels, committees, commissions, and advisory boards such as: Council on Foreign Relations; Pacific Council for International Policy; and the Commission on White House Fellowships. She is also a member of the American Bar Association, Mexican American Bar Association of Los Angeles, and the Los Angeles Bar Association.

Muzette Hill is a lawyer in the Office of the General Counsel of Ford Motor Company. She represents Ford on all emissions-related warranty issues on both the state and federal levels. She also consults with and advises the business clients, providing input in all phases from design and cycle planning through defect reporting and handles all issues addressed under Ford's Global Recall Process. She advises Ford and its subsidiaries on global insurance and risk management matters, including property and casualty issues, commercial general liability, product liability and issues arising from mergers and acquisitions, divestitures and spin-offs. Ms. Hill is on the Advisory Board and faculty of the Practising Law Institute, on the ABA's *The Brief* Editorial Board, a former President and member of the Board of Directors of the Cook County Bar Association, a former Chair and member of the Board of Directors of the Chicago Committee on Minorities in Large Law Firms, and a Co-founder and former President and member of the Board of Directors of the Black Women Lawyers Association of Greater Chicago. Ms. Hill, a Registered Professional Liability Underwriter, received her B.S. in Journalism from Northwestern University in 1978 and her J.D. in 1982 from Boalt Hall School of Law.

Angela Langford Jacobs practices law in Coral Springs, Florida. She is a third-generation graduate of the University of Florida in Gainesville, earning her bachelor's degree in journalism and communications in 1975. She received her J.D. in 1979 from the University of Florida College of Law. After graduating from law school, she worked with a state agency in Florida for eight years and later for a law firm in Sacramento, California. Beginning in 1988 she began a private practice in Tallahassee, Florida, until moving ten years later to South Florida. After 20 years of litigation, she now limits her cases to no more than 15 per year. As a Solo Practitioner, the majority of her cases are in criminal defense trials and appellate cases in state and federal court. When her calendar permits, she also represents clients in personal injury and employment discrimination cases. Ms. Langford Jacobs is the mother of two. Her daughter, Zandria, attends law school at American University in D.C.

Andrea Johnson is a Visiting Professor at Chicago-Kent College of Law, a Full Professor at California Western School of Law, and Director of the Center for Telecommunications and Intellectual Property in San Diego. Ms. Johnson is a graduate of Howard University and Harvard Law School. In 1996, she taught the first distance-learning class at an American Law School, linking sites using the Internet and videoconferencing. She develops and produces a web-based curriculum called "CyberWorkbooks" that combines the pedagogy of education, the efficiency of technology, and the theatrics of entertainment for a new industry of electronic content called Edutainment.

Marie-Flore V. Johnson has been an Associate in the corporate department of Dorsey & Whitney LLP since April 1999. She practices in the areas of general corporate law, international and technological licensing. Before that she was an Associate in the trial department from 1996–99 and practiced in the area of general litigation law. She received her J.D. from the Boston University School of Law in 1996. She also attended the Université des Sciences, Pierre and Marie Curie until 1986 and graduated with honors in computer science. She studied law at the Université de Paris II School of Law where she received a Diploma of Legal Advanced Studies in International Law in 1983 at the Université de la Sorbonne School of Law, where she graduated with honors in international business law.

Valerie R. Johnson is currently a Staff Attorney at the Legal Aid Society in Rochester, NY. Before her current position she served as a Staff Attorney at Shapiro & DiCaro from 1997–99. Prior to that she had her own private practice from 1989–96. Ms. Johnson was educated at the Rochester Institute of Technology and the University of Connecticut School of Law. She was admitted to the bar in New York in 1996 and in Connecticut in 1989. She maintains bar memberships with the American Bar Association, Monroe County Bar

Association, Greater Rochester Association for Women Attorneys and the Women's Bar Association of the State of New York. She is also a member of the Board of Governors for Our Lady of Mercy High School and the usher board for the A.M.E. Zion Methodist Church. She is divorced with one daughter and one grandson. Her hobbies include "grandmothering," writing, reading, jogging, and traveling.

Linda Yayoi Kelso is third-generation Japanese American. She is a Partner with the Jacksonville office of Foley & Lardner, a firm with more than 700 attorneys, based in Milwaukee, Wisconsin, with 14 offices nationwide. Ms. Kelso heads the Jacksonville office's securities law practice. She grew up in Palo Alto, California. Ms. Kelso graduated with great distinction with an B.A. in history from Stanford University and holds an M.A. in history from the University of Wisconsin. She graduated with high honors from the University of Florida College of Law in 1979, and has been in private practice in Jacksonville, Florida, ever since. Her practice includes public and private offerings, counseling public companies in connection with their periodic reporting to the Securities and Exchange Commission, and business combinations for public and private entities. Ms. Kelso has served on Florida Bar Association subcommittees that have prepared proposed revisions to Florida's securities act and partnership act for submission to the state legislature.

Eileen M. Letts was born in Lansing, Michigan. She received her J.D. from IIT Chicago-Kent College of Law in 1978. She received her B.A. from Ohio State University in 1975. Ms. Letts's first job after graduation was as a Judicial Law Clerk for the Honorable Glenn T. Johnson, Justice of the Illinois Appellate Court. She is currently a Partner at the law firm of Greene and Letts in Chicago, Illinois. Ms. Letts's activities in the legal community include: First Vice President, Chicago Bar Foundation; Executive Committee of the Legal Clinic for the Disabled; member of Economic Club of Chicago; member of the Illinois Supreme Court Committee on Character and Fitness; member of the 1996–97 Magistrate Merit Selection Panel for the Northern District of Illinois; Co-chair, American Bar Association Section of Litigation, Minority Trial Lawyer Committee; and Chair, Chicago Bar Association Special Committee on Minority Federal Jury Service.

Susan D. Liebson has practiced law at Atlantic Richfield Company (ARCO) for more than 18 years. Before that, she was a Litigation Associate at Loeb & Loeb in Los Angeles. Since joining ARCO in 1981, Ms. Liebson has practiced primarily in the transportation division, specializing in marine law and serving as ARCO Marine, Inc.'s (AMI) Chief Counsel for the past 10 years. She is a key member of AMI's management team and combines her legal advice with a strong understanding of the shipping business. Ms. Liebson received a B.A. *magna cum laude* from the University of Southern California in 1975. In 1978, she received her law degree also from the University of Southern California and in 1983, completed her MBA with a major in finance. Ms. Liebson's outside activities center around her family. She resides in Manhattan Beach with her husband Don, son Kevin and twins Brian and Jason. She actively volunteers at the boys' school, serving on the Meadows School Site Council, chairing the PTA Media/Library Committee and coordinating Scholastic Books orders for the kindergarten.

Charisse R. Lillie is a Partner in the law firm of Ballard Spahr Andrews & Ingersoll, LLP, in Philadelphia. She is a member of the Employment and Labor Law Group of the litigation department of the firm. Prior to joining the firm, Ms. Lillie's legal experience included positions as Trial Attorney, U.S. Department of Justice, Civil Rights Division, Deputy Director, Community Legal Services, Inc., Professor at Villanova Law School, Assistant United States Attorney for the Eastern District of Pennsylvania, General Counsel to the Redevelopment Authority of the City of Philadelphia and City Solicitor of the City of Philadelphia. In addition, Ms. Lillie has been a member of many civic commissions, including the Independent Charter Commission, the Philadelphia Criminal Justice Task Force, the MOVE Commission and the Philadelphia Election Reform Task Force. She is a member of the Forum of Executive Women, and serves as President of the Board of the Juvenile Law Center. She is also a member of the Board of Trustees of The Franklin Institute. Ms. Lillie is the recipient of numerous honors and is a former President of the Philadelphia Chapter of the Federal Bar Association. She served on the Board of the Pennsylvania Intergovernmental Cooperation Authority (PICA) from 1993 to 1998. She served as Chair of the Board of Governors of the Philadelphia Bar Association in 1995. She serves as Chair of the

American Bar Association Commission on Racial and Ethnic Diversity in the Profession and as Co-chair of the Racial Bias in the Justice System Committee of the Philadelphia Bar Association. She also serves on the Supreme Court of Pennsylvania Committee on Racial and Gender Bias in the Justice System. She was elected to the American Law Institute in 1995. Ms. Lillie was included in both editions of *Philadelphia Magazine*'s "Best Lawyers in Philadelphia" in 1999 and 1994. Ms. Lillie received her B.A. in 1973 from Wesleyan University— *cum laude*; her J.D. 1976 from Temple Law School—Dean's Honor List; and her L.L.M. in 1982 from Yale Law School. Ms. Lillie was law clerk to the Honorable Clifford Scott Green, U.S. District Court for the Eastern District of Pennsylvania, 1976-1978. She is Deputy Chairman of the Board of Directors of the Federal Reserve Bank of Philadelphia and serves as Vice-Chairman of the Personnel Committee and a member of the Budget and Operations Committee.

Antoinette Sedillo Lopez received her bachelors degree, *magna cum laude*, from the University of New Mexico in 1979. She graduated from U.C.L.A. Law School in 1982. After clerking for the District of Columbia Circuit Court, she joined the law firm of Modrall, Sperling, Roehl, Harris and Sisk, P.C. She joined the faculty of the University of New Mexico Law School in 1986. Ms. Lopez has published various articles in national law journals and has spoken on topics in her areas of expertise to regional, national, and international audiences. She has published a six-volume anthology, *Latinos in the United States: History, Law and Perspective*. (Garland Press). She is the series editor for the Garland series, *Latino Communities: Emerging Voices-Social, Cultural, Political and Legal Issues*. Ms. Lopez has chaired many committees and boards. She served as President of the New Mexico Hispanic Bar Association in 1995. She served as State Director for Clinton/Campaign in 1996. She has represented a mayoral candidate in a case involving campaign spending limitations and has worked on several political campaigns. Her recent publications include "Tracking Children on the Net" published in the *Family Advocate* and "A Comparative Analysis of Women's Issues: Toward a Contextualized Methodology" in the *Hastings Women's Law Journal*.

Margaret K. Masunaga is a third-generation (sansei) Japanese American attorney practicing on the big island of Hawaii in the Kona

Branch of the Office of the Corporation Counsel for the County of Hawaii. Before her position in the public sector, she was an Associate at the law firm of Goodsill Anderson Quinn & Stifel. She received her bachelor's degree at the University of California at Berkeley and obtained her J.D. in 1987, at the University of the Pacific, McGeorge School of Law in Sacramento, California. Ms. Masunaga is active with the American Bar Association, presently as a Delegate-at-Large to the House of Delegates, and formerly serving as Hawaii State Bar Association Representative to the House of Delegates. She previously served on the Young Lawyers Division Executive Council representing Hawaii and Alaska and the YLD Liaison in the Council of the Family Law Section, Special Committee on Youth Education for Citizenship. She presently serves on the Standing Committee on Gavel Awards, as Co-chair of the ABA Hawaii Membership Committee, and as Co-chair of the Family Courts Committee of the ABA Family Law Section. Ms. Masunaga is the Co-president of the West Hawaii Bar Association, and served on the Board of Examiners and the Judicial Performance Committee of the Hawaii Supreme Court. She is currently on the Board of Governors of the Hawaii Community Foundation. She also serves on the Board of Directors of the Legal Aid Society of Hawaii, Kona Hongwanji Buddhist Church, Lions Club of Kona, and Interim Commissioner of the Hawaii State Commission on the Status of Women.

Gloria J. Matthews is an Attorney with McDermott, Will & Emery, specializing in commodity, securities and commercial litigation, transactional work, and regulatory matters. She graduated from Northwestern University School of Law in 1978. Ms. Matthews worked as Senior Staff Trial Attorney for the Commodity Futures Trading Commission, Division of Enforcement; at Bellows & Bellows (commercial law firm); ContiCommodity Services, Inc., as Assistant General Counsel; and at Geldermann, Inc., as Executive Vice President and General Counsel. Her board memberships and/or corporate directorships include the Board of Directors of the Women's Treatment Center, the Ancona School Advisory Board, and the Illinois Institute of Technology Graduate School of Finance.

Vanzetta Penn McPherson, a native Montgomerian, is a U. S. Magistrate Judge for the Middle District of Alabama in Montgomery,

Alabama. For 18 years before her appointment to that position in April 1992, she practiced law as an Associate at a Wall Street law firm for one year, as an Assistant Attorney General for the State of Alabama for two years, and as a private practitioner for 15 years in Montgomery. The focus of her private practice was constitutional and employment litigation and domestic law. Ms. McPherson was educated at Howard University (B.A.,1969), Columbia University (M.A,, 1971), and Columbia Law School (J.D., 1974). She is a member of the Alabama and New York bars, the American Bar Association, and a life member of the National Bar Association, the NAACP, and the National Council of Negro Women. She is also President of Montgomery's Federal Bar Association, a Master Bencher in the Montgomery Inn of Courts, and a past President of the Alabama Black Lawyers Association. Ms. McPherson formerly chaired the Family Law Section of the Alabama State Bar, and she now serves on the board of the Bar's journal, *The Alabama Lawyer,* and on the board of the state's prestigious Alabama Shakespeare Festival. She is a frequent speaker at state and national bar conferences. In 1989, she cofounded, with her best friend (also a lawyer), Roots & Wings, A Cultural Bookplace. Ms. McPherson's husband, Thomas McPherson, Jr., is an employment law Mediator and a retired Deputy Director of the Equal Employment Opportunity Commission. They have four children.

Eileen D. Millett is General Counsel of the Interstate Sanitation Commission. In this position, she is responsible for litigation to abate and control water pollution in the tidal waters of New York, New Jersey, and Connecticut. In conjunction with the federal government and other environmental agencies, her commission inspects large corporations and the waters they use to ensure that particular standards are met. Ms. Millett appreciates the autonomy and flexibility her position affords in allowing her to choose direct courses of action. Ms. Millett views the practice of law as being in a constant state of evolution where individuals have the ability to affect its course. The 1974 Syracuse Law Graduate was Assistant Counsel to the New York State Department of Environmental Conservation, Assistant Attorney General in the New York State Department of Law, Assistant Deputy Commissioner of the New York City Police Department, and Inspector General for the New York City Department of Investigation. Ms. Millett is divorced and resides in Brooklyn, New York, with her son.

Patsy Takemoto Mink has been a Democratic Member of Congress since 1990 and previously served in the position from 1965 to 1977. She has served on the Education & the Workforce Committee, the Sub-Committee on Early Childhood, Youth and Families, and the Government Reform. Other committees on which she has recently served include the Sub-Committee on Postsecondary Education, Training, and Lifelong Learning; Sub-Committee on Criminal Justice, Drug Policy & Human Resources; and the Sub-Committee on Government Management, Information and Technology. Ms. Takemoto Mink's other congressional activities include serving as the Democratic Regional Whip from 1997 to 1998; as a Member of the Congressional Asian Pacific Caucus, 1994 to the present (Chair, 1995 to 1998); and as Co-chair of the Education Task Force. Ms. Takemoto Mink also served as Assistant Secretary of State, OES, Department of State from 1977 to 1978; as National President, Americans for Democratic Action from 1978 to 1981; and as a Democrat on the Honolulu City Council from 1983 to 1987 where she served as Chair from 1983 to 1985. Ms. Takemoto Mink was valedictorian of her 1944 Maui High School class in 1944, received her B.A. in 1948 from the University of Hawaii and her J.D. from The University of Chicago Law School in 1951. She is married to John Francis Mink and has a daughter, Gwendolyn Rachel Mink.

Kathryn Kimura Misna is a Managing Counsel with McDonald's Corporation and is the Group Leader of the Marketing/Advertising Practice Group, which is responsible for overseeing the legal support of the marketing and advertising activities conducted by the 25,000 McDonald's restaurants worldwide. Her work involves the negotiation and drafting of relationship and license agreements, the review of advertising claims, the review of promotion marketing programs, as well as the management of government and regulatory enforcement activities. She recently celebrated 22 years with the company. Ms. Misna is a contributing author to the 700-page *Sales Promotion Handbook*, a leading reference on the subject of promotion marketing, a past Chair/President of the 700-member Promotion Marketing Association, a member of the Women's Advertising Club of Chicago, the Asian American Bar Association, the Northwestern University Council of 100—a network of 100 professional women who mentor undergraduate women, as well as the Board of the Japanese

American Service Committee. Ms. Mlsna earned a B.S. and J.D. from Northwestern University and its school of law, is married, and the mother of three children.

Verna Myers was born and raised in Baltimore, Maryland. She attended Barnard College, Columbia University, and Harvard Law School. After graduating from law school, Ms. Myers joined the law firm of Testa, Hurwitz & Thibeault in Boston, where she practiced corporate law. Ms. Myers resides in Newton, Massachusetts, with her husband and son. She is the Principal of Verna Myers & Associates, a diversity management consulting firm that advises private law firms, government agencies, educational institutions, and non-profit agencies on diversity-related issues. She focuses primarily on helping organizations establish comprehensive and systematic efforts to promote diversity and inclusion. She is a member of the Massachusetts State Democratic Party, Newton Ward One Democratic Committee, the Newton Women's Commission, the New Covenant Christian Church and the Massachusetts Black Lawyers Association. Ms. Myers is also on the Board of Directors of FamiliesFirst Parenting Programs and the National Conference for Community and Justice—LeadBoston Community.

Peggy A. Nagae was born in Portland, Oregon, and raised on a truck farm in Boring, 25 miles southeast of Portland. She now lives in Eugene, Oregon, with her husband, Charles G. Bigelow and two daughters, Aspasia, and Kelsey. In 1973, she graduated, *cum laude*, from Vassar College with an B.A. in East Asian Studies and a J.D. with honors from Northwestern School of Law at Lewis and Clark College in 1977. Her first job out of law school was through the Reginald Heber Smith Community Fellowship Program. She was placed at Multnomah County Legal Aid and worked there for two years. In 1997, Ms. Nagae returned to school, this time to the University of Santa Monica, where she graduated with an MA in Spiritual Psychology in 1999. Ms. Nagae has served as a Consultant since 1988. She has owned her own consulting business, which specializes in the areas of change management, organization healing, and leadership development. Ms. Nagae has been involved in civic and organizational groups since graduating from law school in 1977. Some of her more recent civic and professional affiliations include:

Board member, National Asian Pacific American Legal Consortium, 1997 to present; University of Oregon School of Law, Board of Visitors, 1999–present; Presidential Appointment to the Civil Liberties Public Education Fund, 1996–1998; Vice-Chair, ABA Commission on Racial and Ethnic Diversity in the Legal Profession, 1992–95; President, National Asian Pacific American Bar Association 1991–92; curriculum committee member, Leadership Tomorrow (Seattle, WA) 1992–95; and University of Washington School of Law, Board of Visitors, 1990–93.

Christine K. Noma's early years were spent in Marin County, California. She moved to San Francisco when she was 11 years old, where she attended junior and senior high school. She attended college at the University of California, Berkeley, and then went to law school at Hastings College of the Law in San Francisco, where she graduated in 1982. She is a Partner specializing in environmental law at the firm of Wendel, Rosen, Black & Dean. Ms. Noma has served as a Director of the Asian American Bar Association of the Greater Bay Area and as President and Board Member of Legal Assistance for Seniors in Oakland, California. She has also been active in evaluating candidates for judicial appointment, having served two years on the State of California Judicial Nominee Evaluation Commission and three years on Senator Barbara Boxer's Judicial Advisory Committee for the Northern District of California. Ms. Noma is the mother of two sons, whom she shares the joy of parenting with her husband, Stephen Y. Fong. She had a dream when she was pregnant, and knowing that she was having a boy, of raising the most wonderful, considerate, compassionate and feminist son, ever. And that dream holds true today for both her children.

Kimberly Jade Norwood was born and raised in Harlem, New York City. She completed her undergraduate work at Fordham University in 1982, and graduated from the University of Missouri-Columbia School of Law in 1985. While at the University of Missouri, she became the first black person to become a member of the *Missouri Law Review*. After graduation, Ms. Norwood clerked for the Honorable Clifford Scott Green, a U. S. District Court Judge in Philadelphia for a year. After her clerkship, she joined the litigation department at Missouri's then largest law firm, Bryan, Cave,

McPheeters & McRoberts. In 1990, Ms. Norwood left the firm and joined the law faculty at the Washington University School of Law. In 1996 she became the first black person to receive tenure at the law school. At Washington University, she teaches an array of courses including torts, civil procedure, products liability, advanced civil procedure, pretrial practice and procedure, and the civil justice clinic. She is married to Ronald Norwood, a partner at Lewis, Rice & Fingersh, a St. Louis-based law firm. They have four children.

Angela E. Oh served as a Presidential Appointee to the President's Initiative on Race, an initiative that was introduced by President Clinton in the summer of 1997. As an outgrowth of that effort, Ms. Oh continues to be engaged in writing and public lectures concerning the future of race relations throughout the nation. Her most recent essay, *Moving Beyond Self-Interest*, is part of a book entitled *True to Ourselves—A Celebration of Women Making Difference*, published by the League of Women Voters (1998). Ms. Oh joined U.C.L.A. in January 1999 as a Lecturer, Visiting Scholar and Lawyer-in-residence. Between June 1987 and July 1998, she was a Trial Attorney and Partner at Beck DeCorso Daly Barrera & Oh, a firm specializing in state and federal criminal matters. Ms. Oh currently serves as a Commissioner on the Los Angeles City Human Relations Commission. In addition, she is a member of the Board of Directors of Lawyers Mutual Insurance Company, a Trustee of the Asian Pacific American Women's Leadership Institute, and Board Member of the Korean American Family Service Center, a domestic violence prevention program that serves Korean immigrant families.

Sandra R. Otaka received her B.A. from the University of California, Berkeley, in 1984 and her J.D. from the U.C.L.A. School of Law in 1987. Since May 1990 she has worked as the Section Chief, U.S. Environmental Protection Agency in Chicago. From 1987-1990, she was a Litigation Associate at Sidley & Austin and from 1985-1986 she served as a Law Clerk for San Fernando Valley Neighborhood Legal Services, Inc., in Pacoima, California. In 1999, Ms. Otaka received the City of Chicago Human Relations Award and the U.S. EPA, Region 5, *Women Who Have Put Their Stamp on EPA* Award. She holds the following positions: Chair, Asian American Advisory Committee to State Comptroller Dan Hynes; Chair, Chicago Bar Association, Council on

Minority Affairs; Member, Cook County Commission on Human
Rights; Member, Character and Fitness Committee of the Illinois
Supreme Court; Vice President, Japanese American Service
Committee; Member, Board of Directors, Past Vice President, Asian
American Bar Association of the Greater Chicago Area; Founding
Member, Asian Pacific Employee Council, Region 5, U.S. EPA.

Shelly Ann Panton grew up in Lucea, Jamaica, population 2,000. She
left Jamaica at age 15 and moved to Mount Vernon, New York. Ms.
Panton attended Mount Vernon High School for her senior year,
before heading off to Ithaca for four years at Cornell University. After
graduating from college, she worked for the Mount Vernon
Methadone Treatment Program. One year later, she enrolled at
Howard University School of Law. After Howard, Ms. Panton moved
to Minneapolis to join the law firm of Dorsey & Whitney. She practiced as an Associate there for about two years before moving home
to Mount Vernon, NY. She worked in Dorsey's New York office for a
few months before accepting a teaching position in Japan for a year.
Ms. Panton is currently working as a Placement Director at the Offices
of Special Counsel in New York. She doesn't think she will ever return
to the practice of law.

Rachel Patrick began her professional career as an English Teacher
after receiving her B.S. from the University of Illinois, Champaign,
Urbana. She later received a M.S. in Education from Chicago State
University. After 12 years of teaching in the inner city of Chicago, Ms.
Patrick decided to attend law school. She received her J.D. from
DePaul University of Chicago, College of Law. Immediately after law
school, she served for two years as a Law Clerk to the Honorable
George Leighton, who was then a Judge of the U.S. District Court,
Northern District of Illinois. Upon completion of the clerkship, Ms.
Patrick pursued her lifelong goal of serving the public by working in
the area of public interest law. She was the Staff Director for a legal
services project for the elderly and a Special Assistant to the
Commissioner of Corrections. Ms. Patrick has been employed with
the American Bar Association in several public interest positions for
the past 19 years. Initially, she was hired as the *Pro Bono* Coordinator
for the Legal Services Division. Thereafter, she became the Director of
the Public Interest Program for the Young Lawyers Division. Ms.

Patrick served the Association for 12 years as the Director of the ABA Commission on Opportunities for Minorities in the Profession. She currently serves the Association as the Staff Director of the ABA Council on Racial and Ethnic Justice.

Georgette C. Poindexter (known to her friends as Gigi) is a 1981 graduate of Bryn Mawr College and a 1985 graduate of Harvard Law School. She is an Associate Professor of Real Estate at the Wharton School and an Associate Professor of Law at the University of Pennsylvania Law School where she holds the Pietro and Elvira Giorgi Appointment in Law and Business. Before joining the University of Pennsylvania faculty in 1992, she was in private law practice in New York and Philadelphia. Ms. Poindexter is widely published in the field of real estate and local government law. Her scholarly work has appeared in, among others, the *University of Pennsylvania Law Review*, the *Boston University Law Review*, and the *University of Connecticut Law Review*. She lectures nationally on topics in commercial real estate and is a member of the editorial board of *The Practical Real Estate Lawyer*. In 1996, she was elected as a member of the American College of Real Estate Lawyers. Other honors include Wharton teaching awards in 1994 and 1997. She lives with her husband, Tim, and son, Colin, in suburban Philadelphia. When she is not being a wife, a mother, or a Law Professor, she enjoys playing piano and curling up with a novel that has no redeeming literary value.

Cynthia F. Reaves is a Member of the firm and Shareholder of Epstein Becker Green, P.C., resident in the Washington, D.C. office, where she specializes in corporate transactional, tax-exempt organization, and managed care law. Ms. Reaves provides advice and strategic planning counsel with respect to obtaining and maintaining tax-exempt status, corporate mergers and acquisitions, and joint venture and affiliation issues. Before joining the firm, Ms. Reaves worked as a Management Consultant specializing in strategic organizational change within complex corporate structures with an Ann Arbor-based consulting group. While in Ann Arbor, Ms. Reaves also served as the Corporate Vice President and then Chair of the Board of Directors of a multimillion dollar nonprofit corporation. Most recently, Ms. Reaves served as an Adjunct Professor of Law at George Mason University School of Law in Virginia. Ms. Reaves earned her law degree from Georgetown

University Law Center (J.D. 1988) and her undergraduate degree from the University of Michigan (B.A. 1983). While in law school, she served as Managing Editor of the *Tax Lawyer*, a publication of the Tax Section of the American Bar Association. In her spare time she serves as an Advisor for the Small Business Administration and as a member of the Board of Directors of the Women's Business Center, a national non-profit organization. She is active in her community and served as a co-project manager for the Jimmy Carter Work Project, a part of Habitat for Humanity, to develop low-income housing in Washington, D.C.

Amalia S. Rioja serves as Deputy General Counsel to Illinois State Comptroller Daniel W. Hynes. In this position, she is the top legal advisor in the Chicago Office. Prior to joining the Comptroller's Office, Ms. Rioja was a member of the legal staff of the Mexican American Legal Defense and Educational Fund, where she litigated civil rights cases, primarily in the areas of employment and education. Ms. Rioja also has litigation experience in the private sector, where she worked at two prestigious Chicago law firms, Baker & McKenzie and Grippo & Elden. Ms. Rioja earned her J. D. from Northwestern University School of Law and her B. S. in journalism from Northwestern University's Medill School of Journalism. In 1998, Ms. Rioja was appointed to Mayor Richard M. Daley's Advisory Council on Latino Affairs and Cook County State's Attorney Richard Devine's Commission on Juvenile Competency. In addition, Ms. Rioja serves on the Young Professionals Board of the Chicago Council on Foreign Relations, the Executive Committee of the Chicago Bar Association's Alliance for Women, and serves as Co-chair of Heartland Alliance's Midwest Immigrant and Human Rights Leadership Council. Ms. Rioja also serves on the board of directors of the Hispanic Lawyers Scholarship Fund of Illinois, the AIDS Legal Council of Chicago, and Personal PAC. In 1996, Ms. Rioja was appointed an Illinois Delegate to the Democratic National Convention. Ms. Rioja is married to Martin R. Castro, Esq., and they reside in Chicago, Illinois.

Patricia Weston Rivera was born in Newark, New Jersey, and still resides in the Garden State. She attended colleges in New Jersey, including Essex County College where she earned an associates degree in 1970, and Kean College where she received a baccalaureate in elementary education in 1972. Ms. Rivera was awarded a J.D. in

1978, from Rutgers University. Her first legal position was as Staff
Attorney, Union County Legal Services. She is currently an Assistant
Prosecutor for the County of Essex and is assigned to the Adult Trial
Section where she litigates felonies. Her professional affiliations
include membership in the National Bar Association, the National
Black Prosecutor's Association, and the Garden State Bar Association.
Her civic affiliations include the African American Cultural Committee
of the Montclair Art Museum, the New York Arts and Entertainment
Alliance, and just to keep her grounded, the Ebony Ladies of
Literature Reading Group.

Dorothy Roberts is a Professor at Northwestern University School of
Law, with joint appointments as a Faculty Affiliate of the Department
of Sociology, a Faculty Fellow of the Institute for Policy Research, and
a Faculty Affiliate of the Joint Center for Poverty Research. She
received her B.A. from Yale College and her J.D. from Harvard Law
School. Professor Roberts has written and lectured extensively on the
interplay of gender, race, and class in legal issues concerning reproduction and motherhood. She is the author of *Killing the Black Body:
Race, Reproduction, and the Meaning of Liberty* (Pantheon, 1997),
which received a 1998 Myers Center Award for the Study of Human
Rights in North America, as well as the coauthor of casebooks on
constitutional law and women and the law. She has published more
than 50 articles and essays in books, scholarly journals, newspapers,
and magazines, including *Harvard Law Review, Yale Law Journal, The
University of Chicago Law Review, Social Text,* and *The New York
Times.* Her influential article, "Punishing Drug Addicts Who Have
Babies: Women of Color, Equality, and the Right of Privacy" (*Harvard
Law Review,* 1991), has been widely cited and is included in a number of anthologies. She serves as a Consultant to the Center for
Women Policy Studies in Washington, D.C., and as a Member of the
Board of Directors of the Public Interest Law Center of New Jersey
and the National Black Women's Health Project. Her current projects
concern race and child welfare policy.

Covette Rooney has been a Federal Administrative Law Judge with
the Occupational Safety and Health Review Commission in
Washington, D.C., since January 1996. Before this appointment, she
was a Federal Administrative Law Judge with the Social Security

Administration from October 1994 until January 1996. Her educational background includes her graduation from Colgate University. She
was a member of the first class of women admitted to Colgate
University in Hamilton, NY (1974); and a graduate of Temple
University Law School, Philadelphia, PA (1977). Upon graduation
from law school, she clerked for the Honorable Paul A. Dandridge in
the Philadelphia Court of Common Pleas (September 1977 to March
1979). She then went on to work as a Trial Attorney for U. S.
Department of Labor (April 1980 to January 1992) and eventually was
named a Regional Counsel for the Mine Safety and Health
Administration (January 1992 to September 1994). Since her appoint-
ment as Judge, she has been a member of the Judicial Division of the
American Bar Association and the Federal Administrative Law Judge
Conference. Among her many honors, she was inducted into her high
school's 1996 Hall of Fame (Overbrook High School, Philadelphia,
PA), and received an Outstanding African American Award from the
Hattiesburg, MS, School District in 1995. She is presently a member
of the Board of Greater Metropolitan Washington Area Planned
Parenthood. She is single and a resident of Mitchellville, MD.

Mara E. Rosales serves as General Counsel for the San Francisco
Airport Commission and is the Director who manages the San
Francisco International Airport, a $438 million operation. The San
Francisco International Airport is the fifth busiest airport in the country
and the eighth busiest in the world. Before joining the San Francisco
City Attorney's office in 1983, Ms. Rosales was a Staff Attorney with
the California Supreme Court for one year. She is a 1982 graduate of
the University of California Hastings College of the Law. She is a
Governing Board Member of the ABA Forum on Air and Space Law.
Ms. Rosales is a native of San Francisco, California, and the daughter
of immigrant Nicaraguan parents. She currently lives in San Francisco
with her son and daughter.

Dovey J. Roundtree is a pioneering Civil Rights Lawyer, Army veteran,
Ordained Minister and the winner of the 2000 Margaret Brent Women
Lawyers of Achievement Award given by the American Bar
Association. The founding Partner of the Washington, D.C. law firm of
Roundtree Knox Hunter and Parker, Ms. Roundtree served for 35
years as the General Counsel to the National Council of Negro Women

and as Special Consultant for Legal Affairs to the African Methodist
Episcopal Church. One of a group of black women selected by Dr.
Mary McLeod Bethune to integrate the Women's Army Corps at its
inception, Ms. Roundtree attended Howard University Law School on
the GI Bill and went on to break legal ground in both civil and criminal
law. Her 1955 bus desegregation victory before the Interstate
Commerce Commission, *Sarah Keys v. Carolina Coach Company*,
stands as a milestone in the legal battle for civil rights, and her criminal
defense work in Washington D.C.'s all-white judicial system during the
1960's broke barriers that enabled other black attorneys to follow in
her footsteps. Her achievements and spirit have inspired a host of
young women attorneys as well as Cicely Tyson's portrayal of the central character in the television series *Sweet Justice*. Ms. Roundtree is
retired from active legal practice but maintains an active role in church
and community affairs pertaining to the welfare of children.

Wendy C. Shiba is Vice President, Secretary, and Assistant General
Counsel of Bowater Inc., in Greenville, SC. It is a worldwide producer
of wood fiber products and the largest manufacturer of newsprint in
the United States. Ms. Shiba was born in Cleveland, Ohio. She
received her B.S. with high honors, from Michigan State University,
with a major in social science and minor in mathematics. She earned
her J.D., *cum laude*, from Temple University School of Law where she
graduated first in her class and was articles editor of the *Temple Law
Review* and a member of the Moot Court Board. During the year following graduation, she was Law Clerk to Justice Stanley Mosk on the
Supreme Court of California. Before joining Bowater in 1993, Ms.
Shiba was Corporate Chair of the City of Philadelphia Law Department
where she managed all non-litigation legal matters for the city. She did
this while on sabbatical from her position as a tenured Associate
Professor of Law at Temple University School of Laws. From 1980 to
1985, she was an Associate specializing in corporate law with
O'Melveny & Myers in its Los Angeles and New York offices. She has
served as an Arbitrator for the Philadelphia Stock Exchange and is coauthor of the reference book, *Pennsylvania Corporation Law and
Practice*. In Greenville, SC, Ms. Shiba serves on the boards of directors
of the Legal Services Agency of Western Carolina, the Greenville Little
Theatre, and the Campaign Cabinet of the United Way of Greenville
County. Previously, in Philadelphia, she served on the boards of

Community Legal Services, the Public Interest Law Center of Philadelphia and the Legal Clinic for the Disabled, and was President of the Asian American Bar Association of the Delaware Valley. In the Philadelphia Bar Association, she was Chair of the Commission on Judicial Selection and Retention and Chair of the Committee on Minorities in the Profession, Subcommittee on Legal Education and Admission to the Bar.

Beverly McQueary Smith teaches contracts, torts, environmental law, consumer law, race and American Law, and legislation at Touro College: Jacob D. Fuchsberg Law Center in Huntington, New York. She serves or has served on several boards, including the Jersey City Medical Center, the Minority Environmental Lawyers Association, Southern Africa Environment Project, Consumers Union—the publisher of Consumers Reports. Since 1988, she has been a member of the Board of Governors of the National Bar Association (NBA). She is the Chair of the Southern Africa Environmental Project and of the newly formed National Campaign on Black Health. Since the fall of 1999, she has served as a board member of the New York County Lawyers Association and the Council on Legal Education Opportunity. Ms. McQueary Smith served as President of the NBA in 1998 after serving as Vice President in 1995 and as President-elect in 1997. As President of the NBA, she represented some 18,000 black lawyers, judges, legal scholars, and law students throughout the Untied States and, increasingly, the world. Ms. McQueary Smith is a member of the American Law Institute, and in November 1997, became a Commissioner of the New York State Ethics Commission for the Unified Courts System. She has published a host of articles on a wide variety of topics and delivered papers at professional and continuing legal education programs in the United States and abroad. She also served as an official election observer during the 1994 South African elections. She has a B.A. from Jersey City State College, a M.A. from Rutgers, a J.D. from New York University School of Law, and a Master of Laws degree from Harvard Law School.

Elicia Pegues Spearman is a graduate of Wellesley College and Case Western Reserve University, School of Law. Ms. Spearman began her legal career with a clerkship in her home state, Connecticut. After her clerkship, she represented plaintiffs in employment discrimination matters. After moving to the Washington, D.C., area in 1993, she first-chaired personal injury and employment cases for the Washington Metropolitan Area Transit Authority and amassed a 15/1 trial record. Later she defended the Federal Bureau of Investigation in individual and class-action employment litigation cases across the country. Ms. Spearman is currently the Associate Counsel at the Children's National Medical Center and represents management in labor and employment litigation matters. From 1997–99, Ms. Spearman served as the President of the Greater Washington Area Chapter, Women Lawyers Division of the National Bar Association. This organization primarily consists of African American female attorneys in the D.C. metropolitan area whose primary goal is to give some of their time and legal expertise back to the community. Before serving as president of GWAC, Ms. Spearman chaired numerous committees and tutored elementary school children in Southeast, D.C. She is also an active member of Alpha Kappa Alpha Sorority, Inc., is married to Livie V. Spearman, III, and resides in Olney, Maryland.

Nkechi Taifa serves as Director of the Equal Justice Program at Howard University School of Law, where she also teaches seminars on racial disparity in the criminal justice system and public interest law. Ms. Taifa has served as Legislative Counsel for the ACLU, Policy Counsel for the Women's Legal Defense Fund, and Staff Attorney for the National Prison Project. For several years she was a Private Practitioner maintaining a general criminal and civil law practice in the District of Columbia, as well as employment discrimination law. She is a 1984 graduate of George Washington University Law School, and a 1977 graduate of Howard University. Ms. Taifa serves on the Board of Directors of the American Civil Liberties Union of the National Capital Area, the D.C. Prisoners' Legal Services, Inc., the D.C. Bar's Public Service Activities Corporation, the Washington Council of Lawyers, and the Bureau of Rehabilitation, Inc. She is past section Co-chairperson of the D.C. Bar Section on Criminal Law and Individual Rights, and the National Conference of Black Lawyers Criminal Justice Section. She also serves as Legislative Subcommittee Chair of the National Coalition of Blacks for Reparations in America. Nkechi Taifa is the published author of two books for children, *Shining Legacy: Storypoems and Tales for the Young, So Black Heroes Forever Will be Sung;* and *The Adventures of Koj.*

Macarena Tamayo-Calabrese is the Special Assistant to the Executive
Director of the American Bar Association—the national voice of the
legal profession and the largest professional membership organization
in the world. She is responsible for special projects, among them are
writing speeches, researching a host of legal and non-legal topics, and
conducting various technical legal assistance programs in developing
countries. In addition, she manages the International Liaison Office—
the first point of contact for foreign and international bars and
lawyers. She holds the highest position of any Hispanic at the
Association. Prior to joining the ABA in 1995, Ms. Tamayo-Calabrese
was a practicing attorney in Chicago. She was the Managing Attorney
at Lacasa and Associates, a law firm concentrating its practice in
immigration and family law. Ms. Tamayo-Calabrese and her work
have been featured in The Wall Street Journal, the National
Immigration Forum Publication, and the Chicago Daily Law Bulletin.
She has appeared as a guest speaker in WGN-TV Channel 9, WGBO
Channel 66, WSNS Channel 44, and *The Law is for You*, a Chicago-
based cable network. She was the invited speaker at the American
Bar Association's Annual Meeting Opening Assembly in Navy Pier.
Ms. Tamayo-Calabrese received a B.A. from Loyola University of
Chicago and a J.D. from Hofstra School of Law.

Debbie D. Thompson is a native of Burlington, N.C., where she graduated with high honors from Hugh M. Cummings High School and
attended the University of North Carolina at Chapel Hill on a full
scholarship. She was the recipient of the College of Arts and Science
Excellence in Academics Award. In 1989, she received her B.A. in
Psychology and Communications. In 1992, she received her J.D. from
Wake Forest University School of Law in Winston-Salem, N.C. While
at Wake Forest, she was a member of the Student Trial Bar Team and
a reporter for *The Jurist* magazine. Ms. Thompson has worked with
the Georgia Commission on Equal Opportunity and as a Prosecutor
with the Fulton County Solicitor General's Office, where she was the
first recipient of the Prosecutorial Excellence Award. She was of Chief
Counsel with the Georgia Secretary of State's Office—Securities and
Business Regulations Division. Ms. Thompson is currently Staff
Attorney with the U.S. Securities and Exchange Commission—Atlanta
District Office. Ms. Thompson serves on the boards of directors of the
Boys and Girls Club and Our House, Inc. and is on the executive board

of the United Way Volunteer Initiative Program. She is a member of the Georgia Association of Black Women Attorneys and Delta Sigma Theta Sorority, Inc. Ms. Thompson is also is a part-time professional model. She resides in the Atlanta suburb of Smyrna, Georgia.

Vickie E. Turner was born in Gainesville, Georgia, and has practiced extensively in the litigation area over the last 17 years in San Diego, California. She is a Partner with the Wilson, Petty, Kosmo & Turner LLP law firm. Her practice emphasizes the defense of clients in general business litigation, product liability, warranty, and First Amendment rights. She is a Master in the Louis M. Welsh American Inns of Court. She was the 1996 President of Lawyers Club and the 1994 president of the Earl B.Gilliam Bar Association. She is the recipient of the 1999 San Diego County Bar Association Award for Outstanding Service to the Legal Profession. In addition, she is an active member of the National Bar Association and received an outstanding service award in 1998, for participation with the organization. Formerly a Partner at Luce, Forward, Hamilton & Scripps, Ms. Turner served as Chairperson of the product liability practice group. She was selected as one of California's Most Outstanding Lawyers by California Law Business and appointed by U. S. Senator Barbara Boxer to the Southern District Judicial Appointment Advisory Committee. In addition, Ms. Turner has also been a Judge Pro Tem for the Small Claims Court and is a frequent Adjunct Professor at the University of San Diego School of Law teaching trial advocacy skills to law students. She received her J.D. from the University of San Diego School of Law in 1982 and is currently an active member of its alumni board.

Rena M. Van Tine graduated from Oakland University in 1982, and from New York Law School in December 1985. Ms. Van Tine worked at Albert Speisman & Associates, a small law firm in Chicago. Her general practice included real estate closings, wills, and criminal and civil litigation. She joined the Cook County State's Attorney's Office in April 1987, and worked in several branches of the criminal division. In 1992, she transferred to the medical litigation division where she represented several major hospitals and their physicians and nurses in medical malpractice cases. In 1996, she was recruited to serve in the newly formed Complex Litigation Division where she represented Cook County in complex and high profile civil matters. In January

1999, she became Special Counsel to Illinois State Comptroller Daniel W. Hynes. Ms. Van Tine is currently the President of the Asian American Bar Association of the greater Chicagoland area. She also serves on the Executive Committee of the Alliance of Bar Associations, which conducts evaluations of judicial candidates. She is a member of the Women's Bar Association of Illinois and is an active participant with the Strategic Planning Committee and the Judicial Reception Committee. She is a Co-founder and Director of WILPOWER (the power of women in law), which is the political action committee of the WBAI. In addition, she belongs to the Chicago Bar Association, the Illinois State Bar Association, the Cook County Bar Association, the Black Women Lawyers' Association, and the American Inns of Court. She chairs State's Attorney Richard A. Devine's Asian American Advisory Council. She was a member of Vice President Al Gore's Illinois Steering Committee in his run for the President of the United States. Ms. Van Tine assisted in establishing the first and only free legal clinic for the Indo American community. She has also set up health workshops for children from Cabrini Green housing project in Chicago.

Raquel Odila Velasquez held on to the hope of getting a college education during the 20 years she raised a family and worked as a secretary. The opportunity presented itself in 1978, when she enrolled at the University of New Mexico. She graduated with honors in 1982, and was genuinely surprised when the University of New Mexico School of Law accepted her while she was still an undergraduate. Prior to pursuing her undergraduate studies, Ms. Velasquez was active in community activities. She served in both local and state offices of the League of United Latin American Citizens and participated in the organization's national convention. A member of the Methodist Church, she served on local and district boards of the church's Rio Grande Conference. While receiving her law school education, Ms. Velasquez served as an officer of the University of New Mexico Chapter of the Delta Theta Phi Law Fraternity International. When she graduated from law school in 1985, Ms. Velasquez received two awards: the Community Service Award by the Mexican American Law Students Association, and the Dean's Award. Her current position with the New Mexico Human Services Department, Child Support Enforcement Division provides her with the opportunity to interact with the 19 Pueblo tribes in her state, as well as two Apache tribes and Navajo Nation courts in New Mexico. She has served on the Board of Directors of the New Mexico Hispanic Bar Association for several years, and as a Faculty Member at a Continuing Legal Education Conference sponsored jointly with the Juarez, Mexico Bar Association. In the past she served on the board of the New Mexico Women's Bar Association Oral History Project.

Jacqueline A. Walker is a Sole Practitioner who handles general civil matters. Ms. Walker's practice includes representation of clients in probate, real estate, employment discrimination, bankruptcy, contracts and personal injury, as well as other litigation matters. She presides over administrative matters as a Hearing Officer for the Chicago Police Board and the Illinois State Police Merit Board, and serves as an Arbitrator for the Circuit Court of Cook County. She also serves as a Conciliator for the Cook County Commission on Human Rights. Ms. Walker received her J.D. from the American University, Washington College of Law in Washington, D. C. She has an undergraduate degree from Bowie State University in Bowie, Maryland, and a Master's Degree in Education from Howard University, in Washington, D.C. She also received a Diploma in 1986 from the National Institute for Trial Advocacy. Her previous positions include being a member of the Board of Directors of the National Bar Association (NBA), Chair of the Women Lawyers Division of the NBA; member of the American Bar Association Standing Committee on Judicial Selection, Tenure and Compensation; member of the Chicago Bar Association.

Laura A. Wilkinson joined the antitrust practice group of Rogers & Wells LLP in Washington, D.C., as Counsel in 1996. Before joining Rogers & Wells, Ms. Wilkinson served as Deputy Assistant Director of the Bureau of Competition of the Federal Trade Commission, where she oversaw one of the Bureau's litigation divisions and was responsible for merger enforcement in a wide range of industries, including the defense and pharmaceutical industries. Ms. Wilkinson graduated from the University of Pennsylvania in 1982, with a degree in Economics, and from Cornell University's Johnson Graduate School of Management in 1985, with an MBA. She obtained her law degree from Cornell Law School in 1986, with a concentration in business law and regulation. Ms. Wilkinson is admitted to practice in the

District of Columbia and New York. She is an active member of the American Bar Association, the National Bar Association, and Alpha Kappa Alpha Sorority, Inc., and is an Adjunct Professor at Howard University School of Law.

Donna M. Wilson is an Attorney with Polsinelli, White, Vardeman & Shalton, P.C. in Kansas City, Missouri and concentrates her practice in land use and public law. She represents developers and land owners at all levels of government. Ms. Wilson received her B.S. and J. D. from Howard University where she served as Symposium editor of the *Howard Law Journal.* Ms. Wilson's civic activities include serving as Commissioner, Landmarks Commission of Kansas City; Board Member, Blue Hills Homes Corporation; Board Member, Legal Aid of Western Missouri; and Member, Mayor's High Five Education Advisory Board.

Sheila Wilson-Freelon is Vice President and Senior Attorney at Morgan Stanley Dean Witter in Riverwoods, Illinois. Ms. Wilson-Freelon graduated from the University of Mississippi, where she was a "University Scholar." (B. A. political science, *cum laude* 1979). She attended Northwestern University School of Law in Chicago, along with her late husband, Jeffery O. Freelon, Sr., founder of Freelon and Associates law firm. Ms. Wilson-Freelon began her career with a judicial clerkship in the Illinois Appellate Court. She then worked in the labor and employment law section of the Chicago Transit Authority Law Department for approximately five years. She began working in the law department of the Quaker Oats Company in 1990, as an In-house Labor and Employment Counsel. Throughout her legal career at Quaker, Ms. Wilson-Freelon has served in a number of non-legal functions, related to the areas of diversity and social responsibility. Ms. Wilson-Freelon is a member of Grant Memorial AME Church where she has served as Choir Director, Legal Advisor and Secretary to the Board of Directors of Grant Child Care Program, Legal Advisor to Grant's Board of Trustees, and guest speaker for Grant's Baccalaureate Sunday Services. She is a member of the American Bar Association, National Bar Association, and the Cook County Bar Association. She has two children, Kira and Jeffery Jr. In her leisure time, Ms. Wilson-Freelon is an avid reader and gardener and lover of antiques.

Professor Adrien Katherine Wing received her J.D. from Stanford Law School in 1982. She also holds a B.A. with high honors from Princeton and an M.A. from U.C.L.A.. After her law school graduation, she was an International Lawyer in New York City for five years. She worked four years with the Park Avenue firm Curtis, Mallet-Prevost, Colt and Mosle, where she was the only black woman on legal staff. She spent an additional year with the small firm Rabinowitz, Standard, Boudin, Krinsky and Lieberman. Ms. Wing joined the faculty at the University of Iowa College of Law in 1987, where she teaches constitutional law, critical race theory, human rights, and comparative law subjects. Author of more than 40 publications, she is Editor of *Critical Race Feminism: A Reader* (NYU Press 1997).

Karen Wong is Vice President and General Counsel for United Savings and Loan Bank in Seattle, Washington, where she practices banking, real estate, and corporate law. She is a Board Member of the Law Fund and serves on that organization's endowment committee. She is also a Board Member of the Virginia Mason Medical Center and serves on the Employee Benefits Committee. She is President of the Robert Chinn Foundation, a non-profit that supports the Asian Resource Center. She handles all fundraising and money manage-ment matters for the foundation.

Kathleen J. Wu is a real estate lawyer with the Houston-based law firm of Andrews & Kurth. She is currently the Managing Partner of the firm's Dallas office, as well as a regular columnist for *Texas Lawyer* newspaper, where she writes about issues affecting women in the legal profession. She is a regular commentator on the local National Public Radio affiliate. She received her law degree from George Washington University's National Law Center in 1985, and was a *cum laude* graduate of Columbia University's Barnard College in 1982. She lives in Dallas with her husband, lawyer Mark Solomon, and her son, Grant.

Sandra S. Yamate, a Sansei (third generation American of Japanese ancestry), is best known for her interest in and advocacy for authentic multicultural, particularly Asian American, children's literature. In 1990, she and her husband started Polychrome Publishing to publish multicultural children's books. Polychrome books have been showcased by *Teaching Tolerance Magazine* as exemplary examples of multicultural children's literature. Ms. Yamate is also the Director of the American Bar Association's Commission on Racial and Ethnic Diversity in the Profession. In that capacity she works to develop increased opportunities for minority attorneys and monitors the progress of the legal profession in its efforts to achieve greater racial and ethnic diversity. Previously, Ms. Yamate was the Executive Director of the Chicago Committee on Minorities in Large Law Firms. Ms. Yamate is a founding member and past President of the Asian American Bar Association of the Greater Chicago Area. She was the first central region Governor for the National Asian Pacific American Bar Association and the immediate past President of the Japanese American Service Committee. She is the Co-chair of Asian Americans for Inclusive Education and has been working to incorporate Asian and Asian American Studies into school curricula. Ms. Yamate is a former trustee and chaired the first National Summit for the Asian Pacific American Women's Leadership Institute; and a former Member of the Board of the Asian American Institute. Ms. Yamate is a recipient of the Asian American Bar Association's Hall of Fame Award; the Chicago Kent College of Law Outreach Award; the Asian American AIDS Foundation's Community Service Award; the Asian American Coalition's Community Service Award; the Asian American Institute's Milestone Maker Award, and the Chicago Bar Association's Vanguard Award for her efforts to build bridges among different racial and ethnic groups. She was named a *Neighborhood Hero* by the *Chicago Sun-Times*; one of *40 Under 40* by *Crain's Chicago Business*; one of 100 Women Making A Difference by *Today's Chicago Woman*, and one of the five most distinguished Asian American women leaders by *V Magazine*. She received the Asian American Coalition's Pioneer Award for her many accomplishments on behalf of the community. A native of Chicago, Ms. Yamate earned her B.A. from the University of Illinois at Urbana-Champaign, where she was elected to Phi Beta Kappa and graduated *magna cum laude* in history and *cum laude* in political science. She received her law degree from Harvard Law School. Ms. Yamate and her husband, Brian Witkowski, an architect, live in Chicago.

Loria B. Yeadon is Assistant General Counsel—Intellectual Property for AlliedSignal Inc. of Morristown, New Jersey. Her responsibilities include handling Intellectual Property matters, including patents, copyrights, licensing, enforcement, acquisitions and e-commerce for strategic business units in AlliedSignal Aerospace. Prior to joining AlliedSignal, Ms. Yeadon served as Senior Counsel for Telcordia Technologies, Inc. (formerly Bellcore) in Morristown, New Jersey. She is a Board Member for the New Jersey Corporate Counsel Association and serves as Co-chair of its Intellectual Property Committee. She is also a member of the Industrial Advisory Board for the School of Engineering and Applied Sciences at the University of Virginia. Ms. Yeadon received a B.S. in Electrical Engineering, with distinction, from the University of Virginia, M.S. in Electrical Engineering from Georgia Institute of Technology, and J.D., *magna cum laude*, from Seton Hall School of Law. Ms. Yeadon was raised in Kenbridge, Virginia and currently resides in West Orange, New Jersey, with her husband, Joseph, and their two daughters, Lorial and Jemma.

Alice Young is a Partner in the New York office of Kaye, Scholer, Fierman, Hays & Handler, LLP. and Chair of the firm's Asia Pacific Practice Group. For 25 years, she has concentrated her practice on corporate law and international business and has been based in New York, Hong Kong, and Tokyo. She frequently lectures on current law, business, and foreign policy issues and has appeared on CNN, *The News Hour* with *Jim Lehrer*, the *Charlie Rose Show*, ABC's Nightline, Fuji TV, and China Television Network on these subjects. Ms. Young was named by *Crain's* in its list of Top 100 Minority Executives, and by *Avenue Asia* magazine as one of the five most influential Asian American Corporate Lawyers in the U.S. In 1992, she received from the New York Women's Agenda a Star Award for outstanding corporate and civic achievements. She is listed in *Who's Who of American Women*, *Who's Who in American Law*, and *Who's Who of Asian Americans*. She serves as Trustee of the Aspen Institute, Vice Chairman of the Committee of 100, Director of the Yasuda Bank and Trust Company (USA), Advisor to the Harvard Asia Law Society, and a Member of the Council on Foreign Relations, National Asian Pacific American Bar Association, and Asia Society. She is a graduate of Yale University and Harvard Law School. She is married and the mother of two teenagers.

Multicultural Women Attorneys Network

The Multicultural Women Attorneys Network (MWAN) was created in 1989 by the Commission on Racial and Ethnic Diversity in the Profession and the Commission on Women in the Profession. MWAN's objectives are to: identify issues which multicultural women lawyers view as important; explore possible solutions to these issues; and educate the American Bar Association as to its role and responsibility to address these issues.

During its first years in existence, MWAN conducted roundtable discussions around the nation and held two regional conferences to discuss the status of multicultural women attorneys in the profession. The information and research that flowed from that work culminated into two reports: *The Burdens of Both, the Privileges of Neither* and its supplement, *Report on the Experiences of Native American Women Lawyers*. As explained in the reports, MWAN found that multicultural women lawyers encounter persistent, pervasive, and unique barriers to career opportunity, growth, and advancement. MWAN continues to create programs and publications that examine and break down those barriers. For more information, visit www.abanet.org/minorities/mwan/dsdd.html.

1999-2000 MWAN COMMITTEE MEMBERS
Karen Clanton, Chair
Beverly Poole Baker • Patricia Diaz Dennis • J. Cunyon Gordon
Tanya Lee • Verna Myers • Angela Oh • Amalia Rioja

Commission on Racial and Ethnic Diversity in the Profession

The Commission on Racial and Ethnic Diversity in the Profession (formerly known as the Commission on Opportunities for Minorities in the Profession) has been at the forefront of promoting diversity in the profession since its inception in 1986. The ABA President appoints the Commission's Chair and 14 members to implement projects and programs that fulfill the ABA's Goal IX, which states, in part, "To create full and equal participation in the legal profession by minorities."

The Commission's primary goals include: assisting minorities in their legal education and admission to the bar; developing career and employment opportunities for lawyers of color; promoting the appointment of minorities to the judiciary and to judicial clerkships; and increasing the involvement of lawyers of color in bar associations at the national, state, and local level, and with minority specialty bars. The Commission also publishes a quarterly newsletter and other publications that report on the status of minorities in the profession.

COMMISSION
On
WOMEN
In The
PROFESSION

Commission on Women in the Profession

The Commission on Women in the Profession was created in 1987 to assess the status of women in the legal profession and to identify barriers to their advancement. Hillary Rodham Clinton, the first Chair of the Commission, issued a groundbreaking report in 1988 showing that women lawyers were not advancing at a satisfactory rate.

Now in its second decade, the Commission aims not only to report the challenges that women lawyers face, but to bring about positive change in the legal workplace. As the national voice for women lawyers, the Commission is helping to forge a new and better profession that ensures that women have equal opportunities for professional growth and advancement commensurate with their male counterparts. Drawing upon the expertise and diverse backgrounds of its 12 members who are appointed by the ABA President, the Commission develops programs, policies, and publications to advance and assist women in public and private practice, the judiciary, and academia.

Statistics and Facts

On Multicultural Women in the Law and Data Collection for *Dear Sisters, Dear Daughters*

Minority women[1] are the fastest growing segment of the legal profession. According to the 1990 Census, 92.55 percent of the legal profession were White (21.56 percent were White women) and 2.89 percent were minority women. While the results of the 2000 Census were not available at the time this book was published, by looking at law school demographics (where the numbers of minorities enrolled has grown from 8.4 percent in 1976-77 to just over 20 percent in 1999-00), we can project that almost 5 percent of the current population of lawyers are minority women and that number is increasing.

In compiling this book, more than 500 minority women who had graduated from law school ten or more years earlier were invited to submit letters offering their advice, insights, and experiences for the next generation of minority women lawyers. In addition, the solicitation was made available through the web site of the Commission on Opportunities for Minorities in the Profession and various Internet listservs.

The submissions were evaluated by the editorial board for this book. Of those selected for inclusion:

- 54 were from African American or Black authors.
- 17 were from Asian American or Pacific Islander authors.
- 10 were from Hispanic or Latino authors.
- 1 was from a Native American author.

---

1. For purposes of this book, the term "minority" was used to represent African Americans, Blacks, Hispanics, Latinos, Asian Americans, Pacific Islanders, and Native Americans. The Commissions recognize that the term "minority" may be perceived as misleading and inaccurate. We are not in disagreement with this perception, but for practical reasons, at this time, we still use the term.

- 24 were from the East Coast.
- 32 were from the Midwest.
- 11 were from the South/Southwest.
- 15 were from the West Coast/Hawaii.

- 12 work in law firms of 10 or more lawyers.
- 10 are partners.
- 0 are associates.
- 2 did not indicate whether they were partners, associates or held another position.
- 6 work as sole practitioners or in small firms of under 10 lawyers.
- 18 work in corporate law departments.
- 3 work as judges or hearing officers.
- 13 work in government (other than as judges).
- 13 work in legal academia.
- 7 work in law-related positions (association work, law firm recruitment, etc.)
- 3 work in non-law-related positions (consultants, investment bankers, etc.)
- 2 are not currently employed.
- 5 did not specify their current employment.

As part of the solicitation, minority women were also invited to complete a short survey. The purpose was to understand their attitudes about the legal profession. They were asked three questions:

1. Are you currently practicing law?
2. If you were given the chance to live your life over, would you become a lawyer?
3. Would you encourage or have you encouraged your own daughter to pursue a career in law?

There were 152 women who responded to the survey. 110 (or just under 75 percent) are currently practicing law; 42 are not and of those 42, all had practiced law at one time or another.

135 women (almost 90 percent) said that if given the chance to relive their lives, they would become lawyers. While they would choose law again, they were not quite as certain they would encourage or have encouraged their daughters to pursue a career in law. 78 said they would or have encouraged their daughters to pursue a career in law (just over 50 percent). While many added comments that it would depend upon the daughter's particular inclinations, there was no clear consensus from the group of respondents about whether the law was a career they wished for their daughters.

Author Index